The Color of the Third Degree

The Color of the Third Degree

Racism, Police Torture, and Civil Rights in the American South, 1930–1955

Silvan Niedermeier

TRANSLATED BY PAUL COHEN

The University of North Carolina Press CHAPEL HILL

This book was published with the assistance of the Authors Fund of the University of North Carolina Press.

Originally published in Germany as *Rassismus und Bürgerrechte: Polizeifolter im Süden der USA 1930–1955* (Hamburg, Germany: Hamburger Edition, 2014). This translation was funded by Geisteswissenschaften International– Translation Funding for Work in the Humanities and Social Sciences from Germany, a joint initiative of the Fritz Thyssen Foundation, the German Federal Foreign Office, the collecting society VG WORT, and the Börsenverein des Deutschen Buchhandels (German Publishers & Booksellers Association).

The University of North Carolina Press has been a member of the Green Press Initiative since 2003.

Library of Congress Cataloging-in-Publication Data

Names: Niedermeier, Silvan, author. | Cohen, Paul (Paul Allen), translator.
Title: The color of the third degree : racism, police torture, and civil
    rights in the American South, 1930-1955 / Silvan Niedermeier ;
    translated by Paul Cohen.
Other titles: Rassismus und Bürgerrechte. English
Description: Chapel Hill : The University of North Carolina Press, [2019] |
    Translation of: Rassismus und Bürgerrechte : Polizeifolter im Süden
    der USA, 1930-1955. Hamburg : Hamburger Edition, 2014. |
    Includes bibliographical references and index.
Identifiers: LCCN 2019027153 | ISBN 9781469652962 (cloth : alk. paper) |
    ISBN 9781469652979 (paperback : alk. paper) | ISBN 9781469652986 (ebook)
Subjects: LCSH: African Americans—Civil rights—Southern States—
    History—20th century. | Police brutality—Southern States—
    History—20th century. | Torture—Southern States—History—
    20th century. | African American prisoners—Violence against—
    Southern States—History—20th century. | Racism—Southern States—
    History—20th century. | Southern States—Race relations—History—
    20th century.
Classification: LCC E185.61 .N4913 2019 | DDC 305.800975—dc23
LC record available at https://lccn.loc.gov/2019027153

Contents

Figures

Abbreviations in the Text

ACLU   American Civil Liberties Union

ASWPL   Association of Southern Women for the Prevention of Lynching

CIC   Commission on Interracial Cooperation

CLU   Civil Liberties Unit

CPUSA   Communist Party USA

CRD   Civil Rights Division

CRS   Civil Rights Section

FBI   Federal Bureau of Investigation

ILD   International Labor Defense

NAACP   National Association for the Advancement of Colored People

USC   United States Code

Introduction

In September 1949, the National Association for the Advancement of Colored People (NAACP) received an anonymous letter that contained a disturbing drawing. It showed a prisoner who was being whipped by three men. He was handcuffed to a pipe near the ceiling to hold his naked body upright. Bleeding wounds were visible on the man's upper body, hips, and thighs. Steel bars in the background and the words "Lake County Jail" in the lower left-hand corner indicated that the scene took place in a jail cell. One of the three men wielding a whip was wearing a police badge and a sheriff's hat (see figure 1). The scene included the following handwritten text: "Then the four men took me to the jailhouse to the top floor. They handcuffed me to a pipe so my feet just touched the floor. Then they pulled my shirt up over my head and pulled my pants down to the floor. Then they took rubber hoses and whipped me till I could feel the blood."[1] The drawing relates to the case of the so-called Groveland Four, in which three African Americans were arrested in Florida in July 1949.[2] A white woman had alleged that she had been raped by four unknown black men.[3] A fourth suspect was shot by a posse shortly after the allegations had been made. During the course of the investigation, the three defendants said that they had been physically coerced into making confessions by local law enforcement officials, who all denied the allegations.

In contrast to other forms of racial violence in the South, the practice of torturing black prisoners and suspects generally took place outside the public eye, hidden from view behind the walls of prisons and police stations. For the most part, its widespread use was officially denied. As a rule, white representatives of the local justice system, judges, district attorneys, and jury members prevented law enforcement officials from being held legally accountable for torturing African American prisoners.

The anonymous drawing in the archives of the NAACP is an attempt to expose the widely concealed violence of torture and highlight it as a flagrant injustice. This is underscored by the specific arrangement of the text and the image. While the caption "A Negro 'Confesses' to 'Rape'" provides an "official" summary of events and, at the same time, calls into question this version by using quotation marks, the drawing itself illustrates the brutal reality of

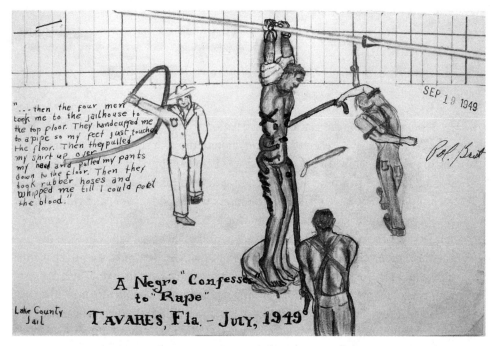

"...then the four men took me to the jailhouse to the top floor. They handcuffed me to a pipe so my feet just touched the floor. Then they pulled my shirt up over my head and pulled my pants down to the floor. Then they took rubber hoses and whipped me till I could feel the blood."

SEP 19 1949

A Negro "Confesses" to "Rape"

Lake County Jail

TAVARES, Fla. - JULY, 1949

FIGURE 1 Anonymous drawing, "A Negro 'Confesses' to 'Rape,' Tavares, Fla.—July, 1949." Library of Congress, NAACP Papers, Group II, Box B-117, Fol. T [1941–1949]. The author wishes to thank the NAACP for authorizing the use of this image.

torture in the jails and prisons of the American South. The juxtaposition of witness testimony and a scene of torture is a visual means of substantiating the allegations of the victim. As such, this drawing is but one example of a multitude of efforts undertaken from the 1930s onward by diverse groups and individuals—including victims, civil rights organizations, and federal agencies—to document and expose police torture and delegitimize its practice.

The Color of the Third Degree provides the first-ever detailed examination of the rampant use of torture on African American suspects and prisoners in the American South between the years 1930 and 1955. It also highlights the initiatives that were launched to curb this practice. In contrast to previous research on the history of the South, which focuses on the height of lynching violence between 1890 and 1930 and the post-1955 phase, in which the civil rights movement galvanized an entire generation, this book delves into the transformations and continuities of racial violence that can be observed during the interim period.[4]

The present study also examines the connection between the quantitative decrease in lynching violence during the 1930s and the use of torture by law enforcement authorities to extract confessions from African American suspects.[5] This gradual decline in racially motivated vigilante justice, and the concomitant use of torture to secure speedy convictions through the criminal justice system, is an aspect of U.S. history that, until now, has been largely overlooked by researchers. In other words, although there were fewer and fewer lynchings, it by no means spelled the end of racial violence.

Furthermore, this book follows up on more recent historical studies on the civil rights movement. Although earlier works point to key events during the mid-1950s—including the landmark U.S. Supreme Court decision in the *Brown v. Board of Education* case; the bus boycott in Montgomery, Alabama, which was sparked by Rosa Parks's refusal to give up her seat to a white passenger on a public city bus; and the case of the brutal murder of Emmett Till—as the starting points of the civil rights movement, more recent research has dated its beginnings to the 1930s and 1940s. In recognition of this new understanding of the long road that activists have traveled, historian Jacquelyn Dowd Hall coined the term "the long civil rights movement" in 2005. Hall stresses that this movement had its roots in the sweeping social, economic, and cultural developments that took place during the New Deal, World War II, and the postwar years. It was this critical phase that gave rise to a broad social movement that was to play a key role in paving the way for the African American civil rights struggle during the 1950s and early 1960s.[6] Although Hall's concept has been criticized for its tendency to give short shrift to the multiplicity and historicity of the black civil rights struggle since the 1930s while overemphasizing the role of the political left during its early phase, I argue that her approach retains its usefulness when used to explain how a local mass-based movement for civil rights gradually emerged in the United States prior to the mid-1950s.[7] Likewise, in her book *At the Dark End of the Street*, historian Danielle McGuire points to the African American protests against sexual violence perpetrated by white men against black women in the South of the 1940s and early 1950s. McGuire shows that these early protests were a catalyst for the civil rights movement that emerged in the 1950s.[8] Following up on this research, the present book highlights the importance of initiatives against torture for the African American civil rights struggle during the phase up to 1955. In doing so, it shows that the court appearances of African American defendants and victims of torture in the South, along with the NAACP campaign against the use of forced confessions as evidence in criminal proceedings, constituted an integral component of "the long civil rights movement." At the same time, it is important to emphasize that they were part of a much longer and continuing struggle for freedom and civil rights by African Americans in the American South and beyond.

In addition, *The Color of the Third Degree* focuses on the torture investigations conducted by federal authorities in the South.[9] In an article published in 2008, historian Christopher Waldrep called the civil rights investigations launched by the U.S. Department of Justice and the Federal Bureau of Investigation (FBI) in the South from 1940 onward a "surprise to historians." The lack of academic debate on this topic has meant that the image of the FBI promulgated by researchers has so far been largely influenced by the bureau's destructive and covert operations that targeted African American civil rights activists from the late 1950s to the 1970s.[10] By contrast, the FBI investigations conducted during the 1940s into cases of torture by law enforcement officials show that federal authorities took action at a much earlier date than previously assumed to defend and protect African American civil rights in the South, albeit—as this book reveals—with initiatives that were limited, both in terms of their scope and rates of success. These investigations are comprehensively documented and analyzed here for the first time.

The present study is based on the extensive archives of the NAACP in Washington, D.C., along with court documents, investigative files, and newspaper reports that have been compiled through research conducted in diverse archives in the South. In addition, I have reviewed and evaluated investigative files of the U.S. Department of Justice and the FBI that date back to the 1940s and early 1950s and are stored in the National Archives in College Park, Maryland. A number of these files were released following applications made under the Freedom of Information Act and have been examined for the first time ever within the context of this study.

Torture as a Subject of Inquiry

Ever since the Enlightenment, state-sanctioned torture has been seen in many parts of the world as an illegitimate act of violence that flies in the face of the self-proclaimed moral image of ostensibly modern societies.[11] Torture is seen as "the most extreme means of violent subjugation and mental annihilation."[12] Its practice goes hand in hand with the destruction of the autonomy and dignity of the victim, and thus stands in stark contrast to the modern concept of humanity.[13]

Although the perception of torture as an illegitimate, inhumane, and backward form of state violence is of far-reaching cultural significance, the practice of torture is still part and parcel of life in many parts of the world.[14] To make matters worse, following the terror attacks of 9/11 in 2001, the relegitimization of torture under the banner of the "war against terror" during the administration of U.S. president George W. Bush (2001–9) revealed that this form of violence is still widely embraced by political actors who seek to rationalize the use of torture and aim to legalize these methods through new interpretations of legal provisions.[15]

The term "torture" generally denotes the deliberate infliction of physical and mental suffering on a person by other persons and thus includes acts of violence by state officials and by private individuals alike. In this book, the term "torture" is used in a narrower sense: to indicate forms of violence used by state and law enforcement officials to acquire information or coerce confessions, based on the definition in the 1984 United Nations Convention against Torture. According to Article 1 of the convention, torture is defined as

> any act by which severe pain or suffering, whether physical or mental, is intentionally inflicted on a person for such purposes as obtaining from him, or a third person, information or a confession, punishing him for an act he or a third person has committed or is suspected of having committed, or intimidating or coercing him or a third person, or for any reason based on discrimination of any kind, when such pain or suffering is inflicted by or at the instigation of or with the consent or acquiescence of a public official or other person acting in an official capacity.[16]

The majority of the cases of police violence against African Americans that are examined in this book correspond to this comparatively narrow definition of torture. Hence, forms of violence were virtually always used that met the criterion of "severe pain or suffering, whether physical or mental," that is "intentionally inflicted" and in all cases served the purpose of coercing a confession and intimidating or punishing individuals for crimes that were allegedly committed. The torture invariably involved individuals of authority, such as police officers, sheriffs, deputy sheriffs, and jail keepers, who were "acting in an official capacity."

Focusing on this form of violence not only helps to restrict the scope of this study but also sheds light on the importance of police brutality in maintaining local racist structures of power and subjugation in the South during the phase before the African American civil rights movement gained momentum.

During the first decades of the twentieth century, police torture was not a specific criminal offense in its own right in the United States. If sanctioned at all, charges were brought within the scope of existing offenses, like "assault and battery" and breaches of police regulations. There were laws on the books in a number of states that prohibited the use of violence to coerce confessions, and anyone found guilty of torturing suspects or prisoners faced possible imprisonment and fines.[17] As investigative reports that date from this period reveal, however, penalties were rarely imposed because district attorneys, judges, and jury members were highly reluctant to limit the power and authority of law enforcement officials.[18]

Newspaper reports and editorials of the day indicate that during the early and mid-twentieth century, the term "torture" had a denunciatory connotation and was a politically sensitive issue in the United States. While the white press in the South generally avoided using the word "torture" in its reporting of cases of police violence during interrogations, the term was purposely used by the black press to expose and denounce the violent abuse of African American suspects, often in a bid to gain public support for the fledgling civil rights struggle.

A more common and prevalent term was "the third degree," which was adopted as police jargon in the late nineteenth century and entered the general American vocabulary in the early twentieth century. Although it was initially used to denote the intensive and lengthy interrogation of suspects by police officers—not unlike the common and somewhat ambiguous "grilling" of suspects—it was reinterpreted in the early twentieth century.[19] Newspapers, works of popular science, and official investigative reports used "the third degree" to describe how lawmen used aggressive psychological and physical interrogation techniques to extort confessions and information from suspects.[20] According to a study that dates from this period, the third degree stood for "the employment of methods which inflict suffering, physical or mental, upon a person in order to obtain from that person information of a crime."[21]

The emergence of this term in everyday language coincided with the widespread use of police torture and forced confessions throughout the United States, which eventually sparked a national debate on police brutality and a reform of law enforcement practices during the 1920s.[22] In 1931, President Herbert Hoover (1929–33) established the National Commission on Law Observance and Enforcement, unofficially known as the Wickersham Commission, which reported that "the third degree" was used "throughout the country," particularly in large American cities like New York, Chicago, Detroit, and Los Angeles.[23]

As historians Marilynn Johnson and Elizabeth Dale have shown for New York City and Chicago, the pervasiveness of the third degree in both cities during the 1920s and 1930s increasingly captured the attention of the American public. In New York, bar associations, judges, newspapers, and civil rights organizations like the American Civil Liberties Union (ACLU) criticized with growing vehemence the arbitrary and brutal violence used by police to coerce defendants into making confessions and demanded a legal reform of the arrest, arraignment, and detention process. In addition, the ACLU supported torture victims by helping them file charges against police officers, although these cases generally did not result in convictions.[24] Police officials denied the existence of the third degree and warned that any legal restrictions of police work would lead to a rise in crime. Marilynn Johnson posits that these initiatives significantly curbed the use of torture in New York during the 1930s. However, Elizabeth Dale has shown that in Chicago, the pattern of torture merely changed during this phase. In reaction to mounting public and judicial criticism, police torture increasingly took place in secret. Furthermore, there was a growing tendency among police to use methods that left no recognizable physical marks on their victims.[25]

These two studies reveal that in American cities, both black and white suspects were physically abused and forced to make confessions. In 1930, a New York legal aid organization called the Voluntary Defenders Committee listed 289 cases in which suspects complained of police brutality during interrogations. The majority of the presumptive victims were poorly educated white males under the age of thirty, and 41 of them were born outside the United States.[26] The data collected by the Voluntary Defenders Committee also shows that a disproportionately high percentage of African Americans were physically abused by police in New York. In fact, 36 percent of victims were African American men, although the black population of New York City was under 5 percent in 1930.[27]

The practice of torture in the South reflected even greater racial discrimination against blacks. The report by the Wickersham Commission highlighted numerous cases from southern states in which police officers and sheriffs used batons, fists, and whips to extort confessions from black suspects. The report also documented the use of the so-called water cure on black suspects, a forerunner to waterboarding that U.S. soldiers used during the Philippine-American War (1899–1902). The water cure consisted of tying suspects flat on their backs and using a hose to force water into their mouths or noses until they provided the requested information and made a confession.[28] Furthermore, the report mentioned torture methods on African Americans that included the use of electricity. One of these involved an improvised electric chair, which was used until 1929 by the sheriff's office in

Helena, Arkansas, to extract confessions.[29] The report also pointed to individual cases of police torture of people of Mexican origin and white suspects.[30]

The cases collected by the Wickersham Commission indicate that the vast majority of victims in the South were African Americans—primarily men but also women.[31] Moreover, they show that police torture of African Americans in the South was already commonplace before 1930. Diverse historical studies confirm that this practice can be traced to the days of slavery.[32]

The Wickersham report and other studies at the time came to the conclusion that the practice of police torture was characterized by the fact that it was carried out in locations that were not open to the public. These reports noted that the legal struggle against torture was extremely difficult because law enforcement officials generally denied its use, and when complaints were filed, they were usually based solely on the statements of the presumptive victims.[33] These documents point to a connection that is constitutive for the modern history of torture: its key characteristics in the twentieth and twenty-first centuries are the aspect of secrecy and spatial concealment combined with the legal ban of its use, which is anchored in national and supranational legislation and international conventions. As with other forms of state violence, torture is relegated to "other spaces" that are beyond the public eye.[34]

Likewise, police torture of African American suspects and prisoners in the South of the early and mid-twentieth century took place in spatial seclusion. Archival files often mention "small cells" in concealed areas of police stations, sheriffs' offices, and jails, including basements, side wings, and the upper floors of buildings. In other cases, suspects were brought to remote locations outside the station house. Although law enforcement officials generally denied ever employing violent interrogation techniques to coerce confessions, a close look at individual cases reveals that the local rumor mill gave residents of communities in the South ample informal knowledge about the use of torture in their towns and cities.

The concealment of torture had far-reaching consequences for the black population. It facilitated the prevalence of this type of violence and its "routine" use, even for relatively minor offenses like theft, public disorderly conduct, and violations of the segregation regulations.[35] It also meant that convictions were often made on the basis of forced confessions. As will be shown, this practice had particularly devastating consequences when suspects were forced to make confessions within the context of capital crimes. In numerous cases, this resulted in death sentences. The official denial of torture by law enforcement officials and the discriminatory structures of the criminal justice system in the South made it extremely difficult for black defendants to substantiate their allegations of torture and prevent their looming convictions.

Violence and Visibility: A Historical and Cultural Analysis of Torture

Against the background of the concealment of torture in the South, the theoretical and methodical approach of this study focuses on the relationship between violence and visibility. It highlights the extent to which the deliberate concealment of torture helped support the racist system of subjugation in the South and affected the abilities of victims to take a stand against this form of violence.

Studies on the history and sociology of violence have revealed that the public display or strategic concealment of violence has highly diverse and extremely powerful implications.[36] As works like Michel Foucault's *Discipline and Punish* have demonstrated, the abolition of public torture and the emergence of the modern death penalty in the nineteenth century entailed a "new restraint" toward the body of the condemned. Foucault notes that modern death penalty rituals are characterized by the "disappearance of the spectacle" and "the elimination of pain."[37]

The continued existence of the death penalty in the United States shows that the institutionalization of punishment does not necessarily lead to its gradual disappearance. Instead, the relative invisibility of violence and pain in the modern ritual of the death penalty allows the execution of condemned offenders to be cast as a rationalized, regulated, strictly scientific act that does not appear to fly in the face of the professed image of a civilized society. Hence, it is the exclusion of violence from the gaze of the public and the concealment of its grim cruelty that enables the continuity of the death penalty within modern societies.[38] The more recent history of torture reflects this development. Since inflicting unbearable pain stands in stark contradiction to the self-image of modern liberal societies, such acts of brutality are usually accompanied by a "rhetoric of public denial."[39] At the same time, research shows that torture draws its authority and effectiveness from the interplay between official secrecy and a shared knowledge of its use, spread by rumor and innuendo.[40]

This raises one of the key questions of the present work—namely, how the concealed use of torture on African Americans helped sustain the white population's claim to supremacy in the South. Within this context, this book also explores whether there was a connection between the largely secret practice of torture in the South during the 1930s and 1940s and the decline in the number of lynchings of African Americans during this period. Did the concealed use of torture serve to sustain the racist power structures that had previously been maintained by lynching violence? And what specific form of repression did law enforcement officials exercise by carrying out hidden acts of torture?

Furthermore, this book explores why it was only in exceptional cases that the torture of African Americans came to the public's attention in the South, and what implications this had for the anti-torture initiatives of the victims, civil rights organizations, and federal authorities. The starting point here is a reflection on what forms of violence within a society receive critical attention and can thus be potentially called into question and punished. In other words, what are the conditions that regulate whether certain forms of violence against specific individuals can even enter the realm of social perception? This perspective is based on a concept of visibility that has developed in recent years in the areas of visual culture and media studies but also in gender, queer, and dis/ability studies.[41] What these approaches have in common is that they make use of visibility as a "critical category of cultural and social analysis."[42] In connection with the works of Michel Foucault, visibility is understood here as a "product of power-knowledge dispositifs" and as a "product of discursive, institutional, cultural preconditions."[43]

Applying this discourse-theoretical concept of visibility to the topic of violence leads to the question of what forms of violence and what victims, or groups of victims, manage to become the subject of social debate and representation. Who, under what conditions, is capable of making specific forms of violence visible and, in doing so, either questioning or maintaining their legitimacy? This perspective encompasses the recent work of philosopher Judith Butler, who raises the question of what life within specific "frames" is perceived as "grievable" and what life is not.[44] "Who counts as human? What lives count as lives? . . . *What makes for a grievable life?*" Butler comes to the conclusion that the attitudes that people take on certain forms of violence are characterized by culturally coded patterns of perception that determine which subjects and which lives are "recognizable" within a specific cultural order.[45] Accordingly, not all individuals who are subjected to violence can hope to receive the same degree of attention for the suffering they have endured. Instead, the exclusion of certain people from the dominant social order ensures that violence perpetrated against them is the subject of public debate only in exceptional cases and rarely, if ever, results in criminal prosecution.[46]

This is also reflected by the history of the torture of African American prisoners and suspects in the South, which shows that the difficulties of the victims in opposing this form of violence were inextricably linked to their deliberate and structural marginalization within the segregated culture and society of the South. Accordingly, my study highlights the importance of the act of testifying in a courtroom. In "Can the Subaltern Speak?"—a pioneering text of postcolonial theory—Gayatri Chakravorty Spivak asks whether people in colonial power structures who are viewed as subaltern can, in view of the unequal balance of power surrounding them, make themselves heard when voicing their concerns.[47] Hence, my study asks to what extent the accusations of torture raised by African Americans in the courts of the South were heard—that is, acknowledged as legitimate and potentially true allegations. Whose evidence and whose claims to the truth were recognized as credible or simply denied? Or, in a more general sense, to what extent did categorizations and attributions like race, class, and gender determine the opportunities that existed to expose the violence that was endured, make public allegations, and even mete out legal sanctions?[48]

Likewise, *The Color of the Third Degree* examines how, when it came to African American allegations of torture, evidence was trivialized, denied, and invalidated. Recent studies in the area of cultural science have pointed out that evidence is "not as timeless, entrenched, and everlasting as it might appear at first glance."[49] According to historian John Tagg, evidence must be seen as historically contingent and studied with respect to its connections to social power structures: "The very idea of what constitutes evidence has a history. It is a history which implies definite techniques and procedures, concrete institutions, and specific social relations—that is, relations of power."[50]

This insight is highly relevant for the present study because it helps us understand why African American victims of torture, civil rights organizations, and federal agencies in the period between 1930 and 1955 were rarely capable of holding law officers accountable for their use of torture, even in the face of overwhelming evidence against them. Historian Martha Hodes speaks here of the "power of indifference" that prevented African American victims of police brutality and racist riots from receiving justice and allowed the perpetrators to get off scot-free despite documented proof and the resulting visibility of the violence that had been perpetrated.[51] At the same time, this raises the question of how civil rights organizations and federal agencies endeavored to bring crimes of torture to the public's attention and prove that they had been committed despite all the difficulties involved.

What strategies and media were used to document the concealed and largely disavowed practice of torturing black suspects and prisoners and to produce evidence of the allegations that they raised? How did southern judges, defense attorneys, and juries react to and act upon the evidence produced?

In keeping with these methodical-theoretical considerations, the individual chapters of this book examine both the practice of police torture and the different means of rendering it visible. At the heart of this analysis lies the transition between a close-up perspective on individual cases and an overriding perspective that takes into account the continuities and changes in the use of torture and the efforts to put an end to this practice.[52]

The Structure of the Book

The first chapter of this book examines the connections between the torture inflicted by law enforcement officials in the South during the 1930s and 1940s and the decline in the number of lynchings of African Americans during this period. As will be shown based on a case from Mississippi, the use of police brutality and torture was closely linked to the efforts of state authorities to curb lynching violence. The violent extraction of confessions by law enforcement authorities channeled the white population's need for retribution against African American suspects who were accused of committing serious crimes against whites. Furthermore, this case will be used to illustrate the situational dynamics and orchestration of police torture of African American suspects.

Chapter 2 is devoted to how allegations of torture were dealt with during criminal proceedings. The focus here is on the question of the forms and limits of African American testimony before the courts of the South: What verbal and gestural means were employed by African American defendants to substantiate their allegations of torture? What reactions did their testimony prompt in court, and what influence did this have on the verdict?

Chapter 3 then sheds light on the work of the NAACP, which launched a campaign in the mid-1930s against torture and forced confessions in the South. Based on a number of case studies, this chapter examines the campaign's implications for the African American civil rights struggle in the South. What impact did the NAACP campaign have on judicial procedures? To what extent was the documentation of individual cases of torture by local NAACP activists able to challenge local power structures? And what means did the organization use to help raise the American public's awareness of the phenomenon of police torture in the South?

Chapter 4 deals with the selective public outcry over the use of torture in the case of Quintar South, which dates from the early 1940s in Atlanta, Georgia. Here the book examines the textual and visual representations of the case both in black and white newspapers with a local circulation and in the national black press. What impact did the media uproar have on the routine acts of police brutality and torture against African Americans?

Finally, chapter 5 is devoted to a series of investigations, beginning in the early 1940s, that were launched by the U.S. Department of Justice into cases of police torture of black suspects in the South. Based on several case studies that reach into the early 1950s, this chapter explores the implications of these investigations: To what degree did the FBI investigations render torture and its victims more visible? What reactions did the civil rights cases against law enforcement officials elicit among the white population? And what impact did they have on the lives of African Americans?

The conclusion summarizes the study's findings and outlines the continuity of torture in the United States during the second half of the twentieth century. It closes with a look at the present situation and asks what insights and lessons this book can provide for the current struggle against racism and police violence in the United States.

CHAPTER ONE

Police Torture and "Legal Lynchings" in the American South

On March 25, 1931, nine African American youths between the ages of thirteen and nineteen were detained in Paint Rock, Alabama. The arrests were made following scuffles between the young men and a group of white youths on a freight train, which resulted in several of the whites being thrown off the slowly moving train. Immediately thereafter, the police station in Paint Rock was informed of the incident by telegraph and instructed to apprehend the alleged aggressors. After the train came to a halt in Paint Rock, the youths were seized by a group of white citizens and police officers and brought to the jail in Scottsboro. Shortly thereafter, two white women, who had also been riding on the train, alleged that they had been raped by the African American youths. Rumors surrounding the rape allegations quickly made the rounds, and several hundred white men gathered in front of the jail. According to eyewitness reports, the crowd threatened to break down the gate if law enforcement officials failed to hand over the prisoners. Out of fear of an impending lynching, the sheriff of Jackson County called for support from the National Guard. The authorities in Montgomery agreed to provide the requested military support and dispatched a National Guard unit to Scottsboro. It was a number of hours later before the mob in front of the jail finally dispersed.[1]

Just twelve days later, on April 6, 1931, the trial of the nine defendants began in the courthouse in Scottsboro. According to a number of reports, some ten thousand people traveled to the venue to attend the trial. The defendants were escorted from the jail to the courtroom by 118 guardsmen. Afterward, the soldiers lined up in front of the courthouse to prevent the crowd from forcing its way in.[2]

Despite the dubious accusations of the two presumptive rape victims (in a later trial, one of the women said that she had made up the whole story), eight of the nine defendants were initially found guilty and sentenced to death by electrocution. Only the youngest, thirteen-year-old Roy Wright, received a life sentence. In keeping with the customs of the South, the verdict was pronounced by a jury consisting of twelve white men. The accused were not allowed to meet with their public defenders until the day the trial began.

The announcement of the verdict was applauded by the audience in the courtroom and jubilantly cheered by the thousands waiting in front of the courthouse.[3]

The Scottsboro case—which, through a series of appeals and retrials in the 1930s, went on to become the largest and longest series of trials in U.S. history—is of key importance to this book for a number of reasons.

First, it indicates that the racist structures of the justice system in the South were increasingly becoming the focus of national and international attention during this era. After the trial, the conviction of the so-called Scottsboro Boys sparked massive protests in the United States as well as in many European countries, the Caribbean, Latin America, and other parts of the world. One of the main reasons for this was that the NAACP, the Communist Party USA (CPUSA), and the communist legal aid organization International Labor Defense (ILD) were involved in the appeal proceedings after the verdict and called for worldwide expressions of solidarity for the Scottsboro Boys.[4]

Second, the case illustrates the growing capacity of state and local authorities to enforce their monopoly on the use of force in the South during the 1930s. In contrast to what would have probably transpired during the late nineteenth and early twentieth centuries, the nine defendants were not the victims of a lynch mob. The local police took measures to prevent this, and local justice officials assumed responsibility for sanctioning the crime by condemning the accused in an expedited trial conducted shortly after the arrests. The Scottsboro trial thus represents a prime example of the replacement of lynching violence by the institution of the criminal justice system. A number of contemporary observers summarized this development by referring to the court proceedings against the Scottsboro Boys as "legal lynchings." Although the term was initially used by the ILD to draw public attention to the racist procedures used during the Scottsboro trial, it was quickly picked up by civil rights organizations and newspapers to denounce the discriminatory treatment of African American defendants by the criminal justice system of the South.[5]

Third, the Scottsboro trial is an example of the continuity of racial violence within the justice system of the South. Looking back on the ordeal, Clarence Norris, one of the nine Scottsboro Boys, said that after their arrest, they were repeatedly subjected to brutal treatment to intimidate them in the run-up to the trial: "We were . . . handcuffed and beaten. There was nothing we could do. They beat us with rifle butts and anything they could put their hands on while we was handcuffed together."[6] Roy Wright, the youngest of the Scottsboro Boys, said in an interview published two years after the trials in Alabama that during the court proceedings, he was violently coerced into testifying against his eight codefendants: "The trial stopped awhile and the deputy sheriff beckoned me to come out into another room — the room back of the place where the judge was sitting — and I went. They whipped me and it seemed like they was going to kill me. All the time they kept saying, 'Now will you tell?' and finally it seemed like I couldn't stand no more and I said yes."[7] In the 1930s and 1940s, law enforcement officials in the South often resorted to physical and psychological coercive means to force African American suspects to make statements and confessions and secure their convictions in subsequent trials. As will be shown over the following pages, police torture was a dark side to the gradual decline in lynching violence in the South.

Violence and the Culture of Segregation (1865–1930)

Numerous historical studies have shown that the history of the American South is intricately linked to the phenomenon of violence. This is true for both the slavery era and the period following the end of the American Civil War in 1865.[8]

The defeat of the South during the Civil War resulted in the abolition of slavery. With the end of the war, the former slaves received civil rights (1868). Furthermore, African American men were granted voting rights in 1870. Union army troops were stationed in the southern states to guarantee that these rights were enforced. During the Reconstruction era, the black population of the South strove for education, political influence, and economic independence. But their hopes of equal participation in political, social, and economic life were not fulfilled. On the contrary, with the withdrawal of Union troops in 1877, twelve years after the end of the Civil War, the brief phase of social participation for the black population came to an abrupt end. The failure of Reconstruction paved the way for the rise to power of defenders of the traditional order of the Old South and radical proponents of white supremacy, who assumed economic, social, and political control and pursued the renewed disenfranchisement of the African American population.[9]

With the aid of the so-called Jim Crow laws that were passed during the late nineteenth and early twentieth centuries, racially segregated areas were established in official buildings, libraries, parks, restaurants, train stations, and public means of transportation.[10] This segregation of the public sphere made the subordinate social position of African Americans in daily life highly visible and palpable, as historian Robin D. G. Kelley has pointed out: "Jim Crow signs, filthy and inoperable public toilets, white police officers, racial epithets, dark bodies standing in the aisles of half-empty busses, were daily visual and aural reminders of the semicolonial status black people occupied in the Jim Crow South."[11] Furthermore, segregation regulations institutionalized a separate and exceedingly unequal school and university system that was based on "racial" criteria and massively restricted the economic, social, and political opportunities of blacks. The passage of discriminatory voting laws meant that the voting rights of black men were gradually rescinded. A wide range of regulations passed to exclude black citizens from the electoral process, jury duty, and political office ensured that they were forced out of key areas of public and political life. In 1896, the U.S. Supreme Court's landmark decision in *Plessy v. Ferguson* upheld the segregation laws of the South.[12]

In the wake of these developments, a racially structured and profoundly unjust social order took shape in the American South during the late nineteenth century. The lives of African Americans were extremely regulated, and any infringement of legal directives or racially coded rules of conduct was sanctioned with severe punishment. According to historian Grace E. Hale, this led to the formation of a "culture of segregation," in which "racial difference" was incessantly proclaimed and maintained.[13]

At the same time, the gradual emergence of a black middle class and the ongoing demands of African Americans for equality constantly challenged and called into question the notion of white supremacy. One consequence of this was that beginning in the late nineteenth century, the white population of the South increasingly resorted to violence to bolster its claims of white dominance and black subservience. According to historian William Fitzhugh Brundage, white supremacy was a continually contested terrain in which African Americans actively resisted their disenfranchisement. Racist violent practices on the part of the white population were of constitutive significance for this daily struggle. Like no other form of disenfranchisement or oppression, the deliberate violation of the physical integrity of black citizens had the ability to render tangible and symbolically express the absolute claim of white superiority and black inferiority.[14]

During Reconstruction, it was primarily members of the Ku Klux Klan who used violence in a bid to prevent the black population from exercising its newly obtained political rights.[15] In addition, the social system of the Jim Crow South received instrumental support from the justice system and law enforcement agencies. Courts sentenced convicted African American offenders to draconian punishments to maintain racist social structures. Sheriffs and city police officers did their part by violently punishing violations of segregation regulations and implicit racial hierarchies.[16] In a study published in 1944 titled *An American Dilemma*, renowned Swedish sociologist Gunnar Myrdal described the role of police officers in the South as follows: "[The policeman] stands not only for civic order as defined in formal laws and regulations, but also for 'white supremacy' and the whole set of social customs associated with this concept. . . . It is demanded that even minor transgressions of caste etiquette should be punished, and the policeman is delegated to carry out this function."[17] As state representatives of white supremacy, sheriffs, deputy sheriffs, and city police officers occupied a prominent position within the social order of the South. Their actions were aimed at maintaining the prevailing status quo and protecting the privileged economic, social, and political standing of white citizens. Police violence against African Americans played a key role in achieving these objectives. It also served to intimidate the black population and relegate those blacks who were suspected of offenses or showed "signs of insubordination" to their designated "place" within the segregated order.[18] In 1940, African American civil rights activist W. E. B. Du Bois gave the following description of the brutal reign of law enforcement officials: "These districts are not usually protected by police — rather victimized and tyrannized over by them. No one who does not know can realize what tyranny a low-grade white policeman can exercise in a colored neighborhood."[19] But violence against African Americans was more than just an integral element of police tactics to maintain the racist social order.[20] Within social surroundings, too, physical violence was a widespread and everyday means of dealing with conflicts, for example, in family relationships, but also beyond this realm as a means of informally punishing and disciplining subordinates and schoolchildren. Police violence against black prisoners and suspects tied into both this culture of private violence and the traditions of violence surrounding slavery and vigilante justice in the South.[21]

The use of police violence was also linked to spatial and socioeconomic factors. As sociologist Arthur F. Raper found in his unpublished study on the southern police system, African Americans in urban environments were most often victims of deadly police violence. Cities like Birmingham, Jacksonville, and Atlanta had a high potential for conflict, fueled by the steady stream of white and black workers moving to the cities and the ensuing competition between these two groups. Police departments reacted to this situation with a wide-ranging system to control the African American population that included curfews, high incarceration rates, and a large degree of physical violence.[22]

In rural regions, whites had a far greater position of power over the black population, although despite increasing migration to the North from 1930 onward, blacks often represented the majority of the population in the districts of the Black Belt.[23] Bolstered by the legitimization that they received from local white voters, sheriffs and the deputy sheriffs under their command enjoyed a virtually unchecked position of power, as witnessed by the disproportionate number of African American citizens who fell victim to police violence, even for seemingly minor transgressions.[24]

An even more salient feature of the Jim Crow system in the South was the phenomenon of lynching violence, which culminated between 1880 and 1920. Although murders by lynch mobs were widespread in all parts of the United States until the early twentieth century, some 3,900 people lost their lives this way between 1882 and 1946 in the South alone. This means that more than 80 percent of the approximately 4,700 lynchings in the United States in this period took place in the South. Even though members of many different social and ethnic groups, including whites, fell victim to lynchings, these mob killings were first and foremost a manifestation of racism against blacks. In more than 80 percent of all documented lynchings in the South, the victims were African Americans, usually men, although women were also lynched. The murderous frenzy reached its peak in the 1890s, when an average of 104 blacks were killed each year by lynch mobs.[25]

These lynchings often occurred in public places, like market squares, where members of the local white population actively took part in mutilating and murdering the victims. They were often staged according to a carefully orchestrated script and acted out in front of hundreds, if not thousands, of spectators. Hale summarizes the course of a so-called spectacle lynching as follows:

> The well-choreographed spectacle opened with a chase or jail attack, followed rapidly by the public identification of the captured African American by the alleged white victim or the victim's relatives, announcements of the upcoming event to draw the crowd, and selection and preparation of the site. The main event began with a period of mutilation—often including emasculation—and torture to extract confessions and entertain the crowd, and built to a climax of slow burning, hanging, and/or shooting to complete the killing. The finale

consisted of frenzied souvenir gathering and display of the body and the collected parts.[26]

The main characteristic of spectacle lynchings was that the acts of physical violence against black victims were carried out openly and generally exhibited to the public.[27] This led to the unfurling of a "spectacle of violence," in which people from all walks of life took part. The use of modern technologies and media, such as the preparation and sale of lynching photographs and the announcement of lynchings on radio stations, serves as an indication that this seemingly archaic ritual was closely connected to the emerging consumer society in the South.[28]

The lynchings served the purpose of constantly reaffirming and performatively demonstrating the purported racial difference between the white and the African American population in publicly visible acts of violence. The ritual of the lynching expressed the notion of an unassailable alliance of the white population of the South, who united against the alleged black criminal to assert their claim of supremacy over the African American population.[29]

The goal was to discipline landless blacks who eked out a living as sharecroppers and constituted the majority of the population in many rural regions of the Deep South. Likewise, lynchings served the function of channeling the multitude of frightful images and stereotypes that spread among the white population of the South after slavery was abolished. Now that blacks were no longer restrained by the yoke of slavery, many whites felt that they had to use all means at their disposal to preserve and protect the purity of the "white race." A particularly prominent role was played here by the widespread image of the lascivious black man who, according to the stereotype, had been unleashed upon the white population after he was freed from the bondage of slavery. During the late nineteenth century, this conjured a hysterical wave of fear of possible sexual assaults upon white women, which found its expression in the terrifying image of the unbridled, brutish, black rapist and the figure of the southern belle—the iconographic incarnation of the "pure" and "innocent" southern woman—who was purportedly the object of the black man's sexual desire.[30]

A wide range of works have shown that categories like race, class, and gender were closely connected with the phenomenon of lynchings.[31] By collectively punishing alleged African American rapists, white men reaffirmed their own masculinity along with their claim to racial purity and white superiority. As indicated in Hale's previously cited description of the spectacle of mob violence, lynchings within the context of rape allegations were often accompanied by the genital mutilation of the accused—a symbolic act committed by the lynch mob with the intention of negating the masculinity of the black victim and, at the same time, celebrating their own white manliness. Moreover, the victim's emasculation expressed an implicit warning to white women that they should under no circumstances violate the strict code of conduct of the patriarchal society of the South. According to historian Jacquelyn Dowd Hall, the nascent rape myth of the late nineteenth century served as an instrument of racist and sexual oppression that was used to regulate the behavior of both black men and white women. It allowed white men to stylize themselves as patriarchs, avengers, and protectors of white women. What's more, the patriarchal defense of "southern white womanhood" went hand in hand with the desire to control the sexual behavior of white women and prevent any possible voluntary liaisons between white women and black men.[32] In contrast to the myth of the black rapist, which was long exploited as a means of justifying the widespread lynching violence against African American men, historical studies have shown that only some of the lynching victims were accused of rape or attempted rape. The alleged murder of white individuals by black perpetrators also evoked the notion of a threatened racial order, which was to be restored through lynching. Furthermore, even petty crimes and violations of the racist code of etiquette could lead to lynchings.[33]

The Decline in Lynchings and the Transformation of Racial Violence

Already during the late nineteenth and early twentieth centuries, African American civil rights activists like Ida B. Wells (1863–1931) and W. E. B. Du Bois (1868–1963) soundly condemned the practice of lynching violence in the South as "barbaric" and "backwards." Furthermore, the NAACP launched a broad public campaign against lynching in the 1910s and, over the following decades, vehemently urged the passage of a law that would allow federal authorities to prosecute lynching cases in the South. Despite these efforts, the legal initiatives of the NAACP failed repeatedly in the U.S. Congress due to resistance from southern senators.[34]

During the 1910s and to a greater degree from 1920 onward, the white elite of the South voiced growing criticism of the practice of lynching. This changed attitude was a result of the economic modernization taking place in the region, which was accompanied by efforts to bolster the business and political ties between the southern and northern states along with an increasing orientation among the southern white middle and upper classes toward the cultural values of the North. Members of the growing white middle class as well as politicians, academics, business leaders, and church representatives began to argue that lynchings called into question the reputation and self-proclaimed progressive character of the New South.[35]

This led in 1930 to the establishment of the Association of Southern Women for the Prevention of Lynching (ASWPL). Under the leadership of Jessie Daniel Ames, these white women activists worked primarily in church circles. In their tireless work against lynching, these women disputed the traditional rationalization of this form of violence as a means of protecting white women and argued that white men were using the "code of chivalry" merely as a pretext to justify violence against African Americans. In doing so, they challenged the racial concepts and sexual fears that had served as the cornerstone for the lynching tradition since the late nineteenth century.[36]

The women who were organized under the banner of the ASWPL used their many contacts via social institutions and churches to win support for their anti-lynching campaign. One measure was to publicly call on white women to dissuade their husbands from taking part in lynching. They also appealed to political officials and law enforcement authorities to take concrete action against lynching violence. For instance, they urged sheriffs to sign a declaration in which they vowed to intercede to prevent lynching, and they endorsed sheriff candidates who publicly spoke out against lynching. The growing public criticism by the white elite and the campaign work of the ASWPL ultimately bore fruit, and sheriffs and police officers increasingly made efforts to avert lynching during the 1920s and 1930s.[37]

Historian Manfred Berg explains this decline in lynching violence as the result of the increasing enforcement of the state's monopoly on the use of force in the South. He backs up this assertion by citing statistical surveys by the Commission on Interracial Cooperation, an Atlanta-based liberal reform institution with primarily white but also black members that, after its establishment in 1919, was dedicated to promoting "interracial" cooperation and had local chapters in several southern states.[38] The data show that 1920 was the first year in which more lynchings were averted than carried out. Between 1932 and 1942, a total of 290 lynchings were prevented by law enforcement authorities.[39] What's more, the absolute number of lynchings continually declined during the 1920s. As previously mentioned, more than one hundred African Americans were lynched every year during the 1890s. During the 1910s, lynching violence claimed an average of fifty-five lives a year and in

the 1920s the annual death toll declined to twenty-five victims. After a renewed increase in lynchings at the beginning of the Great Depression in the
early 1930s, the annual average was still ten victims; however, the numbers sharply declined toward the end of the 1930s.[40]

Studies dating from this period show that sheriffs and police officers were
still tolerating lynchings or even cooperating with lynch mobs during the
early 1930s.[41] The rising number of prevented lynchings beginning in the
1920s, however, indicate that law enforcement authorities in the South were
generally taking initiatives to protect black suspects from being seized by
lynch mobs. The most common method was to whisk the suspects to remote
jails without the public getting wind of the move. This was supported by the
introduction of police cars that, in contrast to trains, made it possible to
transport the prisoners quickly and unobtrusively. In some cases, sheriffs and
police officers used force to stop lynch mobs. Furthermore, local law enforcement authorities increasingly called on state militias to disperse lynch mobs
and subdue local unrest.[42]

This trend does not mean that white southern society had relinquished
its presumptive right to impose harsh punishments on suspected African
American perpetrators. Instead, the growing enforcement of the state's
monopoly on the use of force meant that retribution was increasingly meted
out by the courts. For black defendants who were accused of murdering or
raping whites, this development was a two-edged sword. Although the timely
intervention of law enforcement officials may have saved them from the
clutches of white lynch mobs, they often could hope for little more than a
show trial. As demonstrated by the trial of Arthur Ellington, Ed Brown, and
Henry Shields, which will be closely examined later in this chapter, suspects
were often indicted shortly after their arrest and swiftly convicted and sentenced to death in an emotionally heated courtroom atmosphere.[43]

This development is reflected in numerous research papers. In his study
of the state of Kentucky, historian George Wright comes to the conclusion
that the number of executions of blacks carried out during the first decades
of the twentieth century continually rose, while the number of lynchings
steadily declined during the same period. Likewise, the findings of political
scientist James W. Clarke show a clear correlation in the 1920s and 1930s between the declining lynching violence and the growing number of convicted
African Americans offenders who were executed by state authorities. The
available statistical data on the number of executions carried out in the United
States between 1930 and 1970 also suggest that the dwindling number of
lynchings was tied to the growing use of the death penalty. For example,

there was a sharp increase in the number of African Americans executed for the crime of rape during this period, while the number of lynchings and the absolute number of executions continually declined.[44]

Although there is no conclusive evidence to support the theory that lynching violence was gradually replaced by the death penalty, it can be said that the legal system in the South increasingly assumed the function of maintaining social control over the black population during the early twentieth century.[45] It was now the courts and the state death penalty system that essentially satisfied the white population's need for retribution against African American offenders, which had earlier been expressed through lynching violence.[46]

As mentioned earlier, the term "legal lynchings" was coined in the early 1930s in the wake of the Scottsboro case. In a study published in 1933, sociologist Arthur Raper noted that lynchings were often prevented by making it clear to the public that it could rely on a swift conviction of the alleged offenders. Under such conditions, defendants had virtually no chance of getting a fair and impartial trial. As Raper concluded, "It is not incorrect to call a death sentence secured under such circumstances a 'legal lynching.'"[47]

Historian Michael J. Pfeifer has shown that during the early twentieth century, the raw violence of southern lynch mobs, which the public increasingly viewed as atavistic, was gradually replaced by courtroom convictions and state-sanctioned executions. By campaigning for an "effective" criminal justice system, the proponents of legal procedures slowly but surely gained the upper hand over the supporters of spontaneous forms of violent retribution. Southern politicians who increasingly spoke out against lynching during the 1920s and 1930s saw the swift and efficient use of the death penalty as a key means of curbing "barbaric" and "uncivilized" mob violence. Newspaper articles praised the rapid execution of death penalties as proof that the arbitrary violence of lynchings had been replaced by the rule of law and order.[48]

However, as historian Jürgen Martschukat has pointed out, none of this meant that established racist patterns of thought and action had disappeared. Instead, the growing rejection of lynching violence went hand in hand with efforts to restructure and strengthen the death penalty system. Particular emphasis was placed on the electric chair, which purportedly heralded a more civilized approach to violence, cruelty, and the quest for justice. In contrast to the usual practice of angry mobs exacting violent retribution for alleged transgressions, it promised a state-regulated, quick, and allegedly painless death for execution candidates, the majority of whom were African

Americans. Hence, the introduction of the electric chair helped maintain the racially structured social order of the American South.[49]

The decline in lynchings during the 1930s and 1940s should thus be seen not as an indication of modernization but as a complex and convoluted process that involved the transformation of racial forms of violence. As historian Lisa Lindquist Dorr noted in her study of rape trials of African American men in Virginia between the years 1900 and 1960, the reduction in lynching violence did not put an end to racial violence; instead, it merely "became less visible, routinized, and subordinated to the grim ritual of courtroom procedure."[50]

Furthermore, historian Ethan Blue has shown that the customary periodization of lynching violence, which generally extends from 1880 to the late 1930s, matches extremely well with an interpretation based on the modernization theory of American history during the twentieth century. Indeed, he argues in favor of examining the various forms of state and extrajudicial violence, along with their commonalities and continuities beyond the 1930s, to decipher the key role of violence in the formation of the modern American state.[51] Historian Bruce Baker also surmises that the decline in the number of lynchings was not accompanied by a reduction in violent racist attacks but rather that these acts were "fragmented in many different forms" of violence that enjoyed "varying levels of community sanction."[52]

The NAACP archives consulted within the scope of this study support this supposition. The case files of the NAACP's legal department from the period between 1910 and 1955 provide evidence that suggests that law enforcement officials frequently resorted to torture from the 1930s onward in order to obtain forced confessions and ensure swift convictions of African American defendants. This was the source of numerous complaints filed during the 1930s and 1940s.[53] The cases registered by the NAACP under the category of "forced confessions" point to a connection between the decline in lynching violence and the practice of torture by police. The records document a total of fifty-one cases from the South in which African American defendants accused police officers and sheriffs of using torture to obtain forced confessions between 1930 and 1955. Most of the incidents took place in Georgia (with a total of nine cases), Mississippi (eight), and Alabama (seven), followed by South Carolina (six), Texas (five), Florida (five), and Louisiana (four).[54] In three-quarters of the registered cases, the allegations of torture were made by black defendants who stood trial on charges of raping or murdering white victims. In 43 percent of these cases (a total of 22), they were accused of rape or attempted rape, and in 31 percent (a total of 16), of murder.[55]

Thus, allegations of torture were raised primarily within the context of crimes that traditionally sparked a lynching.[56] These figures reveal a dark side of the decline in lynching. They show that as law enforcement officials gradually enforced the state's monopoly on the use of force in the South, they increasingly relied on methods of torture to obtain forced confessions and secure convictions of suspected offenders.

"A Speedy Trial": The Case of Brown, Ellington, and Shields

The case of Brown, Ellington, and Shields, which was tried in the early 1930s in Kemper County, Mississippi, is particularly well-suited to an analysis of the developments that accompanied the gradual disappearance of lynching. Kemper County, located on the coastal plain of the Gulf of Mexico on the border to Alabama, was a relatively sparsely populated rural area. In 1930, only 888 people lived in the county seat, DeKalb, and the entire county had a population of only 21,881. The closest major town was Meridian, to the south in Lauderdale County. A contemporary observer described Kemper County as even poorer than the poorest areas of neighboring Alabama: "It has poorer railroad connections, fewer miles of improved highways, smaller towns, poorer schools, and cruder human relations."[57] As in other districts of the so-called Black Belt, African Americans constituted the majority of the population. Most worked as sharecroppers on the cotton and corn plantations of white farmers.[58]

While the state of Mississippi holds the sad record of the highest number of lynchings in any U.S. state, with 574 lynchings between 1882 and 1951, on a district level, it is Kemper County that holds this dubious honor: twice as many people were lynched there as the average in other areas of Mississippi. This earned the county the nickname "Bloody Kemper."[59]

In September 1930, two African Americans were lynched after having been arrested on suspicion of robbing a white married couple outside of Wahalak. According to a statement made by the husband, they were attacked and robbed by three black men late in the evening. The husband stated that before the men fled, they had threatened to kill him and rape his wife. During the ensuing search for the perpetrators, the white population requested support from local law enforcement officials and used bloodhounds to track the fugitives from the scene of the crime to their home. Shortly thereafter, twenty-one-year-old Pig Lockett and nineteen-year-old Holly White were arrested and brought to the jail in DeKalb. Two days later, when the suspects were to be arraigned before a local judge, the police car transporting them was stopped and the men were dragged out of the car by a mob of twenty to thirty masked individuals. The two lawmen in the vehicle later maintained that the crowd had overwhelmed them and tied them to a tree, rendering all resistance futile. The mob tied nooses around the necks of the two men and attached the ends of the ropes to a thinner tree, whose treetop had been pulled downward with ropes. Then the tree was released to the point that the accused were pulled up into the air by their necks before they were let down again and asked to make a confession. After the two men refused to confess to the crime, eyewitnesses said that the procedure was repeated until the victims were both dead. No member of the mob faced legal action following these events. As was so often the case with lynchings in the South, the routinely conducted investigation of the incident by a local grand jury failed to produce any results. According to local hearsay, "some young white men around Wahalak" killed the third African American involved in the alleged attack shortly after the arrest of Lockett and White.[60]

The lynching of Lockett and White shows that even during the early 1930s, the white population of Kemper County could still lynch people at will without having to fear any major repercussions from local law enforcement authorities. But it was a different story just three and a half years later with the case of the murder of a white farmer, Raymond Stuart.[61]

On March 30, 1934, sixty-year-old Raymond Stuart was found severely wounded at his home in the town of Scooba in Kemper County. He had received numerous cuts and blows to the body, leaving no doubt that the farmer and landowner had been the victim of a violent crime. Stuart, who was described by local newspapers as a "prominent member of the community," died of his wounds on the way to the hospital, without regaining consciousness.[62]

Immediately after news of the attack broke, a search was launched for the perpetrators. According to the *Daily Clarion-Ledger*—a local newspaper published in Jackson—a crowd of some two hundred people had assembled in front of the victim's home even before the sheriff of Kemper County, J. D. Adcock, arrived at the scene with a number of deputy sheriffs. Bloodhounds were brought in to aid in the search for the killers, but the large crowd prevented the dogs from being able to pick up a scent.[63]

Shortly after the arrival of law enforcement officials, thirty-year-old Ed Brown, a black farmhand on Stuart's farm, was arrested and brought to the country jail in DeKalb.[64] One day later, city police officers from Meridian and deputy sheriffs from the Kemper County Sheriff's Department arrested a second suspect—twenty-seven-year-old Henry Shields, who lived in the vicinity of the Stuart home—and brought him to the jail in Meridian, the administrative capital of neighboring Lauderdale County, some thirty miles away. That very same day, Sheriff Adcock transferred Brown to the jail in Meridian.[65]

On April 2, 1934, three days after the discovery of the mortally wounded Stuart, the local press reported that both suspects had confessed to the murder. During questioning, which was attended by law enforcement officials from the neighboring cities of Meridian and Scooba, along with members of the Kemper County Sheriff's Department, the two suspects purportedly confessed to the murder and provided a detailed account of the crime.[66] The *Meridian Star* reported extensively on the content of the purported confessions. According to the newspaper, the suspects admitted that robbery was the motive for the crime. They had apparently attacked Stuart in his sleep and then hit him over the head with an ax. Before fleeing the scene of the crime, the perpetrators reportedly tried, but failed, to set the victim's house on fire.[67]

The next day, the press broke the news of the arrest of another suspect who also lived near the Stuart home, twenty-year-old Arthur "Yank" Ellington, who shortly thereafter reportedly confessed to taking part in the crime. The three suspects then reportedly repeated their confessions in the presence of the sheriffs of Kemper County and Lauderdale County, Sheriff J. D. Adcock and Sheriff B. M. Stephens, and "even corrected each other" as they told their stories.[68] Local law enforcement officials thus provided extensive information to the public during the course of an ongoing investigation. The confession was announced presumably in a bid to appease the local white community, defuse the volatile atmosphere, and prevent the formation of a lynch mob.

In fact, shortly after the arrests, there were "persistent reports and rumors" that a lynch mob was on its way to the county jail in Meridian to take possession of the prisoners. According to a report in the *Meridian Star*, this prompted the sheriff of Lauderdale County to take "precautionary measures." The article went on to say that the jail was being guarded by a large number of deputy sheriffs who were posted inside and at strategic points outside the building to detect any possible attacks early on and, if need be, repel them. Armed with machine guns, shotguns, and tear-gas grenades, the sheriffs and police officers had reportedly transformed the jail into an "armed fort." The authorities also considered calling in the National Guard for support if the situation should escalate.[69]

Public order was apparently under threat. The local police reacted to this state of emergency by taking two measures. First, they launched a massive mobilization to prevent a lynching. Second, immediately after arresting the suspects, they resorted to means of torture to exact confessions and pave the way for a speedy conviction of the alleged perpetrators.

Furthermore, according to the *Meridian Star*, after the arrest of the three suspects, several unnamed "officials and others" were calling for a "speedy trial for the suspected blacks" as this "would go a long way toward removing any apprehension of attempted violence on the part of the allegedly enraged citizens of Kemper."[70] It is also revealing that even before the trial of Brown, Ellington, and Shields was completed there was talk of a possible execution date should the three defendants be found guilty: "It is believed by officials . . . that if the three blacks are convicted they will be at once sentenced to be hanged at the earliest date allowed under the law. It was thought that the execution could take place on Friday, May 11."[71] After the three suspects were officially indicted by the local grand jury on April 4, 1934, the trial commenced the very next day. To prevent the defendants from being attacked, it was not until the morning before the start of the trial that they were escorted to DeKalb under the protection of numerous police officers and deputy sheriffs armed with machine guns. The court appointed two public defenders as their counsel. After one and a half days of court proceedings, the all-white jury convened for only thirty minutes before it returned its verdict and found the defendants guilty of the murder of Raymond Stuart. Upon receiving the jury's verdict, the presiding judge, J. I. Sturdivant, sentenced the defendants to be hanged. In line with previous speculation in the press, he set the execution date for May 11, 1934.[72] Immediately thereafter, the condemned men were escorted in a police convoy back to the jail in Meridian and placed in the execution cell there.[73]

The *Meridian Star* reported that the witness testimonies and evidence presented by the district attorney had proven without a doubt that the three suspects were guilty. No mention was made of the allegations of torture that the three defendants leveled against the police during the court proceedings. Instead, the newspaper emphasized that the swift action of the judge in arraigning the suspects and expediting the trial had "met with approval of Kemper citizens." The article went on to say that this had dispelled "any apprehension" of possible imminent violent actions by a mob.[74]

In an editorial published two days after the verdict, the actions of the law enforcement agencies were explicitly praised. Under the headline "Kemper Proves Itself," the commentary maintained that the case had been "handled expeditiously," with "due justice to the accused" and due consideration for the "social order." It went on: "Talk of mob violence has been rampant.

Nevertheless, due to the cooperation of Sheriff Jim Adcock of Kemper, and Brice M. Stephens of Meridian, mobocracy has been eliminated and the law has taken its judicial course. Apparently, the negroes have enjoyed a fair, impartial trial." The newspaper went on to say that the Kemper County incident served to prove that "group action [i.e., mob lynching] is unneeded when courts are 'on the job,'—that justice is at least more certain through due 'process of law' than through the uncertainties of mass impetuosity." "Kemper," the commentary added, "proves its fundamental fairness not through mobocracy, but through established agents of justice. A few more like examples of swift and certain retribution—and 'rabble' illegality will disappear throughout the south."[75]

The editorial reflected the opinion that only an unyielding and efficient judicial system could replace the lynchings, and that only the swift sentencing and execution of African American defendants would satisfy the pressing need of the local white population for retribution. The Stuart case thus reveals in an exemplary manner that the intensified efforts to enforce the state's monopoly on the use of force led to a situation in which law enforcement authorities and the courts had to fill a vacuum that was created by the campaigns to curb lynching violence.

A glance at the court transcript in the case against Brown, Ellington, and Shields shows that this development by no means meant that the use of racially motivated violence had abated. On the contrary, as in numerous other cases in the South during the 1930s and 1940s, it was only shortly after the arrest of the three men that the police resorted to methods of torture to force confessions out of the suspects. This came to light during the court proceedings, in which the defendants repeatedly professed their innocence and gave detailed testimony of the torments that they had suffered. Remarkably, several police officers openly admitted during the trial to having beaten the suspects during the investigation. The trial transcript provides an unusually direct insight into the practice of torture: how the African American suspects suffered from it and how local law enforcement authorities sought to legitimize it.[76] The testimonies of Brown, Ellington, and Shields make it possible to analyze torture as a performance in which language and violence were used to proclaim and maintain claims to power.[77]

The Performance of Torture

The trial of Brown, Ellington, and Shields before the Kemper County circuit court began with the statements of a number of witnesses called by the prosecution. After eyewitnesses and physicians had described the physical state of the victim after the discovery of the crime, district attorney John C. Stennis began by presenting as evidence a pair of overalls belonging to Henry Shields that allegedly had traces of blood from the victim. Furthermore, the presumptive murder weapon, an ax that was found not far from the scene of the crime, was entered into the record as evidence.[78] Of key importance to the strategy of the prosecution, however, were the confessions by the three defendants, which were entered into the record over the objections of the public defenders. The lawyers for the defense protested that allowing the confessions to be used as evidence was a violation of the applicable Mississippi laws, which stipulated that a confession had to be made in a "free and voluntary" manner. Judge J. I. Sturdivant had the jury temporarily removed from the courtroom while the question of the legal admissibility of the confessions was discussed. He then called the sheriff of Kemper County, J. D. Adcock, to the witness stand. Adcock testified that the defendants had made their confessions in a free and voluntary manner, although he did admit that Henry Shields had told him that he had been beaten with a strap. "One of the boys, Shields I believe, came in limping, and he kind of got on the box easy and looked like he was excited. I said, 'Henry, sit on that box,' and he said, 'I can't; they strapped me pretty hard.' I said, 'Make yourself comfortable; nobody is going to hurt you at all. All of us are here for your protection.'"[79] Following a question by the defense, Adcock testified that he did not pursue Shields's remark any further.[80] Despite renewed objections by the defense, Judge Sturdivant ruled that the presumptive confessions by Brown, Ellington, and Shields were admissible as evidence.[81] He thus adopted an approach that had been pursued in many other trials of black defendants during the 1930s and 1940s in the South. Confessions were often the most conclusive and, in the eyes of the jury, most compelling evidence presented by the prosecution.[82] This explains why judges presiding over murder and rape trials shied away from excluding questionable confessions by black defendants. In doing so, they apparently reacted to the public's demand for swift justice for the crimes committed, which could be achieved primarily with the aid of confessions.

The judge then summoned the jurors back into the courtroom and called on Sheriff Adcock to recapitulate the confessions of the three defendants in the presence of the jury.[83] Adcock stated that during questioning, the three defendants initially accused each other, but then confessed that they had committed the crime together. He went on to say that Ed Brown and Arthur Ellington seemed particularly relieved afterward: "I asked them if they had told the truth and all the truth, and they said that they had. This little boy on the end, Ellington, I believe he was smiling. He said, 'Yes, sir. I feel a whole lot better.' He asked one of the gentlemen there for a cigarette. I said, 'Any man who tells the truth feels better.' I said, 'What about you, Ed?,' and he said, 'Yes, sir, I feel a heap better.' I said, 'What about you, Henry?' and he wouldn't answer."[84] When the Sheriff from Lauderdale County, Brice M. Stephens, was called to the witness stand, his testimony confirmed Adcock's statements.[85] The prosecution also called the Reverend Eugene Stevens to the witness stand. The cleric testified that at the time of the confessions of the three defendants, he was at the jail at Meridian. Stevens said that all three men had freely and voluntarily admitted to their involvement in the crime, without any coercion. The clergyman made no effort to hide his prejudices against the three defendants, referring to them as "darkies": "The two darkies, Shields and Ellington, went in a side entrance by a chimney, I think. He [Ed Brown] went around and waited in the hall and met them there. You couldn't tell just exactly what part he performed, but he did admit that he struck him [Raymond Stuart] across the shoulders with a stick at some time."[86] According to Reverend Stevens, all three men had confessed to the crime during questioning: "In the main, that is all I heard, that they were the ones that did it and no one else. . . . They said there was no other motive except getting the money."[87]

After the witnesses for the prosecution, Ed Brown was called to the witness stand as the first defendant to testify on the charges brought against him. He denied having anything to do with the murder. In response to the question of why he nevertheless made a confession, Brown testified that after his arrest he had been subjected to violent treatment, above all by Deputy Sheriff Cliff Dial, to force him to admit to the crime:

He told me to come on out here, that he had heard I told I killed Mr. Raymond. I come out of the jail house and I said, "I declare I didn't kill Mr. Raymond." He said, "Come on in here and pull your clothes off; I am going to get you." I said to the last that I didn't kill him. There was two more fellows about like that here and they was whipping me. They had me behind across chairs kind of like that. I said I didn't kill him, and they said put it on him again, and they hit so hard I had to say, "Yes, sir." Mr. Cliff [Dial] said, "Give it [the strap] to me, and I will get it." He took it, and it had two buckles on the end. They stripped me naked and bent me over a chair and I just had to say it; I couldn't help it.[88]

As the court transcript shows, Brown supported his testimony by pointing to the injuries from the blows to his body:

Q: They whipped you hard there?
A: Yes, sir. I will show you. There are places all the way up.
Q: Did you bleed any?
A: Did I bleed? I sure did.[89]

Brown testified that after Dial had forced him to confess, he threatened him with additional beatings if he recanted his statement.[90] Furthermore, he emphatically maintained that he did not kill Raymond Stuart: "If I die right now, I am going to say it: I ain't never harmed Mr. Raymond in my life. If they want to they can kill me because I said that, but I ain't never harmed Mr. Raymond."[91] Ed Brown's testimony indicates that even in the courtroom, he feared for his personal safety.

Afterward, Henry Shields was called to the witness stand. He also testified that after his arrest he had been whipped by Deputy Sheriff Cliff Dial in the Meridian jail. Shields said that due to the relentless whipping, he eventually gave a false confession and declared that he had had a hand in Stuart's murder: "Mr. Cliff Dial and them come back that evening and whipped me. First I tried to tell the truth, but he wouldn't let me. He said, 'No, you ain't told the truth,' and I tried to stick to it. He whipped me so hard I had to tell him something."[92] Ellington, who was subsequently called to the stand, also testified that he was innocent and had been forced to confess. He stated that shortly after word of Stuart's murder started making the rounds, he was seized by a mob of roughly twenty people, several of whom were employees of the sheriff, including the previously mentioned Cliff Dial. He said that the men had tied him to a tree and whipped him.[93] He went on to say that a rope, which had been thrown over a tree limb, was then tied around his neck, and the members of the mob pulled him up in the air twice to force him to divulge information about the murder.[94] In response to a question by his lawyer, Ellington backed up the allegations by pointing to the scars on his neck:

Q: What is the mark on your neck?
A: That's where they pulled me up to the limb twice.
Q: That was done with a rope?
A: Yes, sir.
Q: They pulled you up twice on a limb?
A: Yes, sir.

Q: Did it hurt you?

A: Yes, sir.

Q: When they let you down, could you stand?

A: Yes, sir.

Q: How long did they keep you swinging up there?

A: Not so long.[95]

Ellington testified that despite the prolonged physical abuse, he denied any involvement in the crime, after which the men released him: "They turned me loose and told me to go home, and I could just go home."[96] He said that it was not until the next day that he was arrested by Dial and other law enforcement officials and taken toward Meridian via a detour into nearby Alabama. After they crossed the border to Alabama, he said that the men stopped the car and Dial whipped him so long that he confessed to the crime out of fear that he would have to endure more blows:

A: They took me out and whipped me again and told me to tell what I knowed about it.

Q: Who did?

A: Mr. Cliff.

Q: What did you tell him?

A: I had to tell him. He asked who had the chisel, and he said I had it. I told him I didn't, and he kept on beating me until I had to say I had it.[97]

Arthur Ellington's testimony makes it clear that police officers and local residents worked together to force confessions out of suspects using forms of violence that were reminiscent of the lynching ritual.[98]

The Audience and Language of Torture

While Ellington testified that he had been whipped on the other side of the Alabama state line, Shields and Brown stated that they had been tortured in the Meridian jail. The acts of violence thus occurred in locations that tended to be secluded from the eyes of locals. But police officials were apparently not the only individuals to have knowledge of the torture. A courtroom statement by Henry Shields suggests that segments of the local white population knew about the torture of suspects at the Meridian jail. In response to the question of who saw him in his jail cell on the day of his arrest, he said,

"A lot of people come there."[99] Shields and Brown also testified that the torture sessions were witnessed by a number of Raymond Stuart's neighbors as well as individuals who were unknown to them.[100]

The files in the archives of the NAACP contain numerous references to rumors and unofficial reports of acts of torture taking place outside the public eye.[101] Literary scholar Jan-Philipp Reemtsma has noted that the impact of torture as a method of exerting domination over others is fueled by the dynamic relationship between its concealment and the clandestine knowledge of its use: "A key element of the dissemination of terror is the moment of concealment, yet it cannot be so veiled that it is entirely imperceptible."[102] This also played a role in the torture of African American suspects. While the police—presumably out of fear of legal sanctions or a court ruling that would have invalidated the confessions—went to great lengths to conceal their torture sessions and conducted them in locations that remained beyond the gaze of the public, officials also allowed knowledge of these acts to leak to an audience outside the prison walls. In doing so, they undoubtedly intended to send the message to the local white and black communities that the investigations of the suspects were being pursued with all available means. Likewise, it stands to reason that this informal disclosure of torture practices was calculated as a means of deterring African Americans from committing crimes and demonstrating the state's monopoly on the use of force.

The medium of language played a key role in demonstrations of power and dominance during the torture sessions. A revealing example of this is the statement by Deputy Sheriff Cliff Dial, previously cited from Ed Brown's testimony: "He said, 'Come on in here and pull your clothes off; I am going to get you.'"[103] By commanding the suspect to get undressed, the white officer aimed to establish a hierarchical relationship between himself and the prisoner and, at the same time, asserted his ostensible right to unfettered control over his captive's body. The deputy sheriff's domineering tone set the stage for the claim of white superiority and black servitude right at the start of the brutal interrogation session.

In addition, the subsequent statements by Ed Brown illustrate the closely intertwined nature of language and violence during the torture: "They put me down three times. Two times I said, 'No, sir.' Until the last time I said, 'I ain't never harmed Mr. Stewart in my life.' They said, 'Get down again.' He [Cliff Dial] took the strop away from that little fellow and it looked like he was going to kill me, and I said, 'Yes, sir.' He said, 'What about the lamp?' I said, 'I don't know.' He said, 'Put him down again,' and I said, 'Yes, sir.' He was whipping me so hard I had to say 'yes, sir.'"[104] The verbally and tangibly conveyed absolute authority, including the threats, was an integral component of the orchestration of the torture and directly linked to the use of physical violence.[105] Judith Butler has pointed out that the verbal threat of violence is directly and intrinsically related to its actual use: "The threat begins the action by which the fulfillment of the threatened act might be achieved."[106] This connection is very clearly expressed in an additional statement by the defendant Ed Brown: "He said, 'What did you hit him with?,' and I said, 'Nothing.' He said: 'What did you hit him with, or I will beat you to death.' I said, 'A stick.' He said, 'No,' and I said, 'A foot ax.'"[107] By threatening to kill the suspect if he refused to confess, the deputy sheriff took his claim of superiority over his black victim to a new level. In doing so, he demonstrated the absolute power that he wielded over the suspect's body, whose possible death during the interrogation was not anathema to him.

An analysis of the testimonies of Brown, Ellington, and Shields shows that the torture of African American suspects was an extremely violent and symbolic form of segregation, in which racist claims to power were enacted and affirmed *in actu*.[108] Furthermore, individual statements reveal that the victims experienced the torture as a situation in which they were completely powerless, both physically and mentally.[109] Ed Brown's statement—"He was whipping me so hard I had to say 'yes, sir'"—is a prime example of this.[110]

"We Kind of Warmed Them a Little—Not Too Much": Justifications of Violence

Remarkably, the police officers who were called to the stand to testify made no effort to deny the violence perpetrated during the interrogations and openly admitted to hitting the defendants. They were apparently convinced that the accused would nevertheless be convicted. Moreover, they apparently had no reason to fear any legal consequences for their actions. On the contrary, they indicated that they had acted within the scope of a local system in which physical violence against African American suspects was viewed as an everyday and legitimate means of safeguarding white rule.

One of many revealing examples of this was the testimony of police officer E. L. Gilbert, who, after the testimonies of the three defendants, was called to the stand by the prosecution. In response to a question by one of the lawyers for the defense, he candidly admitted that he had taken part in whipping Ed Brown during the course of the investigation. "We stayed there about an hour and a half I imagine. . . . He was whipped one time but I don't know how many intervals there were. We told him anytime he wanted to talk, we would let him up, and he got up."[111] This statement contains a rationalization of the torture: Gilbert portrayed it as a standard procedure that the defendant could have brought to an end at any time by making a confession. Deputy Sheriff Cliff Dial spoke even more bluntly about the torments inflicted on the accused. In response to the question of whether the prisoners were beaten during interrogations, he said, "We kind of warmed them a little — not too much."[112] In doing so, Dial mockingly attempted to trivialize the treatment of the men in his custody and, at the same time, conveyed the message that law enforcement officials felt perfectly entitled to discipline African American suspects with physical violence and "make them talk." This was confirmed by an additional statement in which he commented on the "questioning" of Arthur Ellington:

Q: . . . Did you strap him some?
A: Yes, sir. He denied it. He said that Ed and them were in it but that he stood around and held the light; and then he finally told what I thought was the truth about the thing.[113]

It appears that Dial saw the use of violence against the black suspects as the only means of bringing out the alleged "truth." Equally revealing is his statement about the actions of the mob that had gathered in front of the house of the murdered Raymond Stuart after the crime had been committed. In response to the question of whether Arthur Ellington had been whipped by the members of the mob, he responded, "Not too much for a negro; not as much as I would have done if it was left to me."[114]

In this statement, he revealed the racial stereotype — already widespread during the nineteenth century — of the African American as an inferior and subhuman being with an "unpredictable" and "recalcitrant" character whose will can only be broken through corporal punishment. His words also reflect the common notion during the slavery era that African Americans had "callous" and "insensitive" bodies and, accordingly, could only be brought under control with violence. As late as the nineteenth century, physicians from the South had maintained that due to their alleged racial inferiority, blacks felt less pain than whites. As historical studies have shown, many slave owners used this notion to justify the physical disciplining and punishment of slaves.[115] Cliff Dial's testimony indicates that even in the 1930s, police officers and sheriffs justified the use of torture by referencing racial stereotypes that can be traced back to the age of slavery in the South. It is also worth noting that the law enforcement officials used whips during the torture — a weapon that was the preferred means of punishing and disciplining slaves during the age of slavery. The use of the whip was therefore highly symbolic and emblematic of the white officers' claim to power over the black suspects.[116]

As the result of the court proceedings against Brown, Ellington, and Shields shows, the candid admissions of law enforcement officials remained, at least for the time being, without consequences. After the conclusion of the proceedings, the lawyers for the defense called on the judge to instruct the jurors on the question of the legal admissibility of the confessions. The judge then told the jurors that they could recognize the so-called confessions as evidence only if they were not the result of "threats, coercion, force or intimidation." Despite these instructions, the jury found the defendants guilty of murder. As local newspapers reported, work immediately began on the construction of gallows in the courtyard of the Kemper Country jail.[117]

And yet it was possible to avert the execution of the three defendants. In February 1936, the U.S. Supreme Court reversed the death sentences of the three defendants. Earlier, the Mississippi Supreme Court had affirmed the convictions on appeal. As will be shown in chapter 3, the hard work and dedication of two Mississippi lawyers — John Clark and Earl L. Brewer — and the legal department of the NAACP ultimately led to the U.S. Supreme Court's review of the case.

THE CASE OF Brown, Ellington, and Shields documents the violent dynamics that tended to emerge as state authorities increasingly asserted their monopoly on the use of force in the South. While law enforcement officials used diverse methods to prevent suspects from being lynched, they also relied on means of torture to ensure that alleged culprits were convicted by local courts. This torture demonstrated the white law enforcement officers' belief that they were entitled to wield absolute power over the black suspects in their custody. At the same time, it aimed to appease the local white population's persistent thirst for vengeance, which was increasingly curbed by efforts to suppress the rule of mob law. Furthermore, the case shows the difficulties that black defendants faced when they attempted to level allegations of torture before the courts of the South. They were accorded subordinate positions, as was particularly apparent in murder and rape trials. Chapter 2 focuses on these situations by examining the means used by African American suspects to substantiate allegations of torture during their trials.

CHAPTER TWO

Torture and African American
Courtroom Testimony

In late November 1941, Walter White, who was the head of the NAACP at the time, received a letter mailed from a prison in the port city of Mobile, Alabama. It was written by Curtis C. Robinson, a twenty-year-old African American who had just been convicted, along with eighteen-year-old Henry Daniels Jr., of raping a white woman and had been sentenced to death by a local court. Robinson wrote that the unjustified allegations of rape had landed him in a hopeless situation: Dear Sir, . . . I'm accused of attacked a white woman here in Mobile, Ala. which I am not guilty of. My people [were] unable to provide me an attorney. So you can understand what I went up against accused of a crime like this one in the south. I didn't have a chance without proper defence. So I was found guilty of criminal[ly] attacking a white woman, which God in heaven I didn't do. I, Curtis Robinson, knowing the law of the south against a colored man attacking a white woman."[1] Robinson's letter illustrates the ongoing explosive nature of racial and gender discourse in the American South during the early 1940s. Indeed, his mention of "the law of the south" clearly indicates that rape allegations against African Americans continued to be ruthlessly sanctioned, which placed black defendants in a highly precarious position in court. This is most clearly expressed in the last paragraph of the letter, in which Robinson appealed to the NAACP officials for legal support: "If I was guilty I wouldn't ask no one['s] help. But as I'm not guilty of the crime, I feel I have a right to live, and also a right to ask someone to help me as I'm unable to help myself."[2]

Robinson's letter bears witness to an understanding of his own powerlessness in the face of a justice system in which black defendants had no chance of receiving a fair and impartial trial. It also documents his efforts to make his claims of innocence heard and to challenge the court ruling. As will be shown, during his trial, Robinson sought in vain to prevent his looming conviction by maintaining his innocence in court and leveling allegations of torture against the police.

The present chapter examines the testimonies of African American defendants and the degree to which their statements were recognized by the courts of the South. In doing so, the text draws inspiration from the ideas of Gayatri Chakravorty Spivak that were outlined in the introduction, namely the extent to which subalterns can "speak" or make themselves heard, and it addresses this by examining how much validity was ascribed to the statements of various individuals in the court cases studied here. Which witnesses were believed and which were not? How did the courts react to African American defendants and witnesses, and what patterns and frameworks were apparent in these reactions?

Racism and Discrimination in the Courtroom

Like many lynchings, trials of blacks who were accused of raping or murdering whites generally followed a specific format. Rather than serve the purpose of justice, these court cases set the stage to publicly degrade the alleged perpetrators and reaffirm racist hierarchies and the patriarchal white gender order. These trials were often of a highly emotionalized character, as reflected in the defamatory statements of district attorneys and the threats by the local white population to lynch the African American defendants. A report from the year 1940 describes the atmosphere in these trials as follows: "One has only to visit a Southern community at a time when some Negro is on trial for the rape or murder of a white person to obtain a vivid picture of the hate and passion and desire for vengeance which is often aroused in the hearts of Southern whites. . . . The air is charged with an undercurrent of tension and there is a feeling of suspense, as if some exiting incident may occur at any moment."[3] In an essay from 1947, British author Rebecca West calls the trials of black defendants in the American South "operas" and draws attention to their performative dimension.[4] Judges, defendants, lawyers for the defense, district attorneys, and juries assumed different roles in these theatrical spectacles. American sociologist Guy B. Johnson summarized the predicament of African American defendants as follows: "When a negro goes into court, he goes with the consciousness that the whole courtroom process is in the hands of the 'opposite race'—white judges, white jurors, white attorneys, white guards, white everything."[5] Judges, district attorneys, and juries served as protectors of white supremacy. They strove to sanction with utmost severity any presumed infractions of the racist power structure of the South. In doing so, racist and gender-coded standards of conduct were invoked and performatively confirmed during the court proceedings.[6] Based on rape trials of African Americans in early and mid-twentieth-century Virginia, Lisa Lindquist Dorr has shown that determining the legal "truth" in these court cases was only of minor importance. "Though [those] legal trials ostensibly sought to ascertain 'The Truth,' in reality they functioned as ritualistic spectacles that diffused the furor usually awakened by the alleged assault. Trials themselves were public performances in which white juries usually . . . acted out their roles as the protectors of white women adhering to a script of sexual and racial ideologies made familiar through Southern rhetoric."[7] African-American defendants played a subordinate role in such trials. As Gunnar Myrdal noted in his previously mentioned study from 1944, a white man's testimony was ordinarily granted "greater reliance" than that of a "Negro." In doing so, the courts followed "an old tradition in the South, from slavery times," when a black person's testimony against a white man "was disregarded." White judges justified their "partisanship" by pointing out that in their experience, blacks were often "unreliable" when they took the stand. Myrdal went on to say that this also fit into a particular "pattern of thinking," whereby it was "dangerous for the social order to allow Negroes to vindicate their rights against white people."[8]

Myrdal's findings reveal the fundamental hurdles faced by African American defendants when they sought to present their view of events in the courtrooms of the South. Nevertheless, an analysis of court transcripts shows that African Americans actively resisted legal discrimination by demanding that their procedural rights be respected. In contrast to lynching rituals, court proceedings at least offered an institutional framework in which defendants had an opportunity to challenge the charges brought against them, even if such legal action generally could not avert their conviction. This is particularly evident in court cases in which black defendants alleged that they were subjected to brutal treatment in order to force them to confess. As will be shown here, the case of Dave Canty illustrates this in exemplary fashion.

"All These Scars, There and There": Testimony of Torture in the Trial of Dave Canty

The starting point for the Dave Canty case was the robbery of two nurses in the Alabama capital of Montgomery on March 19, 1938, in which forty-eight-year-old Eunice Ward was killed and her sister Lillian Ward severely wounded. As Lillian Ward recounted after the attack, she and her sister were taking a drive when they were attacked by an unknown black assailant. The man demanded their pocketbooks, but when he found that they contained only a few dollars, he flew into a rage and hit Eunice over the head with a heavy object that had been lying on the ground. Lillian Ward said that she then struggled with the man and was hit a number of times and attacked with a pocketknife before he fled.[9]

Immediately after news of the robbery broke, a statewide search was launched for the assailant, involving police and sheriff departments from across Alabama and teams with bloodhounds, and Governor David Bibb Graves (1927–1931, 1935–1939) offered a reward for the fugitive's capture.[10] Six days later, twenty-six-year-old Dave Canty was arrested in Mobile.[11] According to the *Montgomery Advertiser*, Canty was transferred that very same day to Kilby Prison, the state penitentiary near Montgomery, apparently to prevent him from being lynched.[12] The defendant was later shown to Lillian Ward, who was still in the hospital, but she could not be sure whether Canty was the perpetrator.[13] Three days later, the *Advertiser* reported that three white boys who lived in the neighborhood of the robbery had witnessed a black man fleeing the scene at the time of the crime. During a lineup at Kilby Prison, the boys identified Canty as the individual.[14]

On April 4, 1938, the *Advertiser* ran a front-page story announcing that after hours of questioning at police headquarters in Montgomery, Dave Canty had confessed to the robbery of the two nurses: "Fidgeting nervously in a chair in the basement of police headquarters, after several hours of questioning, Canty suddenly motioned to the group of officers surrounding him and said that, if he were returned to Kilby Prison . . . he would have something to say about the case. The officers took Canty to Kilby immediately and there, in the office of the chief deputy Warden, . . . he admitted responsibility for the crime and scrawled his signature at the bottom of a written confession."[15] The newspaper also published the confession, which was apparently leaked to the press by the investigating officers:

The confession was given as follows: *"On Saturday afternoon, March 19, 1938, about 4 o'clock just before a heavy rain came up . . . , I went by the side of the car where the two ladies were and grabbed the big lady (Miss Eunice Ward) and got the pocketbook. And after I got the pocketbook . . . , I pushed the other lady away and got $5.65 and threw the pocketbook down on the right side of the car. When I hit the lady on the head with an insulator, the little lady (Miss Lillian Ward) fought me, she hit me and I hit her and shoved her down and run. I'm gone and broke and run. I run . . . up to the Central of Georgia Railroad to Fifth Street—from there to Mulberry and caught the bus. I got off the bus on the corner of Dexter and Lawrence Streets.*

(Signed) Dave Canty."[16]

According to the *Advertiser*, Canty signed the confession in the presence of numerous witnesses.[17] The local authorities and representatives of the press thus went to great lengths to announce to the public that rapid progress had been made in the investigation, presumably—as in the previously analyzed case of Brown, Ellington, and Shields—to satisfy the white population's desire for revenge. After W. T. Seibel, the district attorney of Montgomery, swiftly filed charges, the trial of Dave Canty was held in the Montgomery Circuit Court from June 1, 1938, to June 4, 1938. Canty was represented by two white attorneys, Edward W. Wadsworth and Alex C. Birch.[18]

Reporting by the local press shows that the Canty trial was a public spectacle that captivated the attention of the local white population. "Throughout the day the courtroom was packed with many spectators standing. The crowd seemed more interested in hearing the evidence of Miss Lillian Ward than any of the other witnesses. . . . Miss Ward was not required to take the regular witness stand but sat in a chair on the floor just in front of the court bailiff. Her words were clear and distinct. Once or twice during her testimony Judge Carter allowed a brief recess which seemed to aid her composure."[19] The theatrical dimension of the trial is also clear from the description of Dave Canty's appearance in court:

> Another capacity crowd attended yesterday's session, many spectators having been forced to stand. Scores of others were turned away, as was the case on the preceding day. The crowd was orderly, but occasionally Judge Carter had to threaten to clear the room unless laughter and unnecessary noise ceased. When Cantey took the stand late in the afternoon, the crowd surged as close to the defendant as it was possible to get. Strict silence was maintained throughout his testimony, everyone present intent on hearing every word.[20]

After he was called to the witness stand, Canty testified that he had been tortured during the police investigation and forced to make a confession. He said that a number of officials, including Montgomery chief of detectives Paul Rapport, detectives A. C. Dennison and A. Chancellor, and police officer Tom Carlisle, had beaten him shortly after his arrest in Mobile and after he was transferred to Kilby Prison:

> They taken me down to the jail, and Mr. Rapport and Mr. Dennison— the one that wear the glasses—they left the jail, and that other man, the big fat one, and Mr. Carlisle and the others they taken me back in the room and hit me back there in the back room, and they put a

clamp on me and taken me back there. They cursed and punched me and beat me, and they say "Boy, what you done?" I say what you all talking about, and they beat me. One of them, that fellow standing at the middle door, he say, "All right I will kill you." After awhile, Mr. Rapport came and when they came in he told me, "I want you to be quiet all the way to Montgomery." He said, "Don't start nothing." . . . I was brought to Police Headquarters in Montgomery and they stopped a little while and carried me out to Kilby. I stayed there that Sunday, and that Monday Mr. Dennison and Mr. Chancellor came out, and took me in one of the rooms there, and they and Mr. Carlisle got one of them there straps and whipped me.[21]

Canty also gave detailed information on the diverse locations and chronology of the alleged torture, named the individuals involved, and repeated verbal statements by law enforcement officials. With this degree of detail, he evidently intended to substantiate the veracity of his allegations of torture. He also used physical gestures, as clearly shown in the following passage from the court transcript: "Mr. Dennison took me by my head right by the side of my face, like this, (demonstrating) bam!, and he beat me, bumping me head like this (indicating) and his hands slipped off my head, and he mashed them I think."[22] Canty's attempt to use various means of communication to back up his allegations is evident in yet another area of the court transcript, in which he provides a detailed description of the brutal treatment that he received in the Alabama state penitentiary:

They took one of those things that squeezes on your hands and twists down like this (indicates), you can see the hole right here (indicating place on his hand) and right here (indicating the same hand), and they squeezed up on me just as tight as they could. . . . [Mr. Chancellor] hauled off and hit me in the mouth, and as he struck me with his fist, he say "Mr. Carlisle, come over here, I want you to do something, you are the biggest, the hardest," and he walks over there where I was . . . and says, "I am going to show you all something," and he came over and jerked my leg, and puts both foots on my foot and he scotched my head like this (showing to the jury) and he said, "All right, I am going to show you." He twisted my leg just as far as he could get me, and I fell on the floor, and when I come back to, that is the way they left me.[23]

The supplemental information added to the transcript in parentheses demonstrates the diverse nonverbal means that Canty used in the courtroom to substantiate his claims of torture. In another passage it becomes clear that, in compliance with a request by his lawyers, he also demonstrated the alleged traces of violence on his body:

Q: Take them over there (to the jury) and show them to the jury.
A: (Witness went before the jury and showed scars he said the officers put on him in beating him on both his legs and knees. Also scars on his hands.) All these scars, there and there.[24]

During further testimony, it becomes clear that this type of statement and self-presentation was, if nothing else, a source of irritation for the district attorney, as Canty once again showed his scars to the jury.

A: Both my hands were freshly wounded when you (Mr. Wadsworth) and Mr. Birch came to see me and I showed you my mouth where the sore was fresh. I showed you this scar where they beat me and kicked me, I haven't showed it to you all (to the jury).
MR. WADSWORTH: That's all right, show that, I would like to have you show them.
THE SOLICITOR: I don't object if he wants to strip and show us everything on him.[25]
(The Witness exhibits scars to the jury.)
[A:] These places were fresh when I showed them to you and Mr. Birch.[26]

While the district attorney intended to ridicule the presentation of the scars, he reacted with open aggression at another moment in the testimony. When he insinuated that Canty was lying under oath about the alleged traces of torture, it came to the following exchange:

Q: Didn't you show the jury some scars that had been on your leg a long, long time, and wasn't put there by any beating of the officers?
A: I ain't showed nary a scar that had been on my leg a long, long time.
THE SOLICITOR: Don't pull your pants up, I didn't want to see your ugly legs. Nobody wants to see your leg. Pull it down.[27]

The degrading manner in which the district attorney instructed Canty to pull down his pants leg again and keep his "ugly legs" covered suggests that he viewed the man's conduct in court as an affront. Canty's use of vivid descriptions and a range of physical gestures to substantiate the allegation of torture was apparently seen by the district attorney as a provocative act with which the black defendant had abandoned his assigned position as a passive and subordinate figure in the courtroom.

Canty's defiant attitude was also apparent in an article published in the *Montgomery Advertiser*, in which his testimony was described as follows:

> Cantey told the jury he was beaten severely four days in succession at Kilby Prison because he would not say he killed Miss Ward and injured her sister. . . . The witness said the lash and other weapons of torture were applied at police headquarters a few days after he had been beaten at Kilby. He showed the jury what he said were scars from the whippings, most of them being on the legs below the knees. . . . Dave described the alleged whippings with gesticulations which he said the officers went through in punishing him. He frequently stood and on a few occasions walked to the rail in front of the jury box.[28]

Furthermore, it was reported that a number of veteran police officers told reporters that they doubted the veracity of Canty's allegations of torture: "Veteran officers said . . . that 'Cantey's tale about the beating he suffered' was 'the most fantastic account of the "third degree" they had heard from the lips of any defendant or witness.'"[29] Following Canty's testimony, the district attorney called numerous witnesses to the stand to rebut the allegations of torture. All the witnesses said under oath that Canty had voluntarily made his confession, without being subjected to force or coercion. Prison guard J. H. Lindsey, for instance, testified that the defendant was in his charge for "safe keeping" and that he "heard no licks, and saw no signs of a beating, contusion or bruises on this negro," adding that Canty "did not complain" to him about being harmed.[30] Likewise, police officer Carlisle, who had earlier been named by Canty as one of the individuals involved in meting out the torture, resolutely rejected the allegations. In response to the question of whether he had hit Canty, he testified, "I have never beat him or struck him, and saw no one else do so."[31]

In his concluding remarks, District Attorney Seibel emphatically urged the jury to find Canty guilty of the charges brought against him. Over the objections of the defense, he exclaimed that the "monster" who was responsible for these crimes had to be punished, and admonished the jury not to believe the defendant's allegations of torture or his claims of innocence: "I suppose if there is a man in that Jury [who] believed that story that the defendant told on the stand, he ought to have his brain taken out and weighed or have his brain examined. Because, if you believe that, you will believe anything."[32] The members of the jury evidently agreed with the prosecution. After a three-day trial, Canty was declared guilty and sentenced to death by electrocution.[33]

THE CONVICTION OF Dave Canty illustrates the fundamental limits of African American testimony in the courts of the American South. As in many contemporary trials of African Americans who were accused of murdering or raping whites, detailed allegations of torture had no impact on the verdict. Instead, they were dismissed as an attempt by the defendants to avoid punishment. At the same time, this case documents the diverse ways in which black defendants attempted to level allegations of torture and proclaim their own innocence despite the legal discrimination they suffered.

These observations are conceptually important because they expand our understanding of the repressive context of the justice system in the American South in the phase before the rise of a mass-based civil rights movement. They reveal that the process of establishing the truth was a hotly contested endeavor in which African American defendants used diverse means to raise their voices against the inferior position that had been assigned to them and attempted to make heard an alternative interpretation of events, even if their interventions generally had no influence on the final verdict.

This finding ties in with recent works in the area of black cultural studies that have called for an examination of demonstrations of black resistance and black cultural identity, along with their historical roots and political implications.[34] Dave Canty's testimony clearly shows that defiant actions by African Americans are evident even within the repressive context of the justice system of the South. In that sense, his testimony can be interpreted as a verbal and physical manifestation of black resistance—a rebellion against the imposed marginalization and voicelessness of African Americans within the racist structures of the justice system.[35]

Furthermore, the case of Dave Canty provides insight into the highly unequal framework within which the statements of white and black witnesses were interpreted by southern courts. In the following section, this phenomenon will be subjected to a more detailed examination based on the previously mentioned Daniels-Robinson case.

Torture and Hierarchies of Credibility: The Daniels-Robinson Case

The trial of Henry Daniels Jr. and Curtis C. Robinson was sparked by news of the rape of twenty-six-year-old Zeola Mae Armstrong in Mobile, Alabama, on August 19, 1941. Only a few hours after the case became public, police arrested a number of African American suspects, including eighteen-year-old Henry Daniels Jr. and twenty-year-old Curtis C. Robinson. Three days later, the *Mobile Register* reported that the two prisoners had confessed to the crime. To avert any attacks by the local white population, immediately after the arraignment the two suspects were transferred to the Alabama state penitentiary—the previously mentioned Kilby Prison in Montgomery—located some 150 miles away.[36] Three months later, the trial of Daniels and Robinson was held in the circuit court in Mobile. Since neither they nor their families had sufficient funds to pay for legal assistance, the court appointed three public defenders to represent the two defendants.[37]

Court transcripts reveal highly divergent versions of "the truth" of the case. While the witnesses for the prosecution corroborated the charge of rape and referred to the overwhelming evidence of the defendants' guilt, the two men emphatically proclaimed their innocence and insisted that they had been forced to make false confessions.[38]

District Attorney Bart B. Chamberlain opened the proceedings by maintaining that the two defendants had already expressed on a number of occasions their desire to have sexual intercourse with a white woman.[39] This immediately brought into play the powerful stereotype of the depraved black rapist with an irresistible urge for sexual contact with white women—an image that remained widespread in the South from the late nineteenth century onward.[40]

The examination of the witnesses began with Zeola Mae Armstrong, who was asked to recapitulate the sequence of events.[41] Armstrong described the rape in great detail. She said that the two defendants dragged her into an alley, hit her in the face with their fists, and dealt blows to other parts of her body. Despite her attempts to resist and flee, she said the two men threw her to the ground, held her there, and raped her. According to the court transcript, Armstrong identified the two defendants, Robinson and Daniels: "I know that [the defendants] are the two men who raped me and I cannot be mistaken about them as the light was shining on them and I could see them."[42]

During subsequent proceedings, physicians, toxicologists, and a number of police officers involved in the investigation made reference to the comprehensive body of evidence against the two defendants. The substantiation of the charges by numerous white male experts appeared to be aimed at addressing any possible doubts about the testimony of the female victim. As a result, Armstrong was increasingly sidelined during the trial. Particular attention was accorded to the results of the gynecological examination of the victim, which, according to toxicologist Nelson E. Grubbs, revealed traces of sperm. Furthermore, the clothing of the defendants and the victim were presented as evidence that, according to the testifying investigating officer, showed indications of the physical struggle between them during the rape.[43]

Moreover, the charges were backed up by the alleged confessions of the two defendants. Although their lawyers raised the objection that the confessions had been made "involuntarily" and were thus legally null and void, Judge David H. Edington admitted them as evidence.[44] In doing so, he adhered to the same legal practice that had been used in the case of Brown, Ellington, and Shields, as well as in the trial of Dave Canty. The purported confessions were then read by District Attorney Chamberlain. According to the court transcript, these documents provide a highly detailed description of how the crime was committed, as told from the first-person perspective of the perpetrators.[45] In the last passage of the confessions, the defendants state that their admissions were made voluntarily and were not induced by "threats." In the case of Henry Daniels Jr., this was worded as follows: "I know I am charged with having raped this lady and I know I can be electrocuted for what I have done. . . . No one did anything to make me tell what I have told, nor did anyone make any threats to make me say what I have said nor had anyone offered me anything."[46] Affixed with the handwritten signatures of the defendants, the confessions substantiated the charges of rape against Daniels and Robinson. The detailed descriptions of the motive for the attack and its course of events appeared to be unshakable proof of the accusations, which were further substantiated by the testimony of the victim and the statements of the white male experts.

The testimony of the two defendants, however, expressed another, rival truth about the case. Before the eyes of the judge, the jury, and the audience in the courtroom, Henry Daniels Jr. and Curtis C. Robinson emphatically asserted their innocence and made allegations of torture and forced confessions. Daniels, for instance, testified on the witness stand: "They threatened to kill me if I didn't say what they told me to, and to save my life I signed that confession. I knew if I didn't they would kill me anyway. Four or five people were in the room then. . . . As to whether they did anything to make me sign it, they laid me across a bench and beat me. That man there held me with his foot and hit me in the stomach, this went on for half an hour and then I said I would confess to it."[47] Daniels went on to say that, fearing for his life, he then signed the purported confession.[48] Robinson also testified that he had been tortured by police officers:

[It was] a little cell that they took me into. . . . There was blood on the floor and there was a table in there. . . . You ask me to tell how large it was, if I know. . . . It was as large as this open space here. . . . The table was a wooden table, made like a bench and it was in the middle. As to how long it was, — about from here over there. . . . They beat me then with a rubber hose, they pulled my clothes off and beat me.[49]

The testimonies show that the defendants attempted to substantiate their allegations by providing detailed information on the location and chain of events during the brutal interrogation — for example, by making a comparison between the spatial surroundings of the courtroom and those in the torture cell. Daniels even went so far as to identify one of the individuals in the courtroom as one of his tormentors: "That man there held me with his foot and hit me in the stomach."[50]

Likewise, as the examination continued, both defendants reaffirmed their innocence. Daniels, for instance, repudiated the purported confessions point by point: "No, sir, I did not say to Curtis Robinson that Tuesday, 'Let's get one tonight.' No, sir, when me and Curtis Robinson left his house and went out in the alley, I did not see this white lady coming along the street and I did not say, 'Here comes one. Let's get her.' I never saw this woman until she came to the city jail."[51] Robinson even dramatically underscored his claim of innocence by directly addressing the members of the jury: "Gentlemen of the jury, I didn't rape that lady. I was upstairs with my wife in bed, the same wife who is here today."[52] By combining his claim of innocence with a reference to his married life, Robinson possibly sought to demonstrate his own adaptation to the patriarchal order and segregated society of the South. His appeal to the jury represented an effort to make himself heard as a witness and, contrary to the stereotype of African American dishonesty and degeneracy, be perceived as credible and trustworthy. This is reflected in a further statement by Robinson in which he directed his comments to the presiding judge: "They had beat me up so, I lasted as long as I could, and they was going to kill me. Your honor, I didn't do this thing. I never have thought of anything like that."[53]

The court transcripts make it clear that Daniels and Robinson used a wide range of communicative means and strategies on the witness stand in an attempt to draw attention to a different version of "the truth." Typically enough, however, their claims of innocence and detailed allegations of torture remained without consequence for the time being. After the examination of the witnesses and the final statements by the defense and the prosecution, Robinson and Daniels were found guilty by the jury and sentenced to death by electrocution.[54]

THIS TRIAL'S OUTCOME again reflects the narrow limits of African American testimony in southern courts. The marginalized position of black defendants meant that their testimonies were granted a lesser degree of credibility than those of white witnesses. The convictions of Daniels and Robinson thus provide a prime example of the connection between subalternity and "voicelessness." Ostensibly "credible," "honorable" white witnesses were juxtaposed with the purportedly "unreliable," "deceitful" black witnesses, whose subaltern status was reflected in the virtual impossibility of making themselves heard in court.

The Clemency Inquiry into the Daniels-Robinson Case

The subsequent course of the Daniels-Robinson case, however, reveals ruptures and contradictions within this bipolar framework of white and black testimony. Moreover, this case demonstrates that African American courtroom allegations of torture did not always remain without consequence. After the Alabama Supreme Court confirmed the conviction of Daniels and Robinson on January 28, 1943, their defense lawyers—with support from the national legal department of the NAACP—petitioned for the case to be reviewed by the U.S. Supreme Court. On May 17, 1943, the highest court in the land decided against taking on the case, whereupon the then governor of Alabama, Chauncey Sparks (1943–47), requested a clemency hearing for the two condemned men, which was held at the governor's official residence in Montgomery on June 15, 1943, one day before the official execution date.[55]

After the hearing, Governor Sparks announced before representatives of the press that he had called for an inquiry into the allegations of torture and had delayed the execution of the two appellants. He went on to say that he intended to commute the death sentences to life in prison should the allegations of torture be confirmed. According to the *Montgomery Advertiser*, both Robinson and Daniels had provided him with detailed accounts of their brutal mistreatment. The newspaper article noted that Robinson had pointed to a scar on his head that he said came from a police truncheon.[56] In light of the surprising decision by the governor, even the national African American weekly the *Chicago Defender* reported on these developments.[57]

Segments of the white population were outraged at the governor's decision, as documented by two anonymous letters from the investigation file.

The very fact that a hearing had been held for the two condemned men was viewed as an affront to the racist and patriarchal power structures of the South. One letter writer wrote, "So long as Negroes can attack white women, be found guilty by a jury of twelve men and are sentenced by a competent judge, and then gain mercy at the Governor's hands, there is no need for that law, there is no need for juries nor judges. . . . What excuse will the Governor have now for failing to punish two fiends who admitted attacking a white woman? Are we to have law and order in Alabama or can fiends continue these attacks believing that the Governor will refuse to punish them?"[58] The other anonymous letter characterized the governor's decision as an open invitation to all those who were tempted to emulate the two condemned men: "The police get razzed and the attackers get a reprieve. What a relief this must be to Negroes who may want to try the same thing! What a Governor—what a laugh!"[59]

Within the scope of the investigation, numerous officials involved in the Daniels-Robinson case in Mobile were asked to respond to the allegations of torture. The recorded statements reflect not only the authorities' concern for the possible consequences of the case but also their efforts to cast doubt on the allegations of torture brought forward by the two appellants by referring to their own credibility and the integrity of the other white witnesses. This was particularly clear in the account given by District Attorney Bart B. Chamberlain, who had declared in an affidavit written back in March 1943 that he and a number of other white officials had been in attendance during the confessions: "After convincing evidence was placed before them, one of them confessed and, when his confession was read to the other, he freely and voluntarily confessed. I was present when these confessions were made, and in fact, I obtained them. They were also made in the presence of several police officers and deputies and also Doctor Nelson E. Grubbs, Assistant Toxicologist for the State."[60] After Chamberlain was called on in July 1943 to make another statement on the allegations of torture, he wrote the following: "I state emphatically nothing was done to either of them to obtain a confession. . . . Each of the defendants is as guilty as anyone could be and of the most damnable offense, and their statements or the statement of anyone that they were forced to make a confession is absolutely untrue. . . . There is no question as to the rape having been committed and there is no question as to the guilty persons and there is no question as to the righteousness of the verdict."[61] These letters by the district attorney reveal a strategy that was subsequently pursued by many other individuals who were questioned during the investigation of the torture allegations. They refuted the allegations made by the two defendants by referring to the status and respectability of the white officials who were directly involved in the case against Daniels and Robinson.

For instance, Judge David H. Edington, who had presided over the trial of Daniels and Robinson in the Mobile Circuit Court, emphasized that several respected citizens had been present while the confessions were written down. "High-class men, like Dr. Grubbs and others . . . were present in the office . . . when these negroes made their confessions." The judge also commented that during the trial, he had the impression that both of the defendants had "lied" on the witness stand.[62] In addition, the sheriff of Mobile County, W. T. Holcombe, declared in his statement to the governor that the allegations of the two condemned men were untenable: "In my opinion the physical facts and the undisputed testimony in this case precluded the possibilities not only of there being any truth in the claims of these men, but also show conclusively that the defendants were guilty as charged."[63] He went on to say that modern investigative methods had replaced the use of torture: "As the head of this department I do not tolerate any mistreatment of prisoners in our custody. . . . The so called third degree is, in this county at least, obsolete and is considered stupid by all intelligent and efficient officers. It can be truthfully said that here in Mobile the microscope and test tube and camera . . . have replaced the blackjack and the rubber hose."[64] The documents in the investigation file show that all the white experts involved in the trial categorically dismissed the allegations of torture and forced confessions made by Daniels and Robinson. Many officials also referred to the photographs of the accused as proof of the hollow nature of their allegations.

Photographic Interventions

As stated in the declaration by Sheriff Holcombe, the photographs of the two defendants that were taken shortly after they signed their confessions showed "no evidence or sign of any beating or mistreatment."[65] This opinion was shared by police photographer J. J. Hyde, who apparently took the photographs:

> The two negroes [. . .] made the most brazen confession I have ever heard. Both were perfectly at ease, not nervous or frightened. Before questioning they sat and argued about who hit the white lady first, each accusing the other. The first thing said to them was they were perfectly safe there, and nobody would be allowed to harm them. Not

one person went so far as to speak out of the way to either of them. After they confessed, I photographed them. There was no evidence of any beating on either of them, except one of them had three or four fingernail scratches on his upper breast. The victim told us the night before that she had scratched them.[66]

In alluding to the photographs of the two defendants that were taken just after the confessions were made, Hyde implicitly referred to the presumptive ability of the medium of photography to provide an objective reflection of reality. The "testimony" of photography was aimed at dismissing the allegations of torture by the two defendants.[67]

This is also expressed in the statement by toxicologist Nelson E. Grubbs, who said that during his examination of the two men, he could find no traces of physical violence, with the exception of a number of scratches that had apparently been made by the victim: "Both of them were stripped of all their clothes which I examined in the laboratory there. We saw both of them naked and the only mark of violence on either of them was about four scratches on Robinson's upper chest, that appeared to be fingernail scratches. They were photographed and placed in their cells for the night. The pictures show they were not beaten."[68] Although the photos were mentioned in a number of instances, the investigative file contains no additional indication of the existence of these images. Instead, it contains only two undated police photographs of Robinson and Daniels (see figures 2 and 3) that were attached to a letter by warden E. R. Wilson of Kilby Prison, in which he stated: "I am positive that I did not receive a report from the Night Captain, Deputy Warden or Prison Doctor stating that these men were injured at the time of their arrival. Some two or three days after these men arrived I made a trip to the death cells and at that time they did not complain to me about injuries of any kind."[69]

Although the attached photographs presumably aimed to dismiss the allegations of torture made by the two African Americans, a handwritten commentary written in red on the lower left-hand side of the letter noted that the photographs were taken "several months after they were convicted."[70]

The investigation file of Governor Sparks also contains a number of statements that confirmed the torture allegations of the two condemned men. For example, it includes several letters written by Edgar M. Parkman, the white chaplain at Kilby Prison. Parkman noted in his letter to the governor that due to his daily contact with the two prisoners, he was convinced of their credibility: "Since December 1941, I have been in constant

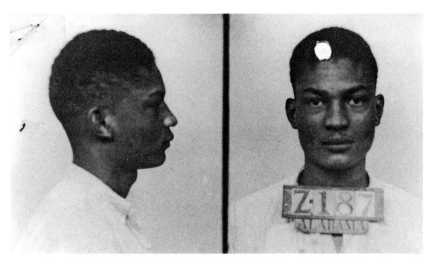

FIGURE 2 Police photograph of Curtis Robinson. Alabama Department of Archives and History, AG, 1943–1947: Sparks, CHCF, Curtis Robinson.

touch with the [two] men. It is my personal belief that they are telling the truth when they claim they had signed a forced confession. I cannot claim infallibility in distinguishing truth from untruth but what they say rings true. Neither of the men has varied in any essential manner during the past twenty months. They have been anxious to supply any information that might throw light on the manner of securing the confession and the circumstances of the case."[71] The chaplain went on to say that he had heard a number of things that would substantiate the claims of the two condemned men, and he made reference to a comment by a white prisoner: "Unfortunately no medical record was kept of the treatment of bruises on Curtis Robinson at Kilby Prison, but Otto George, a white prisoner who then occupied a cell near Curtis Robinson, tells me that Curtis was complaining of injury to his head and eye and that some medical dressing was brought to him by a guard. . . . Otto George also mentioned that conversations he overheard between Curtis Robinson and Henry Daniels led him to believe that they were beaten in order to obtain a confession."[72] The allegations by Daniels and Robinson were most clearly substantiated by fellow African American prisoner Mattie Williams, who said that he had seen with his own eyes how the two men had been tortured:

They called for Curtis Robinson to be brought down from his cell and I heard them say that they were going to beat him until he confessed to

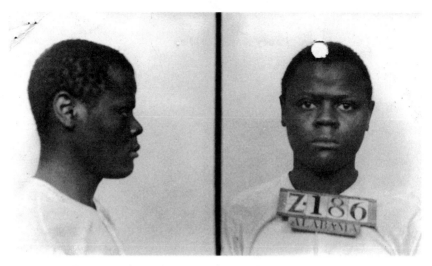

FIGURE 3 Police photograph of Henry Daniels Jr. Alabama Department of Archives and History, AG, 1943–1947: Sparks, CHCF, Henry Daniels Jr.

what he had done. When they brought him down, they took him in a room and took all his clothes off and put him on a table and then they took a rubber hose pipe and beat him. . . . His back was cut and torn and I saw one of the men kicking him off the table and then they threw him back on the table and they said, "We'll kill you, you black son of a bitch, we'll beat until you talk." . . . Another night I saw the same seven policemen drinking whiskey in the back of the jail and then a little while later I heard them call for Henry Daniels to be brought down. They took all his clothes off and put him on this same table where they had beaten Curtis Robinson and they beat him with the same rubber hose pipe. They were all cursing him and one of the men asked if he didn't jump on this white women and he said, "No, sir, I did not." The policeman said, "You're a damn liar, you did do it," and he hit Henry Daniels in the face with this hose pipe and he hit him about his head several times.[73]

With his detailed account of the chain of events and the language used by the torturers, Williams laid claim to a truth about the torture that was diametrically opposed to the assertions of most of the white officials questioned, who denied any use of violence to obtain the confessions.

The documents in the investigation file of the Daniels-Robinson case thus outline a field in which the diverse individuals involved expressed contradictory truths and claims to the truth. At the same time, their credibility was assessed in highly divergent manners. The statements of the white officials were ascribed an authoritative status that was used to reject the torture allegations of the black condemned men as untrue and implausible. References to the prominence and respectability of the questioned individuals—as reflected in the comment about "high-class men"—show that the strategies and rhetoric of producing evidence were directly linked to categories of social differentiation like race, class, and gender. The presumably more credible statements of the white male officials were accorded more weight than those of the witnesses who substantiated the allegations of torture.

The Debate about the Racial Origins of the Plaintiff

The documents in the investigation file also reveal cracks in the image of the credible white witness, particularly when it comes to the "character" and racial identity of the "white" victim. Parole officer W. T. Kemp noted in his report that there were considerable ambiguities about the origins and "race" of Zeola Mae Armstrong: "Zeola has a very dark complexion and has the earmarks of having Cajan blood in her."[74]

This called into question the racial identity of the presumed white victim. "Cajan" referred to a group of people living in southwestern Alabama and southeastern Mississippi, whose ancestry was presumably a mixture of whites, African Americans, and Native Americans.[75] Armstrong's father was reportedly a Cajan, and there had apparently been certain ambiguities with respect to the "race" of individual members of Zeola Armstrong's family: "She had a first cousin, Cleve Orso, who was sentenced to prison from Washington County and was placed with the Negroes at Kilby Prison. There was a question raised at that time about the race of Cleve. I do not know whether he was separated from the Negroes or not while he was in prison."[76] It is also evident in the report that the question of racial origins was directly linked to the character of the rape victim: "Zeola has a reputation for drinking quite a bit. However I am unable to find [whether] she has ever been arrested for this offense."[77] Furthermore, Kemp noted that she was said to have had recurrent contact with an African American woman who ran a brothel in Mobile that was frequented by white men.[78]

The conduct and racial origins of the rape victim were apparently a source of irritation. As Lisa Lindquist Dorr has pointed out, in cases in which southern white women claimed to have been raped by black perpetrators, the respectability and whiteness of the female victims were always carefully scrutinized.[79] Although such trials regularly employed the rhetoric of white male chivalry or the image of the white man as defender of the honor of southern white womanhood, not all rape victims were viewed as worthy of the same degree of protection. Only those women who adhered to the strict rules of racial interaction and respected the norms of appropriate social and gender-specific behavior could expect the highest degree of protection from white men. Hence, white womanhood was not an innate characteristic but rather directly linked to notions of female honor and social respectability.[80]

THE DEBATE OVER the race and character of Zeola Mae Armstrong revolved around the fundamental question of whether she was "white enough" to be regarded as a credible victim who was worthy of protection. These types of frictions within the ostensibly homogeneous white population of the South reveal the fragility of contemporary concepts of race and, at the same time, exemplify that even among the white population, there abounded highly diverse, categorically intertwined, and divergent degrees of perceived credibility.

Any doubts about the credibility of the plaintiff remained without consequence for the two prisoners on death row, however. After consulting the results of the inquiry, Governor Chauncey Sparks rejected the petition for clemency and ordered the immediate execution of the two condemned men.[81] On August 13, 1943, Henry Daniels Jr. and Curtis C. Robinson were executed by electrocution in the state penitentiary of Alabama.[82]

CHAPTER THREE

The NAACP Campaign against "Forced Confessions"

In April 1935, the National Association for the Advancement of Colored People (NAACP) published in its monthly magazine, the *Crisis*, an article on the previously mentioned case of three African American farmhands— Henry Shields, Arthur Ellington, and Ed Brown—who, after being convicted of the murder of Raymond Stuart, were on death row in a Mississippi prison. A photograph on the front page showed the three condemned men in prisoner garb, sitting in front of a light wall and gazing at the camera, with Arthur Ellington in the middle supported by Henry Shields and Ed Brown (see figure 4). The article made the following observation: "Note that Ellington, in the center, is being held up by his two companions. That is because he is nearly dead from the torture he received when a 'confession' was forced out of him. He was beaten and hanged a little at a time to make him confess. As a result his neck is damaged and he is injured so severely otherwise that he cannot sit up alone."[1] The text and image clearly sought to highlight the harrowing ordeal that Ellington had suffered at the hands of law enforcement officials. The article also noted that the two other prisoners, Brown and Shields, had been "brutally" beaten to extort confessions. According to the article, it was only the intervention of the NAACP that had stayed their execution. The article ended with an appeal to all readers to financially support the organization in its efforts to petition the U.S. Supreme Court to review the case: "Funds are badly needed by the national office for this and other legal cases pending. Practically all funds for this case must be raised outside of Mississippi. Immediate action is needed from the public if these three farm workers are to be given a chance at life."[2]

In the wake of the Brown, Ellington, and Shields case, between 1935 and 1955 the NAACP became involved in several dozen cases in which African American defendants in the South had been convicted based on alleged forced confessions. As previously mentioned, these were primarily trials involving charges of rape or murder. During its campaign, the NAACP built on strategies and methods that had previously been put to the test in its struggle against lynching. In articles, press releases, and public

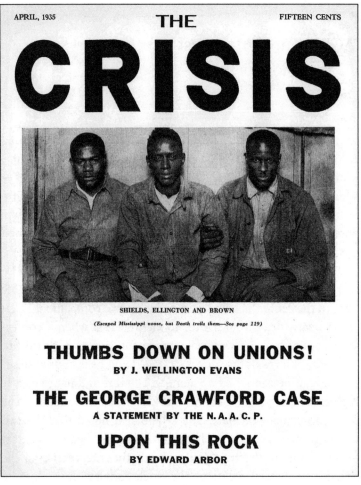

APRIL, 1935   **THE**   FIFTEEN CENTS

CRISIS

SHIELDS, ELLINGTON AND BROWN
(Escaped Mississippi noose, but Death trails them—See page 119)

THUMBS DOWN ON UNIONS!
BY J. WELLINGTON EVANS

THE GEORGE CRAWFORD CASE
A STATEMENT BY THE N. A. A. C. P.

UPON THIS ROCK
BY EDWARD ARBOR

FIGURE 4 Cover of the NAACP monthly magazine, the *Crisis*, April 1935. The author wishes to thank the Crisis Publishing Co., Inc., the publisher of the magazine of the NAACP, for the use of this image, first published in the April 1935 issue of the *Crisis*.

statements, the organization used the allegations of torture made by black defendants as an opportunity to draw attention to the continuing scourge of racism in the South and to garner support for its own civil rights struggle. As will be shown here, one of its key strategies was to document and condemn the widespread use of torture in the justice system of the American South. At the same time, the organization aimed to curb the judicial use of forced confessions in the South and elsewhere by appealing selected verdicts.

The Struggle for Legal Equality in Court

The NAACP was established in 1909 by black and white civil rights activists in reaction to the Springfield race riot one year earlier.[3] Within just a few decades, it grew to become the largest and most influential civil rights organization in the United States. Already by 1919, it had 90,000 card-carrying members. Following a massive increase in membership in the early 1940s, the NAACP had more than 500,000 members in 1946.[4]

Ever since its founding, the organization had led the legal battle to combat discrimination against African American citizens in the areas of education, labor, voting rights, and the judicial system. A main focus of its early activities was to campaign against the ongoing lynching violence in the South, with particular emphasis on convincing members of Congress to approve federal legislation that would allow the U.S. Department of Justice to launch investigations into members of lynch mobs and prosecute such individuals in federal courts. Despite decades of lobbying, these legislative initiatives repeatedly failed in the face of resistance from U.S. senators representing southern states. Nevertheless, through compiling statistics; investigating and documenting cases of lynching; organizing exhibits and protest rallies; and publishing articles, pamphlets, and photographs, the NAACP managed to draw the attention of the American public to the continuing lynching of black citizens in the South.[5]

In the 1930s, the organization increasingly shifted the focus of its civil rights campaign to legal battles in American courts.[6] This development was driven by Charles Hamilton Houston, a prominent African American lawyer who served in the early 1930s as the dean of the law school at Howard University in Washington, D.C., a historically black university. From 1934, Houston worked full time as the special counsel to the NAACP, and in 1936, he hired a former student of his, Thurgood Marshall, as assistant special counsel.[7] Two years later, Marshall, who would become the first African American Supreme Court justice in 1967, succeeded Houston as special counsel to the NAACP.[8]

A few months after his appointment, Marshall published an article in the *Crisis* in which he expounded on the strategy that the legal department of the NAACP would pursue in the future. Under the headline "Equal Justice under Law"—which is the inscription engraved above the entrance to the Supreme Court building in Washington, D.C.—he pointed to the legal achievements of the NAACP. In the thirty years since its establishment, Marshall wrote, the organization had brought thirteen cases before the highest court in the land, adding that in twelve of these trials, the court had decided in favor of the appellant. He said that these decisions were "guide posts" in a sustained fight for the civil rights of African Americans, and noted that these legal victories had broadened the scope of protection guaranteed by the Constitution in the areas of voting rights, equal justice before the law, jury duty, segregation, and equal educational opportunities.[9] Marshall concluded that the legal campaign of the NAACP had thus made a significant contribution to improving the civil rights of blacks *and* whites: "The campaign to secure equal justice in the courts has brought about several precedents which have been of value to all defendants in criminal cases both Negro and white. . . . The opinions in these cases define the civil rights of the Negro as a citizen. In addition, they broaden the interpretation of civil rights for all citizens and extend civil liberties for whites as well as Negroes. The activity of lawyers acting for the N.A.A.C.P. has added to the body of civil rights for all Americans."[10] Marshall's review of the organization's achievements shows that the activities of the NAACP toward the end of the 1930s increasingly focused on courtroom battles in civil rights cases. In the eyes of the proponents of the "legal approach" within the NAACP, this was— particularly against the background of the unsuccessful political lobbying for an anti-lynching law—the only promising means of permanently eradicating discrimination and segregation in the United States.[11]

The archives of the NAACP for the period between 1930 and 1955 document hundreds of reviewed cases in which black defendants alleged that they were discriminated against by the justice system because of their ascribed race. Not surprisingly, a disproportionate number of such allegations were made by defendants who were on trial in the South. The activities of the NAACP legal department primarily targeted the phenomenon of police violence, the discrimination against African Americans during jury selection, and violations of the right to due process and the right to counsel.[12]

The NAACP and *Brown v. Mississippi* and *Chambers v. Florida*

In 1934, the NAACP first took action against the use of forced confessions in the courts of the American South with the case of Brown, Ellington, and Shields. After the conviction of the three defendants by the court in Kemper County, Mississippi, one of their court-appointed lawyers, John Clark, decided to file an appeal in their case and asked the NAACP national office for help. Clark's motion was all the more surprising because he and his wife were politically active in Mississippi and well connected to the state's conservative political establishment.[13] Two of the three other lawyers refused to participate in the appeal, while the third allowed Clark to use his name in the filing but did not want to play an active part in any future proceedings.[14] Apparently, Clark's colleagues believed that their involvement in the appeal could potentially harm their legal careers. The meager financial outlook of the case might have played a role, too. Since the defendants were not able to finance an appeal, Clark wrote to the NAACP national office in New York City to ask for help. Faced with a difficult financial situation, the NAACP sent Clark a small check and decided to wait for the outcome of his appeal before taking further action.[15] In January 1935, the Mississippi Supreme Court affirmed the judgment against the three defendants on the technical grounds that the defense lawyers had made no motion during the trial to exclude the coerced confessions as evidence. One judge, however, wrote a sharp dissent from the majority's decision. Judge William D. Anderson, a longtime Mississippi attorney and former mayor of the city of Tupelo, concluded that the defendants had been "driven to confess their guilt by most brutal and unmerciful whippings."[16] He argued that the proceedings in the trial should be invalidated under the Fourteenth Amendment's due process clause.[17]

Following the decision of the Mississippi Supreme Court, attorney John Clark wrote to the NAACP to urge the organization to handle the case. Clark stated that he could not take the case any further, even though he firmly believed that the three men had been tortured into their confessions.[18] After a physical and nervous collapse, he entirely withdrew from the case. As his wife stated in a letter to Arthur Garfield Hays, longtime general counsel to the American Civil Liberties Union, her husband had received "strong and unjust criticism" for his support of the defendants, adding that the "justice loving, law abiding people" in Mississippi had been in sympathy with Mr. Clark's work "but dare[d] not to express their opinions because of inflamed public sentiment."[19]

Her comment indicates that certain segments of the local white community disapproved of the police's strong-arm methods against the three defendants yet were not able, allowed, or willing to express their disapproval publicly. Another indicator of local whites' empathy toward Brown, Ellington, and Shields is that their case received the support of an even more prominent member of Mississippi's white political elite after John Clark resigned. Mississippi's former governor, Earl Brewer—a widely respected criminal lawyer and a longtime political opponent of the notorious racist Theodore Bilbo—took over the case at the request of Clark's wife and prepared a second appeal to the Mississippi Supreme Court. Brewer appropriated the main argument in Judge Anderson's dissenting opinion to claim that the trial had violated the Fourteenth Amendment due process clause and Mississippi law.[20]

In March 1935, the NAACP announced that it would financially support Brewer and a possible appeal to the U.S. Supreme Court. An article that appeared that same month in the *Crisis* criticized the black community in Kemper County for having remained "silent" on the case.[21] This commentary, as well as the obvious mistreatment of Brown, Ellington, and Shields, evidently galvanized the local black community into action, and a local NAACP chapter in Meridian was organized, numbering 126 members by the end of the month.[22] As in similar cases of civil rights litigation in the 1930s and 1940s, the egregious violation of black defendants' civil liberties, and the NAACP's initiative on their behalf, enhanced local awareness of civil rights and laid the organizational cornerstone for future activism.

At the close of April 1935, the Mississippi Supreme Court again upheld the verdict against the three accused. This time, Judge Anderson and a second judge dissented from the decision, repeating the argument that the verdict had been in violation of the due process clause of the Fourteenth Amendment.[23] Even though Brewer had agreed to work pro bono, the cost for the appeal to the U.S. Supreme Court proved too high for the financially strained national office of the NAACP. As a result, the money was raised with much difficulty by an alliance of several donors and institutions.[24] Of the almost $2,000 raised for the overall cost of the proceedings, the NAACP contributed $690. Another $574.67 was donated by the Commission on Interracial Cooperation (CIC), whose director, Will Alexander, notified the NAACP in May 1935 that his organization would add 50 percent to any funds collected by the NAACP or other sources.[25] J. Morgan Steven, a member of the Association of Southern Women for the Prevention of Lynching, and Theodore D. Bratton, a bishop of the Episcopal Dioceses of Mississippi, collected the remaining $650 needed for the appeal from local white and black communities in Mississippi.[26]

In his appeal before the Supreme Court, Earl Brewer pursued the argument advanced by the two dissenting Mississippi judges: that the convictions of the three petitioners were in violation of the Fourteenth Amendment to the Constitution.[27] The legal department of the NAACP had already tested this line of argument in other criminal proceedings. In 1923, the organization had successfully argued in the case of *Moore v. Dempsey* that the appellants had been convicted in a mob-dominated trial that violated the due process clause of the Fourteenth Amendment. The decision in *Moore v. Dempsey* established a new legal doctrine that affirmed the right of the Supreme Court to intervene in the court proceedings of individual states if it was clear that the Fourteenth Amendment had been violated.[28] Based on this decision, the NAACP managed on two occasions in the 1930s to convince the Supreme Court to reverse the convictions in the trial of the Scottsboro Boys. In *Powell v. Alabama* (1932), the Supreme Court decided, with reference to the due process clause, that defendants charged with a capital crime had the right to retain a lawyer before the beginning of their trial. The ruling interpreted that this right to counsel was enshrined under the Fourteenth Amendment and thus binding for the individual states. In *Norris v. Alabama* (1935), the Supreme Court decided—once again on the basis of the due process clause— that African Americans could not be systematically excluded from the lists of jury and grand jury candidates.[29]

In February 1936, the U.S. Supreme Court announced its decision in the case of *Brown v. Mississippi* to reverse the convictions of Ed Brown, Arthur Ellington, and Henry Shields. In their statement, the justices explicitly criticized the treatment of the three appellants by the criminal justice system of the South. "It would be difficult to conceive of methods more revolting to the sense of justice than those taken to procure the confessions of these petitioners, and the use of the confessions thus obtained as the basis for conviction and sentence was a clear denial of due process."[30] The justices made it clear that the treatment of the three men and the use of their confessions by the court in Mississippi were a clear violation of the right to a fair trial as established by the Fourteenth Amendment of the Constitution. This decision formed the legal basis for the NAACP to bring a number of forced-confession cases before the Supreme Court over the ensuing years.

This legal initiative was boosted by a Supreme Court that, much in accordance with the New Deal policy of the U.S. federal government, extended its oversight over state criminal procedure and challenged the racially discriminatory structures of the southern criminal justice system. Accordingly, between 1936 and 1945, the Supreme Court justices decided in eight instances to review decisions in forced-confession cases that had been tried in the South. In seven of these cases, they overruled the lower-court decisions on the argument that the confessions used as evidence had been extracted by violence or coercion and thus were in violation of the due process clause of the Fourteenth Amendment. In all but one case, the NAACP was directly involved in the appeals process.[31]

The decision on *Brown v. Mississippi* was also noteworthy because of the further rationale voiced by the justices, who said that the treatment of the appellants by the authorities in Mississippi was inconsistent with the self-proclaimed image of the United States as a "modern civilization": "The transcript [of this trial] reads more like pages torn from some medieval account than a record made within the confines of a modern civilization which aspires to an enlightened constitutional government."[32] The criticism of the legal practices of the southern courts was even more explicit in a passage in which the justices referred to the notorious legal institutions of the Star Chamber in England and the Inquisition in other European countries, whose excesses had been overcome with the protections provided by the U.S. Constitution: "Coercing the supposed state's criminal into confession and using such confessions . . . in trials has been the curse of all countries. It was the chief iniquity, the crowning infamy, of the Star Chamber and the Inquisition, and other similar institutions. The constitution recognized the evils that lay behind these practices and prohibited them in this country."[33] With reference to this dark chapter of humanity that many had believed relegated to the history books, the justices of the Supreme Court recognized the police torture in the American South as a backward and barbarous act that called into question the reputation of the United States as a civilized nation. They also made reference to the founding myth of the American nation as a political system that had resolutely disassociated itself from absolutist European monarchies in general, and the British colonial power in particular.

Reports in the national press eagerly seized on this interpretation of the case. For instance, the *Chicago Daily Tribune* published the following commentary: "The opinion has to do with a murder trial in a backwoods region in Mississippi. It reveals a story of stark terror, torture and brutality that eclipses even the horror tales of the middle ages. The rope and the lash are exposed as having taken the place of justice in a part of the land ordinarily believed to [be] inhabited by civilized people."[34] The *Washington Post* condemned the events in Mississippi as a "despicable reversion to savagery," and a number of commentaries emphasized the importance of the verdict for the protection of human rights under the law; for example: "No decision in recent years has been more pointed or emphatic in its demands for observance of the human rights guaranteed to every citizen by the fundamental law."[35]

A number of commentaries also made reference to the national and international debate over the case of the Scottsboro Boys. The *New York Post* compared the treatment of Brown, Ellington, and Shields to this landmark case and called it a "legal lynching," which it said was "an even greater menace than . . . illegal lynching," as "it quiets objection by casting the forms of law around what is really mob murder." The newspaper went on to say that one could only hope that the South would revise this practice in view of the decision in *Brown v. Mississippi*.[36]

The national African American press struck a far more pessimistic tone in its coverage of the *Brown v. Mississippi* case. As the *Chicago Defender* noted three months before the decision by the Supreme Court, the case made it clear that defendants in southern courts—despite the national and international protests surrounding the case of the Scottsboro Boys—still faced widespread discrimination.[37] After the U.S. Supreme Court overturned all earlier decisions in Mississippi, the publishers of the newspaper commented with a good dose of sarcasm that it was "not quite clear to people who live in intelligent communities how members of the 'presumed superior race' can fall so low in the depths of judicial depravity."[38]

The NAACP adopted similar rhetorical language to that of the Supreme Court justices and certain segments of the national press, using words like "civilization" and "barbarity" to express its outrage over the case of Brown, Ellington, and Shields. In an article published in the *Crisis* shortly before the Supreme Court decision, the NAACP summed up the circumstances as follows: "The three farm hands were convicted solely upon a 'confession' which was secured from them by beatings and torture almost unbelievable in a civilized state."[39]

In its legal campaign against police torture, the NAACP thus relied on strategies that it had already put to the test since the 1910s as part of its anti-lynching campaign—namely drawing attention to the widespread prevalence of lynching violence in the South and characterizing it as a barbaric act that stood in stark contrast to the modern and civilized image aspired to by the American nation. Early anti-lynching activists, such as African American journalist Ida B. Wells, had used the concept of civilization in the late nineteenth century to denounce the brutality and inhumanity of lynching in the South.[40]

In contrast to the anti-lynching campaign, however, the NAACP now focused on the discriminatory procedures of the criminal justice system. In a leading editorial in the *Crisis*, the magazine lauded the successful appeal in the case of *Brown v. Mississippi*: "Mississippi has been told by the U.S. Supreme Court that the rack and torture chamber may not substitute for the witness chair. Brown, Ellington, and Shields have a new lease of life and the N.A.A.C.P. has another victory to its credit before the high court."[41]

For Brown, Ellington, and Shields, this "new lease of life" at first meant little more than being spared from their imminent execution. All three remained in jail in Jackson, Mississippi, awaiting their retrial. Eight months later, the three defendants agreed to a plea bargain with the local district attorney. Apparently, Brown, Shields, and Ellington were convinced that the local court would convict them again of murder, no matter how meager the evidence against them. The three were sentenced to prison terms of ten, five, and three years, respectively. Taking into account time previously served, Ellington was finally discharged from prison in May 1937, Shields in February 1939, and Brown in December 1941.[42] As in most forced-confession cases decided by the U.S. Supreme Court during this period, Brown, Ellington, and Shields had to bear the brunt of the successful litigation on their behalf, which made them a renewed target of the state attorneys whose legal work had been reprimanded by the Supreme Court decision.[43]

The reactions to the case of Brown, Ellington, and Shields show that the NAACP effectively used the decision to alert the public to its legal campaign to combat discrimination against African American defendants in southern courts. However, its primary goal was to gradually curb the use of forced confessions as evidence in court, as Thurgood Marshall explained in a letter to a Florida lawyer in July 1942.[44] These efforts soon bore fruit, and in 1940 alone, the NAACP managed to win three cases that it had brought before the U.S. Supreme Court.[45] A particularly important victory that year was the case of Isiah "Izell" Chambers, Jack Williamson, Charles Davis, and Walter Woodward from Florida, which led to a favorable decision by the U.S. Supreme Court in February 1940.

On May 13, 1933, a white resident of Pompano Beach, Florida, was murdered. Shortly thereafter, law enforcement officials in Broward County arrested between thirty and forty black suspects. A number of these men were held for more than a week at the Fort Lauderdale jail and interrogated day and night by white deputy sheriffs, jail keepers, and civilians without being allowed any contact with a lawyer. Four of the suspects—Chambers, Williamson, Davis, and Woodward—were then charged with murder before the local court. During the trial, they testified that they had been whipped and beaten during the interrogations until they finally made false confessions. As proof of their ordeal, they revealed to the court the many scars and bruises on their bodies.[46]

After the conclusion of the proceedings before the Broward County Circuit Court, the four defendants were found guilty based on their alleged confessions and sentenced to death by electrocution. Over the next several years, the Supreme Court of Florida overturned the death sentences of the four men on two occasions. It was not until their third conviction by an all-white jury in Broward County that the Florida Supreme Court confirmed the sentence. Thereafter, the NAACP legal department took up the case and appealed it to the U.S. Supreme Court.

After the first hearing of the case before the Supreme Court in January 1940, Walter White, the longtime head of the NAACP, told a crowd of reporters of "the tremendous importance of carrying these cases involving the protection of basic citizenship rights to the U.S. Supreme Court," adding, "I wish we would have fifty such cases brought before the high court every year. I believe it would strengthen the arms of justice in all parts of the country."[47]

On February 12, 1940, the Supreme Court announced its decision in the case of *Chambers v. Florida*. As in *Brown v. Mississippi*, it nullified the conviction of the four appellants with reference to the due process clause of the Fourteenth Amendment. Although—in contrast to the case of Brown, Ellington, and Shields—the justices could find no clear evidence for the use of physical violence against the four men, they declared that the use of the confessions was unlawful because they "had been obtained by coercion and duress."[48]

The symbolic importance of the decision was underscored by the fact that the Supreme Court justices made the announcement on the birthday of former president Abraham Lincoln (February 12, 1809–April 15, 1865) and thus implicitly commemorated Lincoln's legacy as the "Great Emancipator," who freed the slaves during the American Civil War. The decision explicitly made reference to the discriminatory circumstances of the case and emphasized the obligation of the Supreme Court to shield all American citizens from legal discrimination: "Due process of law, preserved for all by our Constitution, commands that no such practice as that disclosed by this record shall send any accused to his death. No higher duty, no more solemn responsibility, rests upon this Court, than that of translating into living law and maintaining this constitutional shield deliberately planned and inscribed for the benefit of every human being subject to our Constitution—of whatever race, creed or persuasion."[49] Likewise, the justices made reference to the contemporary political developments in Europe and Asia. Five months earlier, World War II had erupted in Europe, and beginning in 1933, American newspapers had reported extensively on the massive curtailment of civil rights in Nazi Germany. "Today, as in ages past, we are not without tragic proof that the exalted power of some governments to punish manufactured crime dictatorially is the handmaid of tyranny. Under our constitutional system, courts stand against any winds that blow as havens of refuge for those who might otherwise suffer because they are helpless, weak, outnumbered, or because they are non-conforming victims of prejudice and public excitement."[50] With reference to the injustices committed by "tyrannical powers," the court demanded—as in *Brown v. Mississippi*—that democratic legal traditions be respected in the United States.

The national press emphatically welcomed the *Chambers* decision. A number of articles emphasized the "historic" relevance of the ruling and pointed to the special importance of the Supreme Court as a haven for civil rights.[51] The African American press in particular emphasized that it was none other than Justice Hugo L. Black, a former member of the Ku Klux Klan, who announced the decision in favor of the black petitioners. The *Pittsburgh Courier* reported that in contrast to the usual practice, Justice Black read the full text of the decision before a "hushed and solemn" audience in the packed courtroom of the Supreme Court.[52] The front-page article said that the decision "on the 131th anniversary of the birth of Abraham Lincoln, the Emancipator," had once again affirmed for the black population the "inviolability of their rights and the protections vouchsafed them under the Constitution."[53]

The *Chicago Defender* extolled the decision as "another step towards the complete emancipation" of the black population in the South.[54] One day after the announcement of the decision, the NAACP issued a press release in which its president, Arthur Spingarn, highlighted the importance of the ruling for blacks and whites in the United States: "No poor man in America, whether white or colored, can lose hope so long as the United States Supreme Court remains a bulwark protecting the constitutional citizenship rights of the under-privileged and defenseless."[55] In an editorial published in March 1940, Roy Wilkins, the editor of the *Crisis*, called the decision a "rebuke to torture." He went on to say that although detaining suspects without a warrant, torturing them, and extorting false confessions was "in vogue in many places in our country," it was nevertheless "part of the routine police procedures" against African American suspects in the South.[56] As with *Brown v. Mississippi*, Wilkins noted that the *Chambers* case illustrated "the tremendous odds against Negroes arrested in a prejudice-ridden local community where they are at the mercy of local officials and local public opinion. They are terrorized and stripped of all their rights."[57]

With commentaries like this, the NAACP emphasized the special importance of its ongoing legal battle against the use of forced confessions—namely, keeping unjustly condemned African American defendants from being executed, and using constitutional law to rein in the racist criminal justice system of the South.

The archives of the NAACP reveal, however, that the organization was not prepared to represent all African American defendants from the South who alleged that they had been tortured and forced to make a confession. Already in 1937, Charles Hamilton Houston had written a letter to a lawyer in Texas stating that the NAACP only supported cases in which there was reason to assume that the defendant was innocent of the crimes that he or she had been accused of and was "a victim of race prejudice." He added that the organization only selected cases that had "elements . . . of general interests to Negroes, affecting their civic, economic, or political life."[58] In the opinion of legal historian Mark V. Tushnet, the NAACP shied away from defending presumably guilty convicted African Americans because it was afraid that such cases would damage its public image.[59]

A wide range of factors—including legal considerations, financial considerations, and the individual circumstances of each case—determined whether NAACP lawyers intervened in a specific case. Indeed, NAACP lawyers justified their refusal to take on certain cases by referring to the organization's limited financial resources to pursue legal experiments or by citing that these cases were not suitable for establishing legal precedents. Nevertheless, such cases were debated extensively. After all, rejecting a case could have dramatic consequences, as the NAACP was often the only institution that could appeal a conviction and potentially prevent the predominantly destitute defendants from being executed.[60]

Numerous cases show that the legal activities of the NAACP were severely impeded by the massive discrimination against African American defendants in southern courtrooms. When contesting their convictions, such defendants could refer only to procedural violations that had been raised at their court hearings. If the defendants or their lawyers had failed to draw attention to such breaches of their rights during the trials, the NAACP lawyers had no legal grounds for justifying a request for the U.S. Supreme Court to review the verdict.

A particularly dramatic example was the case of eighteen-year-old George Edwards Jr., who in early March 1946 was sentenced to death by a court in Leesville, Louisiana, for murdering a white farmer. After his conviction, Edwards sent numerous letters to William Henry Huff, the director of the Abolish Peonage Committee of America in Chicago, who forwarded the messages to the NAACP. Edwards described in great detail how he had been repeatedly tortured before the beginning of his trial and was finally forced to make a false confession. He also pointed out that during the trial, he was represented by white public defenders who had failed to raise the allegations of torture before the court and given him no opportunity to testify on his own behalf.[61] After reviewing the trial transcripts, the NAACP lawyers concluded that there was no basis for an appeal. On May 9, 1946, George Edwards Jr. was executed by electrocution in the prison of Vernon Parish, Louisiana.[62] As NAACP lawyer Robert L. Carter noted in a letter dated May 14, 1946: "[We] went over the record of the case and were unable to find any federal question involved. We attempted to get a further delay in the execution. . . . The stay . . . had been granted, [but] the Governor suddenly cancelled and pushed up the date of the execution. After trying other means of obtaining a stay, we were unable to do anything. Unfortunately, George Edwards has been executed. We regret that we were unable to save this young man's life."[63] The Edwards case illustrates that the defense launched by the predominantly white lawyers for the benefit of their African American clients determined the successful work of the NAACP in forced-confession cases. It was also for this reason that the NAACP could bring only a fraction of the cases submitted to them before the U.S. Supreme Court. However, NAACP activities in these selected cases often had a direct impact on the civil rights situation of African Americans in the South, as shown in the previously discussed case of Dave Canty.

Local Interventions: The Case of Dave Canty

After Canty was sentenced to death by the Circuit Court of Montgomery, Alabama, for the murder of Eunice Ward in March 1938, the NAACP legal department petitioned the U.S. Supreme Court to review the case. In March 1940, the court overturned the death sentence without an oral hearing by pointing to the precedents established with *Chambers v. Florida.*[64]

A close look at developments on the ground reveals that NAACP activities in the Canty case also challenged established local power structures. Only a few days after newspapers in Montgomery published the alleged confession of Dave Canty in early April 1938, William G. Porter—the head of the NAACP branch in Montgomery at the time—informed the national office of the case. Porter said that Canty had been treated "very roughly" to extort the confession.[65] The NAACP legal department asked Porter to provide more information on the case but received no response.[66] One month later, Marshall sent a letter to Dr. E. W. Taggart, the president of the NAACP branch in Birmingham, Alabama, to inform him of the failure to act on the part of the officials in Montgomery and request that he conduct a "preliminary investigation" of the case. Marshall said that the only evidence against Canty consisted of an "alleged confession extorted by force and violence."[67] In view of the specific circumstances of the case, however, Marshall advised Taggart to exercise caution and restraint in pursuing his investigation: "From all indication this case is very important and at the same time is the type of case which is being protected by the authorities to the end that it might be dangerous to make too searching an investigation. We do hope, however, that you will be able to make a preliminary one and let us have your information as soon as possible."[68] At the request of the NAACP legal department, on May 31, 1938, Taggart sent a report to Marshall after having spoken with representatives of a local African American citizens' committee. These were individuals who were active in the Canty case and had visited the suspect in jail following his purported confession. According to Taggart, there was every indication that Canty had been violently forced to make his confession: "They beat Canty into confession. Dave is said by the committee who talked with him that he 'just soon to die one way as another' and signed the confession which the police dictated."[69] Taggart said that the members of the committee had not been allowed to examine Canty for any physical signs that he had been tortured.[70] Moreover, he noted that the suspect had also been subjected to brutal treatment when he was taken to a public witness lineup: "They took Canty back to the scene and had him run handcuffed. Canty stumbled and tripped one of the police between whom he was running, throwing him to the ground. This vexed the officers into kicking and abusing the prisoner."[71]

The results of the investigation conducted by local civil rights activists thus directly contradicted the official denial of all allegations of torture by the local police. Shortly after Canty admitted to committing the crime in April 1938, the *Montgomery Advertiser* ran a story in which police commissioner William P. Screws publicly dismissed the "rumors" that Canty had been physically abused and claimed that no "strong-arm methods" had been used to obtain the murder confession.[72] To substantiate this version of events, the chief investigator of the Montgomery Police Department, Paul Rapport, personally accompanied a reporter from the *Advertiser* to the Alabama state prison and allowed him to photograph the avowed murderer. As the journalist subsequently reported, he asked Canty if he had been physically abused in any way, to which he replied, "No." Furthermore, he wrote Canty showed "no visible sign of a beating."[73]

After the NAACP lawyers received the reports by Taggart, they decided to continue to provide legal assistance. Marshall wrote to Taggart that he personally believed that this was "a very important case" that not only involved "the rights of Dave Canty" but would also "be of benefit to Negroes in the South in general."[74]

Taggart sent a letter to E. G. Jackson, editor of the *Alabama Tribune*, Montgomery's black newspaper, urging him to help revive the existing NAACP branch and foster within the local black community a willingness to unite in the fight against racial injustice: "The people of Montgomery ought [to] see, as a result of this apparent and flagrant miscarriage of justice, that they need to form an organization that has the power and moral courage to raise a voice of protest that will never be hushed against that sort of thing."[75]

The archival records of the Montgomery NAACP branch indicate that "the people of Montgomery" did react to the case. In late May, William G. Porter wrote to Walter White to ask for support in "reorganizing" the NAACP branch in Montgomery by supplying him with campaign literature and sending him the names and addresses of other NAACP activists in the South who might assist him in this undertaking.[76] Six weeks later, Porter reported that the Montgomery NAACP branch was "well organized" and had "taken over the Canty case," having paid $250 to have the briefs filed for its appeal. "If the Montgomery Branch succeeds, you will see a different South in a few years," he optimistically predicted. Porter also noted that despite the expected resistance by the head of the local police department, people were prepared to challenge Canty's conviction. "As you know[,] the commissioner of police is the chief one fighting the case and the one to make the statement that the confession was not made through force. . . . This is going to be a mean case and we are going through with it."[77] In a letter dated November 14, 1938, Porter confirmed his intention to see Canty's case through to "the bitter end," adding, "I know you would love to see us win."[78] Porter was possibly reassured by the rising membership numbers of the Montgomery NAACP branch, which gained fifty new members in July 1938 and thirty-six new members in August 1938.[79]

Thanks to the tireless efforts of local and national NAACP activists, the Montgomery branch collected another $270, which was paid to Canty's lawyer, Edward W. Wadsworth, while Canty's family paid $500 to the lawyer.[80] As many observers had expected, however, the Alabama Supreme Court affirmed the death sentence against Canty in June 1939.[81]

After the verdict, Marshall and Canty's new lawyer, Alex C. Birch, started to work on their appeal to the U.S. Supreme Court.[82] As Canty's execution drew closer, the Montgomery branch's membership rose to about one thousand.[83]

NAACP files also show that the activities of the local branch of the organization for Dave Canty led to alliances with white citizens in Montgomery. In November 1939, T. T. Allen, who in the meantime had replaced William G. Porter as the head of the Montgomery branch, recounted a meeting with a white resident who had assured him of her support:

A Mrs. Rutledge who represents a group of liberal-minded white people here talked with me yesterday. She is also a member of this branch of the N.A.A.C.P. It appears that there is a great number of fair-minded whites who believe that Canty is absolutely NOT GUILTY, and Mrs. Rutledge for some time has shown a great interest in this case and offered to be whatever help she could. She offered to go before the Governor and the Pardon Board to tell them of what rumors are circulating in their circle[;] also they are trying to get affidavits to show that witnesses were frightened into not testifying in the trial.[84]

Alex C. Birch, the white attorney representing Dave Canty, also reported during the trial that many whites in Montgomery had expressed their doubts about Canty's guilt and their disapproval of his alleged torture by the local police: "Many of us think that peace officers are often prone to use third degree methods. It is needless to say that the stamp of disapproval should be placed on such inhuman conduct. There is a limit to human fortitude and endurance, and the innocent will often confess to crimes to avoid further unbearable punishment."[85] The letters and reports cited here indicate that the NAACP activists in the Canty case had raised awareness of civil rights among the local population and, to some degree, among white residents. With their initiatives, the local black activists demonstrated that they were prepared — to the best of their abilities — to take action against the discriminatory treatment of Dave Canty. Their actions were essentially acts of resistance that, however briefly, challenged the local racist power structure.

Further developments in the case show that the activities of the NAACP were not without impact. After the Alabama Supreme Court confirmed the death sentence against Canty on June 22, 1939, Thurgood Marshall and Leon A. Ransom joined Alex C. Birch in petitioning the U.S. Supreme Court to review the case. In their application to the court, they referred to the discriminatory circumstances of the case and the massive allegations of physical abuse that Canty had raised during the trial. As previously mentioned, the Supreme Court reversed the death sentence in March 1940. Yet despite these successes, the NAACP legal campaign had its limits. In July 1942, Dave Canty was again tried on murder charges before the Montgomery Circuit

Court, found guilty once again, and sentenced to life in prison. Out of concern that the case would once again be appealed, the prosecution refrained from presenting Canty's dubious confession as evidence. After the Alabama Supreme Court confirmed the decision in January 1943, the U.S. Supreme Court declined to review the case on May 3, 1943. Canty died several years later in Kilby Prison, Alabama, the same place where the police had allegedly tortured him into his purported confession.[86]

Defended by a Black Attorney: The Case of W. D. Lyons

Whereas the Canty case brought to the fore various forms of black resistance to the practice of torturing suspects to obtain forced confessions, the case of W. D. Lyons, which also dates to the early 1940s, demonstrated both the symbolic impact of the legal activities of the NAACP in a southern court and the changed strategies against the background of World War II.

The case was sparked by a sensational murder and robbery in Fort Towson, Oklahoma, on December 31, 1939, in which a white couple was killed and their house set on fire. Their four-year-old son also died in the flames. The couple's eight-year-old son managed to rescue himself and his one-year-old brother from the burning building.[87] After the governor of Oklahoma received news of the crime, he dispatched a special investigator named Vernon Cheatwood to Hugo, Oklahoma, to solve the case. According to unconfirmed rumors, an escaped white convict had confessed to the crime, but since the governor was going to be up for reelection soon, his office allegedly decided to make another individual responsible for the act in a bid to divert voter attention away from his administration's failure to ensure adequate prison security.[88] On January 11, 1940, the local sheriff's department arrested a twenty-one-year-old African American named W. D. Lyons. A few days later, local newspapers reported that Lyons had confessed to the crime.[89]

In late March 1940, NAACP leader Walter White received a letter from Roscoe Dunjee, the publisher of the African American weekly the *Black Dispatch* and president of the Oklahoma Conference of Branches of the NAACP, requesting that the organization's national office provide financial support in the Lyons case. Dunjee said that he wanted to hire a lawyer for Lyons and have the background of the case investigated. According to his information, Lyons had been subjected to a "terrible flogging" in order to "extort a confession."[90] In another letter written on December 26, 1940, Dunjee urged the national office of the NAACP to become directly involved in the case, which he argued was far more suitable for a legal intervention than the Chambers case, in which the Supreme Court had rescinded the death sentences of the four defendants. He pointed out that in contrast to that particular case, the white community in Hugo, Oklahoma, was very favorably inclined toward the defendant and did not side with the local authorities: "We have the best case to be found in the South in the question of forced confession. . . . My thought is that the national office would do a good job to tie into this case direct[ly]."[91]

Finally, Dunjee suggested that Thurgood Marshall, in his function as the top attorney at the NAACP, should play an active role in defending Lyons in his upcoming trial. He said that such a step would allow the NAACP to take the spotlight and "revive association activity all over the U.S.," adding that Marshall's personal presence in the courtroom would be of great importance to the trial. Once again, he emphasized the positive attitude of the local white population toward Lyons, presumably to convey to Marshall that he had no reason to be concerned for his personal safety.[92]

Marshall agreed to travel to Oklahoma and mount a legal defense for W. D. Lyons by working together with Stanley Belden, the white attorney who had been hired by the local NAACP branch. This was a decided departure from the usual approach adopted by the organization, namely that it only intervened after a black defendant had been convicted.

On January 24, 1941, the NAACP published a press release on Marshall's arrival in Hugo to take part in the trial.[93] Three days later, proceedings commenced against Lyons before the local circuit court. The archives of the NAACP contain numerous personal letters that Marshall sent to Walter White during the trial, documenting both his personal impressions and the impact of his presence in the courtroom.

As Marshall reported, the local population flocked to see the trial of Lyons, without showing any hostility toward the defendant or his legal representatives: "The court room is crowded beyond capacity, the building itself is crowded every day. More than a thousand people from all over the county. Coming in trucks wagons, etc. All of the sentiment is good. No evidence of mob spirit."[94] The very appearance of a black lawyer before the court in Hugo challenged the racially coded role expectations of the white representatives of the justice system and the audience:

When I arrived in Hugo last Sunday night I was not sure what was going to happen. . . . When we walked into court, word got round that "a nigger lawyer from New York" was on the case. Court attaches were very nice and explained that this was their first experience in seeing a Negro lawyer try a case—first time they had seen such an animal. . . . Well, our case was called, I was introduced to the Court and took a seat at the counsel table—the building did not fall and the world did not come to an end.[95]

The exceptional importance of the proceedings, according to Marshall's report, was highlighted by the introductory remarks of the presiding judge and the presence of a number of classes of children from the local white school: "The judge announced that 'two nationalities' were involved and he did not want any disorder in the Court house. . . . On Tuesday, Wednesday and Thursday there were several classes from the local white school in Court. The Judge announced from the bench that they were there and that this was a 'gala day'—can you imagine a Negro on trial for his life being considered a gala day."[96] According to the court transcript, Lyons testified that he had been beaten several times with a blackjack during his interrogation and that the aforementioned special investigator, Vernon Cheatwood, had played a decidedly active role in the torture. "[They] would take me up and bend me across the table and Mr. Cheatwood beat me on the back of the head with the blackjack, and set me back down in the chair and start beating me on my legs again and arms."[97] Lyons said that later in the interrogation, investigators forced him to make a confession by placing a pan in his lap with the bones of the deceased victims of the murder and robbery: "They said they was the bones of Mrs. Rogers, Mr. Rogers, and the baby, and I had never seen any bones of dead people before, had I ever seen dead people before, and I was afraid of those bones on my lap in the pan. Mr. Cheatwood would lay the bones in my hand, such as the teeth and body bones, and make me hold it and look at it, wouldn't let me turn my head away, and beat me on the hands and knees."[98] Out of fear of being subjected to further abuse and intimidation, he said that he shortly thereafter made an initial oral confession of committing the crime and, after being transferred to another jail the following day, testified that he made a second confession in the presence of the investigating district attorney and a stenographer.[99]

The state prosecutor subsequently called a number of deputy sheriffs to the witness stand who all denied the allegations of torture but admitted that Lyons had been confronted with the bones of the deceased. The officers testified that they did this to make him start "thinking about what he did."[100] Afterward, Marshall and Birch called a number of white witnesses to the stand to testify that Vernon Cheatwood had openly spoken to them about the torture of Lyons. Marshall made the following comment on this in his report:

We put on the clerk (white) in the hotel where Cheatwood was staying who testified that Cheatwood came to the hotel the day after the confession and told the porter to go upstairs and get his "nigger beater" which he showed to the people in the lobby of the hotel telling that he had beat Lyons for six or seven hours and made him confess. The father and sister in law [sic] of the deceased woman both testified that Cheatwood had told them he beat Lyons for seven hours from his head to feet. There are some good white people in this world.[101]

The appearance of the African American NAACP lawyer in court and his efforts to defend the procedural rights of Lyons were perceived as an affront to the traditional, racially defined hierarchy of southern courtrooms, and Marshall very effectively used this to his advantage: "I did all the cross-examining of the officers because we figured they would resent being questioned by a Negro and would get angry and this would help us. It worked perfect. They all became angry at the idea of a Negro pushing them into tight corners and making their lies obvious. Boy, did I like that — and did the Negroes in the Court-room [sic] like it."[102] This account illustrates the performative and symbolic dimension of Marshall's courtroom defense. By conducting a cross-examination that called into question the truthfulness of the white witnesses, he broke a long-held taboo, in that the testimony of white witnesses traditionally enjoyed a higher degree of credibility than that of black witnesses. Likewise, with his brash manner of questioning the deputy sheriffs, he overstepped the expected, conventional roles of a black man in court and a black man interacting with police officers, namely that he should behave passively. According to Marshall's reports, the African American members of the audience were particularly aware of the symbolism of these events in the courtroom.[103]

Despite the efforts of Marshall and Birch to call into question the legal admissibility of the confessions, the presiding judge ruled that Lyons's second confession would be accepted as evidence. Based on the interval that had elapsed since the interrogation, he decided that the confession had been made "voluntarily."[104] After the oral proceedings were completed, Lyons was found guilty by the twelve-member all-white jury and sentenced to life imprisonment. However, Marshall viewed the sentence as proof that the members of the jury secretly believed that Lyons was not guilty. He wrote to White: "You know that life for such a crime as that — three people killed, shot with a shot gun and cut up with an axe and then burned — shows clearly that they believed him innocent."[105] He went on to say that this local initiative had put the NAACP "in a perfect position to appeal."[106] Furthermore, he was optimistic that the trial would have a long-term impact on the local white population's awareness of civil rights: "One thing this trial has accomplished—the good citizens of that area have been given a lesson in Constitutional Law and the rights of Negroes which they won't forget for some time. Law Enforcement officers now know that when they beat a Negro up they might have to answer for it on the witness stand."[107] According to legal historian Michael J. Klarman, the presence of black lawyers in southern courtrooms offered positive role models for African Americans and motivated them to protest against their ongoing discrimination in the criminal justice system.[108] Thurgood Marshall's report confirms this assessment. In it, he notes that the intervention by the NAACP had motivated blacks to get involved and fight for their civil rights: "You can't imagine what it means to those people down there who have been pushed around for years to know that there is an organization that will help them. They are really ready to do their part now. They are ready for anything."[109] Furthermore, the activities of the NAACP in the Lyons case aimed to draw the attention of the American public to the continuing discrimination against black defendants by the criminal justice system of the South. Before his departure from Hugo, Marshall suggested in a letter to White that the NAACP uses the Lyons case to launch a national donation campaign. Marshall said that the particular circumstances surrounding the case made it ideally suited to raising money: "We could use another good defense fund and this case has more appeal than any up to this time. The beating plus the bones of dead people will raise money. . . . We have been needing a good criminal case and we have it. Let's raise some real money."[110] In March 1941, the NAACP published a full-page announcement in the *Crisis* calling for donations to mount a defense in the Lyons case. The text under the headline "Tortured with Charred Bones!" includes a photograph of Lyons in prison garb (see figure 5). In the photo, Lyons is gazing off into the distance, and his hands are in cuffs.

In printing the photograph, the publishers of the *Crisis* were relying on a visualization strategy that they had already put to the test in the campaign against lynching violence. Beginning in the 1910s, the NAACP had been using photos of lynchings to publicly denounce rampant mob justice in the South. During the late nineteenth and early twentieth centuries, hundreds of photographs and postcards circulated throughout the South showing members of lynch mobs posing in front of hanging and mutilated African American victims. These images were made to demonstrate the presumed superiority of the "white race" over alleged black offenders who

Tortured With Charred Bones!

THIS man, 20 years of age, was convicted on January 31, 1941, of murdering a white man, his wife and 4-year-old child, on the night of December 31, 1939, near Fort Towson, Oklahoma.

Lyons is supposed to have "confessed" to the crime. The "confession" was secured by placing the charred bones of the dead people in his lap, *and by rubbing Lyon's arm with the teeth and jow-bone of the dead woman!*

Immediately after the crime, committed with a shotgun and axe, with the bodies of the victims burned up as the house was set afire by the killer, a white prison camp convict is said to have made a full confession. His statement that convicts were worked as prisoners by day, but permitted to roam freely at night, was so scandalous politically that it was hushed up and the word went out: "get a Negro and get him quick!"

School Children at Trial

Lyons was arrested, but was held without trial all during the political year of 1940. For four days, beginning January 27, 1941, N.A.A.C.P. attorneys defended him during his trial, which the presiding judge described as a "gala" affair. Schools for white children were dismissed and the youngsters admitted to the courtroom.

Thurgood Marshall, special counsel of the N.A.A.C.P., who went from New York to appear for Lyons, along with Stanley Belden, a white attorney, was the *first* Negro attorney to act in the courthouse in Hugo, Okla., in its entire history.

Lyons was found guilty by a jury with recommendation of mercy. When a white jury in Oklahoma finds a Negro guilty of shooting a white family to death, hacking the bodies to pieces with an axe, and then setting fire to the home and burning the bodies—*and still recommends mercy*—something is rotten in Denmark!

Defense Fund Needed

The N.A.A.C.P. is appealing for funds to carry this case to higher courts and perhaps to the United States supreme court. White and colored people who live near Lyon's home already have contributed $360 to the expenses. It will take about $5,000 to finance the appeal in this case alone.

But, while we are talking about the beauties of democracy and the necessity of strengthening our American system

W. D. LYONS

by giving justice to all, why not make a contribution to this Lyons case a testimony to our faith in democracy and our determination that it *shall* work? Why not a defense fund for all the black men the N.A.A.C.P. is called upon to defend? Why not $10,000?

Contributions should be sent to the

N.A.A.C.P., 69 Fifth avenue, New York, N. Y. Large contributors may indicate that their money is to go to the N.A.A.C.P. Legal Defense and Educational Fund, Inc., and thus it will be deductible for income tax purposes. In any case, checks should be made payable to Mary White Ovington, Treasurer.

FIGURE 5 "Tortured with Charred Bones!," a call for donations to the NAACP in the case of W. D. Lyons, *Crisis*, March 1941, 85. The author wishes to thank the Crisis Publishing Co., Inc., the publisher of the magazine of the NAACP, for the use of this image, first published in the March 1941 issue of the *Crisis*.

had dared to question the "racial order" of the South. By reproducing these photographs in publications, flyers, and public exhibitions and placing them in another context, the NAACP had given these images a new interpretation: instead of serving as proof of white superiority, they were now a visual testimony to the barbarism and backwardness of the white southern population.[111]

The NAACP took a similar approach in the Lyons case. Lacking a photo of its own, the organization used one that the sheriff's department in Oklahoma had taken immediately after the suspect had made his alleged confession. But instead of presenting Lyons as an avowed killer, he was shown within the context of his legal defense fund as a victim of the discriminatory procedures of the southern criminal justice system. As with the lynching photographs, the recontextualization of the photo of Lyons led to a diametrically opposed reinterpretation of its message. Yet in contrast to the images of murdered and mutilated lynching victims, which documented the total powerlessness of blacks within the racist order of the South, the image of Lyons allowed readers to identify themselves with a surviving victim of racist violence and discrimination. In the accompanying article, the publishers of the *Crisis* emphatically pointed to the unusual circumstances of the case in a bid to convince readers to support the NAACP legal campaign: "This man, 20 years of age, was convicted on January 31, 1941, of murdering a white man, his wife and 4-year-old child. . . . Lyons is supposed to have 'confessed' to the crime. The 'confession' was secured by placing the charred bones of the dead people in his lap, *and by rubbing Lyons's arm with the teeth and jawbone of the dead woman!*"[112] Aside from helping Lyons appeal his conviction, the article said that the donations would also help to strengthen American democracy: While we are talking about the beauties of democracy and the necessity of strengthening our American system by giving justice to all, why not make a contribution to this Lyons case a testimony to our faith in democracy and our determination that it *shall* work? Why not a defense fund for all the black men the N.A.A.C.P. is called upon to defend? Why not $10,000?"[113] Whereas the NAACP had used the word "civilization" during the 1930s to draw the public's attention to the scandal of torture in the South, now, against the background of World War II, it embraced the word "democracy." Shortly after the outbreak of hostilities, the NAACP made it clear in public statements that it was prepared to support an entry into the war against Nazi Germany but that it also wanted to build on the developments abroad to advance the struggle for democracy at home, in the United States. In its statements in support of Lyons, the NAACP evidently made reference to president Franklin D. Roosevelt's famous "Four Freedoms" speech of January 1941, in which he announced that the United States would work to secure a world founded on four essential human freedoms. In addition to freedom of speech and freedom of worship, Roosevelt declared that freedom from want and freedom from fear would henceforth be safeguarded by American policy.[114] Particularly after the United States entered the war on

December 7, 1941, the NAACP repeatedly challenged the government by contrasting instances of horrendous racial violence in the South with the proclaimed goals and ideals of U.S. war policy.[115]

This strategy was also recognizable in the ongoing course of the case against W. D. Lyons. After the Oklahoma Supreme Court upheld the life sentence in June 1943, the NAACP made the following announcement in a press release: "The methods used in obtaining the confession in the case have no parallel in American jurisprudence. Such treatment of an American citizen by officers of the State of Oklahoma strikes at the very foundation of the principles of democracy, now threatened from without as well as from within."[116]During the course of World War II, an increasing number of African Americans began to publicly protest against their continuing disenfranchisement, particularly in view of the fact that black soldiers were risking their lives to defend American democracy abroad. By stressing Lyons's status as an "American citizen" and condemning his treatment by the authorities in Oklahoma as an affront to the "principles of democracy," the NAACP called into question America's moral self-image. The message was clear: tolerating torture in the South stood in direct contrast to the foreign policy rhetoric of the United States. As researchers like legal historian Mary L. Dudziak have shown, the NAACP and other civil rights groups pursued this strategy of argumentation during the Cold War by repeatedly pointing to the discrepancy between the democratic vision and ideological claim to global leadership of the United States and the ongoing discrimination against African American citizens.[117]

In the Lyons case, though, this strategy was not crowned with success. To the utter surprise of the NAACP legal department, the U.S. Supreme Court upheld the life prison sentence on June 5, 1944. In the opinion issued by the court, the majority of the justices concurred that due to the circumstances and the amount of time that had elapsed between the alleged physical abuse and the second confession made by W. D. Lyons, his signed statement was admissible evidence. On October 9, 1944, the Supreme Court rejected a request filed by the NAACP to hear the case again.[118]

After 1945: The NAACP and the Case of the Groveland Four

The end of World War II and the victory of the Allies over Germany and Japan meant that the legal battles of the NAACP were increasingly the focus of public attention. This was fostered by the previously mentioned massive growth in membership enjoyed by the NAACP. In 1946, the organization had

500,000 members. Back in 1943, Thurgood Marshall—at the height of the race riots that shook a number of American cities that year—had expressed his deep disappointment over the continuing discrimination against the African American population: "Despite all that has been done by the NAACP and others there have been only a few minor changes. The underlying policy of segregation and discrimination is no better and if anything worse. We are still second class citizens as civilians and second class soldiers and officers in the army."[119] After the end of World War II, however, it became clear that this military conflict had significantly shifted the coordinates of the so-called "race question." This was reflected, for example, in the self-confidence of African American soldiers, who, following their return to the United States, vehemently insisted that their civil rights be respected.[120] Moreover, the war had engendered a situation in which the ongoing discrimination against the black population in the South was perceived as a "national problem."[121] For instance, black civil rights activist and author W. E. B. Du Bois remarked in 1948 that the American nation "is no longer pessimistic on this problem": "Far from believing that black and white cannot live together in peace and progress in one nation, it [the nation] has awakened to the fact that peoples of all colors and races must live together in one world or perish. This gradual realization of a great revolution following two world wars had made our problem of races a burning political question."[122] National awareness of racism in American society was intensified by the ensuing Cold War. The mounting ideological conflicts between the United States and the Soviet Union made the issue increasingly relevant to U.S. foreign and domestic policy.[123] The NAACP capitalized on this changed perception in its campaigns, as the following examples show.

In February 1946, an incident occurred in Batesburg, South Carolina. After being honorably discharged from the military, African American World War II veteran Isaac Woodard was taking a Greyhound bus home to his family. Following an argument between him and the driver, the bus stopped in Batesburg, where Woodard was arrested by Batesburg police chief Lynwood Shull and one of his officers and forcibly removed from the bus. On the way to the town jail, the officers beat him repeatedly with nightsticks and hit him so hard on the head and in the face that he was permanently blinded. The story of this black war veteran, who served four years in the U.S. Army during World War II, sparked an outcry in the national press.[124] A rally in New York City was attended by roughly 31,000 people who gathered to protest Woodard's brutal treatment and the persistent discrimination against African Americans in the South. In July 1946, the U.S. Department of Justice finally launched an FBI investigation into Chief Shull. In November 1946, Shull was acquitted by the U.S. district court in Columbia, South Carolina, and the white audience applauded when it heard the verdict by the all-white jury. Thereafter, the NAACP initiated a tour in which it visited a number of major American cities with the sightless former army sergeant to draw attention to the extreme urgency of the African American civil rights struggle.[125]

The NAACP also played a key role in exposing the blatant injustices committed in the case of the so-called Groveland Four, which was a focus of public attention during the late 1940s.[126] In July 1949, rumors circulated in Lake County, Florida, that a young white woman, seventeen-year-old Norma Padgett, had been raped by African Americans. Shortly thereafter, Charles Greenlee, Samuel Shepherd, and Walter Lee Irvin were arrested by the local sheriff's department. A fourth suspect, Ernest Thomas, was shot by a posse while trying to flee the sheriff's deputies. Immediately thereafter, hundreds of white men gathered in front of the Lake County jail and demanded that the authorities hand over the alleged culprits. Sheriff Willis V. McCall told the crowd that the suspects had been transferred to the Florida state penitentiary. In actual fact, he had temporarily brought them to a hiding place to preempt any action by the mob. The crowd of angry whites then drove to the black neighborhood of Groveland and fired shots into the homes of residents there. A number of houses were set on fire, and many people were attacked on the streets until the entire black population eventually fled the neighborhood.[127]

A few days later, NAACP lawyer Franklin H. Williams traveled to Groveland at Marshall's behest to ascertain the exact circumstances of the case. Williams managed to gain access to the three suspects. In their statements, they recounted that after their arrest they had been tied by their hands to a pipe on the jail cell ceiling and whipped to force them to confess to the crime.[128] Irvin related the events as follows:

> They let us stay in the cell a while and then they came back and taken us down in the hole of a jail. They taken me down first. Three went down with me. There wasn't anyone else down there. They handcuffed me over a pipe. So that my feet could not touch the floor; then they started beating me with a rubber hose. I was bleeding all the time around my head. They kept saying that I was the one that picked the girl up last night and they would beat me until I told them I was the one. . . . They hit me in my nose with their fist and beat me across my

back and chest and they beat me all over, but I had my pants on. . . .
They taken me back down in the hole a second time and beat me
again. I was bleeding pretty bad.[129]

Irvin's account of the events has many similarities with the quote in the drawing received by the NAACP in September 1949 and depicted at the beginning of this book. The statements of the arrested men were confirmed in a
written protocol by Williams, in which he noted the numerous injuries and
wounds that the three suspects had sustained. On Irvin's condition, he wrote:

Note: (observation of following signatories) in various parts of his
head especially in the back there are numerous healing scars, one in
particular is one inch long. On his chest and stomach, there are wide
bruises obviously caused by a stick or other objects lashed across the
chest. On his shoulders, there are similar lash marks. . . . Across his
back there are also scars and lash marks. On his wrist there are healed
scars encircling the entire wrist. On his face (jaw and forehead), there
are distinct bruises, his right jaw appears to be fractured. There is
blood on his pants, especially down the back.[130]

Immediately following Williams's return from Florida, the NAACP organized
a press conference in New York City, where the lawyers presented the results
of his investigation and reported on the massive allegations of torture
raised by the three suspects. The U.S. Department of Justice initiated an
FBI probe into the members of the local sheriff's department, but the investigation was discontinued at the request of the local U.S. district attorney
shortly before the trial of Greenlee, Shepherd, and Irvin. Federal agents were
told that it would be better to postpone the inquiry into the lawmen until after
a verdict had been reached in the case against the three suspects.[131]

In this trial before the court in Tavares, Florida, the local state prosecutor refrained from entering the dubious confessions as evidence. Nevertheless, on September 8, 1949, the jury returned a guilty verdict against Irvin
and Shepherd, and they were sentenced to death by electrocution. Sixteen-
year-old Charles Greenlee was given a life sentence because he was under
the minimum age for the death penalty.[132]

In October 1949, the NAACP published an eight-page brochure on the
Groveland case. The cover with the headline "GROVELAND U.S.A." showed
a photograph of a burning house and was framed by the catchwords "RIOTS,"
"HOME BURNING," "NIGHT RIDING," "TERROR," "HATE," "LYNCH LAW,"
and "KU KLUX KLAN."[133] The NAACP appealed to its readers nationwide to

support the legal initiative in favor of the three convicted men. Particular attention was given to the allegations of torture made by the men, which, as it was emphasized, had first been documented and brought to light by an "on-the-spot investigator" for the NAACP who reported that he had discovered "lash scars on their bodies and cuts on their heads made by these beatings" that were "still clearly visible" two weeks after the alleged confessions. "No doctor had seen the boys when the NAACP attorney interviewed them. They were still wearing the same clothing, dirty, and bloodstained from the beatings, in which they were attired when they were arrested."[134] The brochure emphatically urged readers to make a donation that would serve as their personal contribution to ending racism and discrimination in the United States:

> The cost of the long legal battle for justice in the Groveland case is an estimated $20,000. We cannot meet these expenses without your financial help. What is it worth to YOU to bring freedom to the three victims of bigotry and the "master race" theory in Florida? What is it worth to YOU to scotch the snake of Ku Klux Klan hoodlumism? What is it worth to YOU to make secure the peace of mind of every human being in the United States of America? Every cent you can contribute will bring us closer to our goal. Make the terror of Groveland a thing to be forgotten forever in a world where human dignity and justice reign supreme. Help the NAACP finish the fight. Give what you can today.[135]

The NAACP presented arguments here that were similar to those used fourteen years earlier in their appeal for donations in the Brown, Ellington, and Shields case, namely that the struggle against racism and discrimination in the South could only be won with the support of the population. In contrast to the year 1935, the appeal in 1949 was received by a public that was far more sensitized to these issues. Within just a few weeks, $4,600 in donations had been collected. In addition to the NAACP, the three convicted men received the express support of liberal and socialist groups, like the Southern Regional Council (the successor organization to the CIC), the Workers Defense League, the Communist Party USA (CPUSA), and the Socialist Party of America.[136]

After the NAACP filed a petition to appeal, the U.S. Supreme Court overturned the death sentences of Irvin and Shepherd in March 1951. Justice Robert H. Jackson described the case as "one of the best examples of one of the worst menaces to American justice."[137] While the district attorney of Lake County was preparing to press new charges against the two defendants,

Sheriff Willis McCall shot the two defendants during a prisoner transfer for the second trial, killing Shepherd on the spot and critically wounding Irvin. Although both prisoners were bound with handcuffs, McCall maintained after the shooting that the two men had tried to overpower him and that he had opened fire in self-defense. Irvin said later in a sworn statement that the sheriff had shot them without provocation. Afterward, Irvin was charged in Florida again, convicted of rape, and sentenced to death. The Florida Supreme Court upheld the verdict, and in 1954, the U.S. Supreme Court rejected an application by the NAACP to review the case. On December 15, 1955, Florida governor Leroy Collins commuted Irvin's death sentence to life imprisonment after the NAACP and other national and international organizations publicly campaigned for a reduced sentence.[138]

The Groveland case clearly shows that the NAACP campaign against forced confessions had no immediate impact on the practice of torture by southern law enforcement officials. Furthermore, the organization did not succeed in curbing the commonplace torture of African American citizens who came into contact with the police for committing alleged minor infractions. As police brutality was primarily a matter of state criminal law, it had to be challenged from within by local initiatives. Consequently, the NAACP national office called on its local chapters to address the matter of police brutality through continuous protest and legal action. In a pamphlet published in June 1939, it advised its branches to document and investigate cases of police brutality in their respective communities and press criminal charges "in extreme cases of death or serious injury."[139] Nevertheless, the cases examined in chapters 4 and 5 show that in the 1940s and early 1950s, sheriffs, deputy sheriffs, and police officers generally had to fear no legal consequences for using coercive methods. Moreover, the pervasive torture of blacks by lawmen rarely made headlines. The position of power enjoyed by law enforcement officials in the cities and counties of the South was so strong that the topic was largely ignored by the leading white newspapers, and the implicated officers were, as a rule, not held legally accountable. One exception was the case of sixteen-year-old Quintar South, which was made public in the early 1940s in Atlanta, Georgia. As will be shown, the circumstances surrounding that particular case meant that the torture of African Americans by police would become a topic of public debate in the South, at least for a brief period.

CHAPTER FOUR
Selective Public Outrage
The Quintar South Case

On March 8, 1940, a front-page article in the *Atlanta Constitution* reported on a shocking case of police brutality at the city's police headquarters. Officer William F. Sutherland was accused of torturing a sixteen-year-old black youth named Quintar South with a tacking iron, an electrical device with an iron shoe that police staff used to heat a compound and attach photographs to official documents.[1] The newspaper wrote that the iron was used to coerce South into confessing that he had broken into the gymnasium at Clark University, an Atlanta institution of higher education traditionally attended by African Americans. The article noted that Mrs. C. E. Harrison, a white resident of Atlanta, had brought the case to the attention of the public. A large photo showed police captain C. Neal Ellis and probation officer J. N. Starnes inspecting the victim's wounds. The report extensively cited the comments made by the sixteen-year-old about the events at police headquarters:

> He kept asking me about breaking in the gym and I kept telling him
> I didn't do it and he picked up this thing what looked like a soldering
> iron and plugged it in the wall. . . . Then he hit at me . . . and the
> hot iron hit on my arm and when it come off the skin come off with it.
> I didn't holler, though, and he pushed it against my neck and I didn't
> want him to burn me any more and I told him all right, I was one who
> helped break in the gym.[2]

The article also cited the outraged comments of Judge Garland Watkins of Fulton County Juvenile Court: "If the boy's story is true, no more shameful thing has ever happened in Atlanta. If such an act of medieval torture has taken place, the officer guilty must be found out and punished to the fullest extent of the law."[3] Judge Watkins was not alone in expressing such opinions. The following two days, the *Atlanta Constitution* reported that a number of white organizations—including the Georgia Women's Democratic Club, the Child Welfare Organization, the Georgia Humane Association, and the Georgia Association of Women Lawyers—had demanded a thorough investigation into the allegations of torture.[4] In a public statement, the mayor of

Atlanta, William B. Hartsfield, said that he would not rest until the use of torture methods by the Atlanta Police Department had been put to a stop.[5] Both the *Atlanta Constitution* and the city's second major white daily newspaper, the *Atlanta Journal*, condemned the torture in their editorials.[6] In letters to the editor, numerous white citizens of Atlanta expressed their moral outrage over the events.[7]

The abuse of Quintar South was one of the few cases between 1930 and 1955 in which the torture practices of law enforcement officials captured the attention of the white population in the South. An analysis of the reporting of the case by Atlanta's white press shows that the white population of the South had a highly selective awareness of racial violence, and that public outrage over individual instances of torture could not fundamentally change the widespread indifference toward acts of brutality perpetrated against African Americans.[8] The black press took an entirely different slant on the story of Quintar South. While it was portrayed in the white press as a regrettable isolated incident, black newspapers used it as an opportunity to draw attention to the routine use of racially motivated police violence in the American South.

"Horrible Injustice": The Reporting in Atlanta's White Press

The white press of Atlanta confined its reporting of the South case to a highly specific narrative framework that revolved around the previously mentioned C. E. Harrison, a forty-five-year-old woman who was married to a high-ranking employee of a nationwide telephone company, and who employed the youth in her home.[9] The initial articles in both the *Atlanta Constitution*, which saw itself as the mouthpiece of liberal white middle-class Atlantans, and the rather conservative *Atlanta Journal* repeatedly emphasized that it was only thanks to Harrison's initiative that the case was brought to the public's attention.[10] Hence, the reporting focused on the charitable and noble wife of an upstanding member of white society and her nurturing, almost motherly relationship to the sixteen-year-old South. This was also reflected in the portrayal of the encounter between Harrison and South at the Fulton County juvenile detention center: "Mrs. Harrison, convinced of his innocence after talking with Ralph Robertson, coach at Clark University, visited the boy on Wednesday in his cell. 'I saw the wounds on his arms and asked him how he hurt himself,' Mrs. Harrison said. He replied, 'they hurt me at the police station.' I asked him how in the world it happened, and he said that an officer had burned his arm to make him sign a paper saying he helped break into the gymnasium."[11] In the days that followed, the narrative of the concerned and compassionate rescuer and protector of the young black victim remained the focus of the reporting in the white newspapers. In doing so, it conformed with the prevailing gender and role expectations by evoking the image of the white southern lady, whose main social areas of responsibility included managing a household and doing charity work. This designated feminine sphere of social benevolence also included aiding and caring for those African Americans who adapted their conduct to the social, political, and economic norms defined by the white majority society.[12]

In that sense, Harrison's advocacy of Quintar South also derived from the prevailing racial paternalism of members of the southern white middle and upper classes toward blacks who stood in a dependent relationship to them, such as the employees in their households. It is against this background that we can understand how the South case captured the attention of the white press and white society in general. Only one day after the allegations of police misconduct were made public, the grand jury of Fulton Criminal Court voted to indict William F. Sutherland on charges of assaulting, striking, and wounding Quintar South "with the intent to commit a violent injury upon his person."[13] Both the Atlanta Police Department and the Fulton County Juvenile Court investigated the charges.[14] In its commentary on the South case, the *Atlanta Journal* urged the newly launched investigations to bring to light the "full truth" concerning the events: "If the charges are proved, then punishment sure and swift should follow. . . . Common sense, as well as common humanity, decry such methods, and demand that the brutalities of the so-called 'third degree' be abolished."[15] One day after the publication of the first article on the allegations of torture made by South, the *Atlanta Constitution* as well printed a commentary on the incident. Under the headline "Justice for the Weak," the events that transpired at police headquarters were severely condemned: "If the story . . . proves true[,] . . . an atrocity has been perpetrated upon every decent Atlantan." The article went on to say that "there isn't a decent man or woman in Atlanta who doesn't feel shame." According to the author, the privileged position enjoyed by white Atlantans and their model role for the African American community obliged them to ensure that the case was swiftly and fully resolved: "The boy . . . has received horrible injustice at the hands of a social order created by a race which, because of its dominance, is obligated to protect the weaker ones. . . . There is an ancient phrase, 'noblesse oblige,' which means the obligation of those more fortunate in life to protect the weaker and to live up to their own greater blessings."[16] This passage clearly reflects the paternalistic, self-proclaimed image of members of enlightened white society as benevolent supporters of the "good Negroes"—in other words, those who respected the racist rules and roles of the segregated South.[17] It is also revealing in this context to examine the descriptions of the path in life taken by the young Quintar South, whose employment with a white family helped ensure that his own family could make ends meet: "The very fact that the victim fills a humble role in life makes it imperative, for the good repute and the good conscience of the city, that there be [a] full investigation of the affair."[18] The mention of South's "humble role in life" makes it particularly clear why the case captivated the attention of white middle-class Atlantan society; it was, after all, an ideal opportunity to exhibit moral outrage and paternalistic concern. Furthermore, the editorial in the *Atlanta Constitution* appealed to the animal lovers among its readership and argued that since the white population of Atlanta had in the past repeatedly expressed its outrage over the inhumane treatment of stray cats and dogs, there was most certainly an obligation to resolve this case: "If such torture were perpetrated upon a stray dog or cat of the alleys, an outraged public would demand proper punishment for the one who did it. When the victim is a boy, such as this, there can be no sleep unhaunted by conscience-driven dreams until the wrong is righted."[19] The narrative of the respectable white woman defending the rights of an African American youth who was subordinate to her prompted a flurry of emphatic letters to the editor, which were printed in the *Atlanta Constitution*. A reader named Stockton Hume seized on the events as an opportunity to question the traditional tolerance of police misconduct and brutality:

> In common with other citizens of Atlanta I have been appalled at the report of torture of a Negro boy at the hands of a police officer. If this were an isolated case the punishment of the officer and his permanent removal from the police force might be sufficient, but we read far too often of cases of brutality to prisoners. I believe this to be simply a particularly vicious symptom of a more deep-seated evil. The use of the third degree, raids without warrants, and other illegal devices have been condoned on the grounds that this is the only way the police can keep the criminal in check.[20]

A number of readers congratulated the editors of the *Constitution* for their clear condemnation of the alleged torture. Ettianne Baldwin from Atlanta wrote: "I read with a great deal of pride and interest your excellent editorial entitled 'Justice for the Weak' and I felt that I could not pass up an opportunity to thank you for the same."[21] Stuart R. Oglesby wrote a letter praising the editorial in the *Constitution* for expressing "the sentiment of the good people of Atlanta."[22] A reader from Atlanta named George W. Willingham highlighted the special role of the reporter in bringing the case to the attention of the public: "To *The Atlanta Constitution* and Mr. Martin go the entire credit for relieving Atlanta of a curse with which we have been blighted for a number of years. No praise could be too big for the *Constitution* and its staff."[23]

The letters to the editor show that the case offered Atlantan middle-class white society an opportunity to reaffirm its moral and ethical attitudes toward the African American community. Furthermore, they indicate the special role of the press in spreading the word about this case of torture and rousing public indignation. Indeed, immediately following the initiative by Mrs. C. E. Harrison, the press became active in the case, particularly journalists from the *Atlanta Constitution*, including reporter Harold Martin. In one of the subsequent court cases, Martin recounted his own role in the events. He said that shortly after word got out about the case, the city editor at the newspaper sent him and press photographer H. J. Slayton to the juvenile detention center, where they found Quintar South.[24] With the permission of Juvenile Court judge Watkins, and under the custody of probation officer J. N. Starnes, Martin said that he then brought South to police headquarters, where, with the help of police captain C. Neal Ellis, he gained access to the "alleged torture chamber," the darkroom of the identification bureau. Shortly thereafter, there was a police lineup, and South immediately and without hesitation identified Sutherland as his tormentor.[25]

The natural ease with which the reporters were able to move about in both the juvenile detention center and police headquarters, and address their concerns to the relevant officials, points to well-established and close ties between urban police work and investigative journalism. It is also interesting to note that the photographer from the *Atlanta Constitution* was freely allowed to photograph the alleged weapon and crime scene. As Atlanta police chief M. A. Hornsby admitted a few days after the incident at the city's police headquarters, it was only thanks to the arrival of the journalists that he became aware of the case. Martin's report shows that the local press in Atlanta played a decisive role in bringing the case to the attention of the public.[26]

The imagery of the press photographs used by white newspapers to report on the South case ranged from paternalistic empathy to an implicit fascination with the perpetrated violence. This is evidenced in the previously mentioned photo that was published in the *Atlanta Constitution* on March 8, 1940, which shows Captain Ellis and probation officer Starnes as they

examine the wounds sustained by Quintar South. Ellis is smoking a cigarette as he holds up part of the bandage and observes the wound. In his
right hand, in the center of the photograph, he is holding the alleged
weapon used to inflict the burns. On the left-hand side of the picture stands
Starnes, who is also inspecting Quintar South's wound. South's lips are
slightly parted, and he is gazing toward the camera. His left hand is grasp-
ing the back of a chair while his forearm is being examined.

The national black press attributed great importance to the publication of
this photo. The *Chicago Defender* and *Pittsburgh Courier* emphasized positively
that the white newspapers of Atlanta had run front-page stories on the case
and published a photograph of the alleged torture victim.[27] Both newspapers
also published photographs of the case. While the *Defender* printed a similar photo of Captain Ellis holding the tacking iron while standing in front of
Quintar South, the *Courier* used the same image as the *Atlanta Constitution*
in a photo collage discussed later in this chapter (see figure 7).[28]

The remarkable aspect of its publication in the *Constitution* is that it appears to diverge markedly from the traditional visual discourse of African
Americans in southern white media. Although the widespread lynching
photographs of the late nineteenth and early twentieth centuries had portrayed African American men as presumably inferior and brutish culprits,
Quintar South was shown here as an obvious victim of racial violence, who
deserved the sympathy and support of the white community. The presence of
the two officials appeared to demonstrate the empathy and solidarity of Atlanta's white middle-class society with the presumed victim. This tied in with
the visual strategies of civil rights organizations like the NAACP, which, as
discussed in greater detail in chapter 3, had been using photographs of African American lynching victims since the 1910s to raise awareness and spark
public outrage.

However, a closer look at the staged arrangements of the photograph in
the *Atlanta Constitution* suggests different, contradictory interpretations.
While the image can be interpreted as a visual indictment of the police violence against South, it also reflects the continuity of a white hegemonic gaze,
which is characterized by a difference between the two white observers and
the black youth.[29] Although the three depicted individuals are on the same
plane, South seems to be forced into the background. He is standing along the
wall, with the chair and the right arm of the policeman in front of him. This
makes the two officers appear massive, while South looks passive, as if he
were merely enduring the examination. A number of details indicate that the
motif was produced to satisfy the readers' curiosity and without any particular

consideration for the sensitivities of the victim. First, there is Captain Ellis's burning cigarette in his mouth, which indicates routine and casualness. The ash looks as if it were about to fall on the wound just as the bandage is raised. Second, the alleged weapon in the other hand of the officer doesn't exactly testify to a strong sense of empathy. The tip of the iron is pointing toward South, as if a new wound could be inflicted at any moment. Finally, there is the manner with which the officer is holding up the bandage with the tips of his fingers. This may be a way of demonstrating caution, but it also expresses a distance to the victim and the intention to avoid all direct bodily contact with the teenager. This image reflects in many respects the asymmetrical distribution of power and authority in a torture situation and caters to the voyeuristic tendencies of white readers. In fact, in some ways, the photograph resembles a reenactment of the victim's torment. In contrast to what is proclaimed in the headline "Youth Tells Officer of 'Torture Confession,'" the photograph does not show Quintar South in the act of giving testimony on his ordeal; rather it depicts him as a passive figure who is exposed to the probing gaze of white experts.

The ambivalences of this visual representation of South in Atlanta's white press become even more evident when one compares the image in question with a photograph that was almost simultaneously published in the city's black newspaper.

"Let's Stop Police Brutality": How the Local and National Black Press Portrayed the Case

Under the headline "As Youth Described Police Torture," the *Atlanta Daily World* published a photograph on March 9, 1940, showing Quintar South being interviewed by Emel Scott, a journalist working for the newspaper. The photo caption contained the following description: "Quintar South, 16, of 39 Thayer Avenue is shown in the Juvenile Detention Home as he described to Emel Scott the 'hot iron' torture he charges was inflicted at police headquarters" (see figure 6).

On the right-hand side of the photo, we see Quintar South, sitting on a wooden bench with his forearms and folded hands resting on his thighs. Both the collar of his white shirt and the edge of his bandages are visible above the neckline of his dark sweater. South is gazing at the notepad held by journalist Emel Scott, who is sitting next to him and appears to be noting down his statements. Scott is wearing a suit with a white shirt and tie. He is sitting cross-legged on the bench next to South.

As Youth Described Police Torture

FIGURE 6 "As Youth Described Police Torture," *Atlanta Daily World*, March 9, 1940, 1.

A comparison of this image with the photograph published in the *Atlanta Constitution* reveals a number of differences in the representation of the torture case and its alleged victim. Whereas South was portrayed in this white newspaper as the object of the probing gaze of white officials and experts, and was spatially shifted to the background, the image in the *Atlanta Daily World* expresses, at least on a visual level, an equal relationship between the teenager and the journalist. In addition to Scott and South being shown sitting together on a bench, the frontal perspective of the camera on the two subjects allows them to appear as equal partners. In contrast to the image published in the *Atlanta Constitution*, this photograph has a balance of proximity and distance between the two depicted subjects. Both exude calm, seriousness, and integrity. The photograph shows two subjects in action, one reporting on events, the other documenting what happened. Both Scott and South appear as individuals with whom viewers can identify. This is a far cry from the passive posture that the alleged victim assumed in the photograph published in the *Atlanta Constitution*. Here South is portrayed as an active and self-confident young man who bears testimony to the violent treatment that he received.

Unlike the image in the *Atlanta Constitution*, which focused on South's battered and burnt body, the photographic composition of the image published in the *Atlanta Daily World* highlighted his account of the torture that he suffered. Readers encountered an active individual who testified to the violence that he experienced and, by doing so, stood up for his rights. Hence, this photograph was highly symbolic for the African American community of Atlanta. The message here is that the South case represents the omnipresent threat of police misconduct. Furthermore, the image conveys that African American citizens have the right and the obligation to resist oppression and go public with their accounts of violent abuse at the hands of police.

It is possible that the photograph in the *Atlanta Daily World* explicitly aimed to break with conventional representational practices of the American press, which showed blacks as passive victims of racial violence. As literary scholar Anne Elizabeth Carroll has shown, African American newspapers and magazines resolutely pursued this objective during the first decades of the twentieth century. Publications like the NAACP magazine the *Crisis*, along with black weekly and daily newspapers across the country, assumed the challenge of publishing images that shed a positive light on black people and adding them to the dominant visual discourse. These images were designed to demonstrate the diversity of African American culture and provide readers with alternative and positive role models.[30]

Taking its cue from nationwide black newspapers like the *Chicago Defender*, the *Pittsburgh Courier*, and *Negro World*, the *Atlanta Daily World* (known as the *Atlanta World* from 1928 to 1932) pursued the mission of providing the African American population in the South with its own forum. As publisher Alexander Scott II announced in the editorial of the very first edition of the paper in 1928, "The publishers of *The Atlanta World* have felt the need of a Southern Negro Newspaper, published by Southern Negroes, to be read by Southern Negroes." Scott said that the intention here was to put an end to the existing situation in which news of the black population was solely conveyed "through the optics of a host of prejudiced white papers."[31]

Beginning in March 1932, the *Atlanta Daily World* appeared on newsstands as one of the few black daily newspapers in the United States. As a local newspaper with a rather conservative orientation, most reporting revolved around social and church life, along with reports on sporting events. During the 1940s, the paper supported efforts to register African American voters in Atlanta, informed readers about the role of black soldiers in the U.S.

Army, and reported extensively on the problem of crime in Atlanta's black communities.[32]

Likewise, the newspaper published articles on the widespread discrimination against African Americans in the South, largely focusing on police violence, lynchings, and trials of black defendants. Reports, such as on the trial of the Scottsboro Boys in the 1930s, were used as an opportunity to call into question the stereotypical image of black offenders. In contrast to northern black newspapers like the *Chicago Defender*, the *Atlanta Daily World* eschewed militant rhetoric, opting instead to express moral outrage over the many cases of racial violence in the South. At the same time, the newspaper regularly appealed to its readers to educate themselves further and called on them to maintain their sense of dignity in the face of relentless violence and oppression. This was apparently an attempt to avoid a direct confrontation with the white population of Atlanta and instead, by dint of its ongoing reporting on instances of racial violence and discrimination, bear witness to the extent and persistence of these injustices in the American South. This strategy is also recognizable in the Quintar South case.

In contrast to the white press, the *Daily World* used the case as an opportunity to point to numerous other instances of police violence against African Americans in Atlanta. Already in its first report on the Quintar South case, the newspaper drew attention to the criminal proceedings against two other police officers, who, while arresting a black taxi driver named William Humphrey, had seriously wounded the suspect with nightstick blows to his head and face.[33] The following day, the newspaper reported on the case of twenty-year-old Matthew Hawkins, who stated that Sutherland and a group of other police officers had punched him and whipped him with a rubber hose to force him to confess to breaking into a drugstore.[34] In a commentary on the South case published a few days later, the newspaper called for an end to all forms of police violence: "It is hoped that the . . . investigations . . . will result in an immediate and final death thrust to police brutality in our fair city. Let's stop police brutality in Atlanta for all time."[35]

The reporting on the Quintar South torture case in the *Atlanta Daily World* thus differed markedly from the public outcry over the case in the white press of Atlanta. While articles in white newspapers exuded a mixture of shock and moral outrage tinged with morbid fascination, the *Atlanta Daily World* emphasized the necessity of sustained sanctions for police violence against African Americans and underscored the urgency of reflecting on their position within the segregated social order of the South.

Accordingly, the commentary of March 10, 1940, went on to note the decisive role played by Mrs. C. E. Harrison, pointing out that it was the "kind white employer" of Quintar South who was to be thanked for bringing the incident to the attention of the proper law enforcement authorities.[36] Her role was cited as particularly remarkable in light of several other cases of police brutality that had gone unreported because the persons concerned and their families feared "violent consequences," with which they had been "threatened."[37]

In yet another editorial in the *Atlanta Daily World*, columnist J. P. Reynolds wrote that the South case was a poignant reminder of how powerless the black population was in the face of daily racial discrimination and repression by the local police: "Just suppose this colored boy had not had a white lady come to his rescue? The consequences are that his case would never have come to light and the indicted officer . . . would have been out waiting for the next one."[38]

Whereas Reynolds interpreted the events in the South case as yet another example of the inability of blacks to combat police misconduct and brutality, William A. Fowlkes adopted an entirely different tone in his commentary on March 31, 1940. Fowlkes made reference to current developments in the wake of investigations launched against officer Sutherland by the U.S. Justice Department.[39] Although he admitted that the South case demonstrated once again the powerlessness of African Americans to stop racist violence, Fowlkes argued that the white population alone was not to blame. He pointed to the lack of courage among black citizens to go public about acts of violence for "fear of injury to their business or occupation and so forth. As such they have hurt considerably the chance of any law or any official helping prevent the continuance of brutalities." According to Fowlkes, it was necessary to overcome the victim status by taking part in the political and social life of the community. Instead of continuing to flee to a numbing state of lethargy, he called on the black population to assume its civil and political responsibilities and bring to bear the influence that this generates. "JUSTICE IS ALWAYS DONE THOSE WHO HAVE THE INFLUENCE AND POWER TO SEE THAT IT IS DONE," Fowlkes admonished in his final sentence.[40]

As we can see here, local African American commentators drew widely divergent conclusions on the South case concerning the situation of the black community in Atlanta. The resigned reference to daily violence and abuse stood in stark contrast to the impassioned appeal to seize the initiative in the struggle against a system of racist violence. But both positions avoided

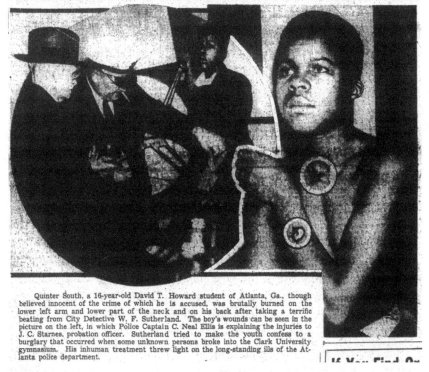

FIGURE 7 "Brutal Cop Beats, Burns 16-Year-Old Student," *Pittsburgh Courier*, March 23, 1940, 1.

explicitly pointing the finger of blame at the white population and the elite leadership of Atlanta.

While leading large-circulation national newspapers like the *New York Times* and the *Washington Post* ignored the South case, the national African American press had already begun to cover the story in March 1940. Once again, photographs played a crucial role in the reporting.[41] On March 23, 1940, the *Pittsburgh Courier* published a front-page article under the headline "Youth Branded with Hot Iron."[42] The story was illustrated with a photo collage under the headline "Brutal Cop Beats, Burns 16-Year-Old Student" (see figure 7). This image consists of a circular cutout from the previously discussed photo by H. J. Slayton published in the *Atlanta Constitution* and a second photograph—presumably also from Slayton or FBI investigators—that shows South bare-chested, with his left arm held at an angle in front of him.[43] The location of the wounds on his forearm and the base of his neck are highlighted by black-edged white rings, and the wounds themselves are outlined in black.

The added markings were apparently intended to stress the particular brutality of the case and serve as an indictment of the ongoing violation of the civil rights of African Americans. As the photo caption noted, the "inhuman treatment" of Quintar South threw light on the "long-standing ills" in the Atlanta Police Department. This visual enactment also played to readers' voyeuristic impulses by shifting the denuded and wounded body of the torture victim to the foreground and placing it on display.

In the article, however, the emphasis was on the positive consequences of the case for African Americans in the South. Thanks to the initiative of the white employer of Quintar South, the newspaper argued, the case had "set in motion the most exciting and thorough-going campaign for a clean-up in more than a generation."[44] In a similar vein, the black weekly newspaper the *Chicago Defender* saw the Quintar South case as an indication of progress: "Atlanta and the South are experiencing one of the most significant episodes in the history of the nation's effort to 'make its democracy work.' Never before has a southern city or state so completely taken up the matter of civil rights and carried it through without respect to race."[45]

In contrast to the articles in the local press, the national black press had an optimistic interpretation of the Quintar South case and argued that it documented a willingness to change on the part of southern whites. Also worth noting here was a new journalistic emphasis against the background of African American participation in World War II. On June 30, 1942, Quintar South was inducted into military service in the U.S. Navy and subsequently served as a seaman with the rank of Steward's Mate, 2nd class, on a U.S. Navy warship in the South Pacific. When he returned to Atlanta on home leave in September 1943, both the *Pittsburgh Courier* and the *Chicago Defender* ran articles on him.[46] At this point in time, two court cases against officer Sutherland in the U.S. federal court in Atlanta had already ended without a result because the jury could not agree on a verdict.[47] Under the headline "Torture Victim Back from Sea," the *Pittsburgh Courier* reported, "Sporting a mustache and whiff of a goatee, and togged down in his snappy navy uniform, 19-year-old Quintard [sic] South, who figured in Atlanta's sensational police torture case last year, breezed in from the sea to tell of his adventures in the South Pacific."[48]

In contrast of the reports from 1940, in which South was first and foremost portrayed as a victim of police violence, he was now presented as a self-confident, good-looking young serviceman in the navy. Although only three years earlier he had been held up by the black press as a symbol of southern racism, now he personified the new self-assurance of African American men who fought for the United States during World War II.[49] The body of Quintar South, which had earlier been branded by the brutality of police torture, had received a makeover of sorts and was now imbued with a new meaning. Instead of highlighting the signs of torture, the report in the *Pittsburgh Courier* pointed to the insignia on his uniform: "He wears three small stars on the upper left of his jacket, a reminder that he has been in three sea battles."[50] This description ties in with the widespread idealization and militarization of the male body during World War II, but it also represents a sea change in the symbolic connotations associated with Quintar South as an individual: from a victim of racist violence to a role model for African American readers across the country.[51] This short story about a serviceman returning from the front can be interpreted as an example of a liberating form of black self-representation.[52] It clearly shows how, emboldened by their participation in World War II, African Americans were increasingly questioning their prescribed status as victims.[53]

The examples of reporting presented here show that black and white newspapers took highly different approaches to reporting on cases of serious police misconduct and abuse in the South. While local black newspapers used the case to highlight the urgency of the ongoing fight against police brutality, the reporting of the white press was much more ambiguous.

The selective media attention and public outcry regarding the case of a young and sympathetic teenager who had become the victim of a shocking form of abuse perpetuated a racist "grammar of representation" that allowed Atlanta's white citizenry to avert their eyes from the routine acts of racial violence perpetrated against other blacks in the city.[54] As subsequent developments in the South case show, the media attention did not sway the widespread ignorance and indifference of the white population of Atlanta with regard to racist police practices, nor did it mean that violent police officers would have to face the consequences of their actions. Although the story immediately sparked public demands for a thorough investigation and criminal prosecution, it never resulted in any legal consequences for the alleged tormentor.

On June 20, 1940—roughly three-and-a-half months after the torture allegations were made public—officer William F. Sutherland stood trial in the criminal court of Fulton County. As the *Atlanta Daily World* reported, South testified extensively on the violence that he had been subjected to at police headquarters in Atlanta. His testimony was confirmed by several of his former fellow prisoners at the police station. Furthermore, South's former employer, Mrs. C. E. Harrison, and *Atlanta Constitution* journalist Harold Martin testified against the police officer. But Sutherland and his colleague M. R. Dodd rejected the allegations as false. Their testimony was supported by statements by a number of police officers who testified on the witness stand that they saw no wounds on South's body during his custody at police headquarters. They also maintained that at no point in time had South indicated to them that he had been burned or tortured. At the end of the one-day trial, after forty-five minutes of deliberation, the jury acquitted Sutherland of all charges.[55] Although South's allegations of torture had prompted a groundswell of protest among the white citizens of Atlanta in March 1940, the acquittal of Sutherland just three months later went uncommented on by the white newspapers of Atlanta. The result of the trial demonstrates the ongoing unwillingness of white jurors in the South to convict police officers on charges of assaulting and physically abusing African American suspects. Jurors and legal representatives were too interested in maintaining the white position of power in their local communities to risk their status by convicting violent police officers.

Sutherland's acquittal by the criminal court in Atlanta did not mean, however, the end of the legal activities in the Quintar South case. Already in March 1940, the U.S. Department of Justice had become active in the case. As chapter 5 will show, the FBI investigations against Sutherland were the first in a series of federal probes launched by representatives of the U.S. Department of Justice to sanction the persistent violation of the civil rights of blacks by law enforcement officials in the South.

CHAPTER FIVE

The Investigations by the Federal Government

In April 1942, U.S. attorney general Francis Biddle (1941–43) issued a press release in the wake of the lynching of an African American man named Cleo Wright in Sikeston, Missouri. Wright, who had been arrested on charges of attacking a white woman in her home in January 1942, was pulled out of jail by an angry mob, tied to the back of a car, and dragged through the streets of Sikeston and into the town's black neighborhood, where he was burnt alive on the street. Shortly thereafter, the U.S. Department of Justice ordered the FBI to conduct the first federal probe of a lynching. In his statement to the press, Biddle stressed that this investigation was essential to America's fight for democracy, especially now that U.S. soldiers were putting their lives on the line abroad: "With our country at war to defend our democratic way of life throughout the world, a lynching has significance far beyond the community, or even the state, in which it occurs. It becomes a matter of national importance and thus properly the concern of the federal government."[1] Biddle's comment reveals the growing interest of the U.S. government in incidents of racial violence from the early 1940s onward. Nearly two years earlier, in March 1940, the Department of Justice had launched an FBI investigation into a police officer who had been accused of violating the civil rights of an American citizen. This was the case described in chapter 4 of Atlanta police officer William F. Sutherland, who had been indicted for burning sixteen-year-old Quintar South with an electric appliance to extort a confession.[2]

The prosecution of Sutherland marks the first in a series of federal investigations of police officers and sheriffs that were pursued in the 1940s and early 1950s in the South. In all of these cases, lawmen were accused of physically abusing and torturing black and, in some cases, white prisoners and suspects in violation of their civil rights. As with the investigations into a number of lynchings during this period, the attorneys working for the Justice Department invoked a number of largely ignored legal provisions from the post–Civil War era. This legislation stipulated that it was within the jurisdiction of federal authorities to prosecute and sanction civil rights violations by police and other state officials, if need be, with fines and prison terms.

The following section will deal with the background of the civil rights initiative launched by the federal government in response to incidences of police torture that occurred in the South. This will be followed by an examination of individual investigations to determine the impact of the efforts of the Department of Justice and the FBI to expose and prosecute cases of police torture. To what extent were the investigations and trials of police officers and sheriffs able to undermine the racist power structure of the South and destabilize the position of power occupied by law enforcement institutions? And what implications did this have for the African American population?

Police Torture and the Initiative Launched by the Civil Rights Section

Since the early twentieth century, the NAACP and other civil rights organizations had endeavored in vain to persuade federal authorities to take action against racism in the South. One of the main demands of civil rights activists was to pass a federal anti-lynching law that would allow federal authorities to prosecute the perpetrators of lynchings in individual states. Despite decades of campaigning, however, the NAACP repeatedly failed to shepherd a bill through Congress. Although during the 1920s, 1930s, and early 1940s the NAACP managed on a number of occasions to convince the members of the House of Representatives to support a federal anti-lynching law, these initiatives failed in the Senate and were rejected by southern senators with the argument that such legislation constituted a violation of state sovereignty.[3]

In view of these unsuccessful legal initiatives, during the 1930s the NAACP repeatedly urged the Justice Department to investigate lynchings, based on laws that had been on the books since shortly after the end of the Civil War. But despite the organization's demands, the Department of Justice under the leadership of Homer S. Cummings (1933–39) rejected all calls to investigate lynching cases.[4] It was not until Frank Murphy was appointed U.S. attorney general (1939–40) that the department began to prosecute individual cases of police violence and mob law in the South.

The federal government's new approach to civil rights had been sparked by the creation of the Civil Liberties Unit (CLU) in February 1939.[5] This recently established section of the Criminal Division was created by U.S. Attorney General Murphy to identify existing legal statutes that would provide a foundation for federal authorities to protect and enforce the civil rights of American citizens.

As political scientist Robert K. Carr and others have shown, the sweeping changes introduced under Democratic president Franklin D. Roosevelt's New Deal were one of the main factors behind the turnaround in the civil rights policy of the federal government that gave rise to the establishment of the CLU.[6] The new economic and social policies designed to overcome the Great Depression led to a significant expansion of the regulatory powers of the U.S. government in the individual states. With the creation of the CLU, which was renamed the Civil Rights Section (CRS) in June 1942, the jurisdiction of the federal government was extended in the area of civil rights. As Attorney General Murphy announced in a radio address in March 1939, the federal government would henceforth steadfastly pursue the goal of safeguarding the civil liberties of all U.S. citizens to the full extent of the law: "The Federal Government today is determined . . . to protect civil liberties by all means available to it. It will not be for this faction or that, this class or that class, this nationality or that one, but for all people. We propose to protect civil liberties for the business man and the laborer alike, for the Jew and the Gentile, and the people of all races and creeds, whatever their origin."[7] Another reason for the civil rights campaign of the federal government was the growing importance of African American voters. Most of these voters had already supported Roosevelt in his 1932 bid for president, but the African American constituency was becoming ever more important due to the steadily rising influx of black migrants from the South to the cities of the North, where many of them were able to register to vote for the first time.[8] Likewise, the new federal civil rights initiative was a reaction to the increasingly vocal demands of the NAACP and other groups for an active civil rights policy by the U.S. government.[9] These groups included the American Civil Liberties Union (ACLU), which had begun to campaign more intensively for the protection of fundamental civil liberties during the 1930s and 1940s. As highlighted in the introduction, the ACLU pointed to persistent violations of civil rights by law enforcement authorities, but the organization focused primarily on northern urban areas like New York City.[10] Many decisions by the U.S. Supreme Court also added momentum to the government's civil rights initiative. As has already been shown in chapter 3, the Supreme Court repeatedly emphasized, particularly during the late 1930s and early 1940s, the necessity of actively protecting the procedural rights of suspects and defendants, as guaranteed under the Constitution.[11]

Furthermore, the federal government's campaign was closely connected to foreign and domestic policy developments within the context of World War II. After the United States entered the war in December 1941, both Japanese and German newspapers and radio stations endeavored to tarnish America's reputation by reporting on numerous cases of racial violence in the United States, including the lynching of Cleo Wright. U.S. government representatives feared that news stories like this would cast doubt on the moral integrity of the United States and the stated goal of the war, namely to defend freedom and democracy.[12] Moreover, there were concerns that a passive attitude by the government toward racial violence could weaken the resolve of the black population to support the war. Frank Coleman, a lawyer working for the CLU/CRS, summarized the fears of the U.S. government as follows: "Stories of lynchings and police brutality . . . would be welcome ammunition to the Axis enemies in their campaign to discredit the self appointed champions of the 'Four Freedoms.' And many considered the weakening of our prestige abroad less serious than the impairment of morale at home. Would not many of our own citizens become cynical and disillusioned about fighting . . . in the name of ideals which even then were being trampled under foot at home by 'village tyrants' and lynch mobs?"[13] When the Justice Department then ordered civil rights investigations, it justified its actions based on the Enforcement Acts of 1870 and 1871 and the Civil Rights Act of 1875, which were passed by Congress after the Civil War to safeguard the newly won civil rights of the African American population.

This legislation stipulated that civil rights violations by state officials could be prosecuted and sanctioned by federal authorities with fines and prison sentences. Title 18, Section 52, of the United States Code (USC) (today Title 18, Section 242) made it a punishable offense for a local, state, or federal official, "acting under color of any law, statute, ordinance, regulation, or custom," to willfully deprive anyone of "rights, privileges, or immunities secured or protected under the Constitution or laws of the United States."[14] Such an offense was punishable by a fine of up to $1,000 and a maximum of one year in prison. Title 18, Section 51 (today Title 18, Section 241) also made it a punishable offense if two or more persons conspired "to injure, oppress, threaten, or intimidate any person . . . in the free exercise or enjoyment of any right or privilege secured . . . by the Constitution or laws of the United States." The maximum punishment was ten years in prison and a $5,000 fine.[15]

As interpreted by the representatives of the CLU/CRS, these statutes allowed federal attorneys to prosecute civil rights violations by officials in individual states—including the illegal use of police force and participation in lynchings—and file indictments in local federal courts. In a memo distributed in May 1940, the Justice Department urged the federal attorneys in all judicial districts to make use of the rediscovered legislation to prosecute civil rights violations and underscored the importance of the USC statutes as a "powerful weapon" to hold police officers and other state officials legally accountable for their actions. At the same time, however, federal attorneys were told not to file any charges without having obtained prior approval from the Justice Department. This allowed the department to retain decision-making power over the launching of federal investigations.[16]

During its first years, the new unit received between 1,500 and 2,500 complaints annually concerning violations of civil rights across the country. However, the uncertain legal situation, the lack of personnel at the CLU/CRS, and limited support from within the Department of Justice meant that FBI investigations were ordered in only relatively few cases. To make matters worse, only a small number of these investigations resulted in trials in federal courts. During the first eight years of its existence, the CLU/CRS filed a total of 178 indictments. In addition to lynchings and cases of police brutality, federal attorneys prosecuted violations of the right to vote as well as infringements of freedom of the press and freedom of religion.[17]

When it came to the area of police brutality, the CLU/CRS confined its activities to carefully selected cases of police violence and torture. In an internal memo from the year 1942, Wendell Berge, the then head of the Criminal Division at the Department of Justice, wrote that so many complaints of police torture were received every year that the department could take into consideration only those that were accompanied by a certified statement from the victim. Furthermore, he noted that the department only dealt with complaints about police violence that were not submitted by "a hardened criminal": "This policy indicates an awareness as to the necessity of police officers some times [sic] using tactics which they would be not so apt to use if they did not have before them a hardened criminal with a long record, or a known suspect who had been involved in many questionable matters over a long period. The Criminal Division thoroughly appreciates that a third degree complaint [by] a victim with a bad record is a very different case from one where the victim is a first offender."[18] This selective policy by the Justice Department indirectly gave law enforcement officers a greater degree of leeway in their handling of suspects who had repeatedly run afoul of the law or were known to the authorities. Consequently, the civil rights initiative did not aim for an across-the-board crackdown on torture practices used by police in the United States. As the memo went on to say, the initiative not only excluded from investigations complaints from so-called hardened criminals but also firmly limited the unit's focus to "cases of outright brutality."[19] Presumably this was an attempt to prevent the civil rights investigations of the federal government in the individual states from all too quickly becoming a target of public criticism, particularly in the South.

The policy of focusing on individually selected cases of police violence and torture meant that the civil rights initiative of the Justice Department only challenged to a very limited extent the widespread use of racially motivated violence by law enforcement officers in the South. As the Sutherland case shows, however, FBI investigations alone represented a challenge to local police power structures.

Exposing Torture: The Case against William F. Sutherland

Already on March 8, 1940, immediately after news broke of the torture allegations made by Quintar South, high-ranking officials at the Department of Justice ordered the FBI to conduct an investigation of the case, and shortly thereafter the local district attorney filed an indictment against Sutherland with the U.S. district court in Atlanta.[20] One of the first steps taken by the FBI office there was to secure the alleged weapon—the previously mentioned tacking iron—at the police station in Atlanta and send it to the technical laboratory in Washington, D.C., for a detailed analysis: "It is requested that the tip of this heating iron be examined for any traces of blood or flesh that may be still adhering thereto. It is also requested that tests be made as to the heating speed of this iron in regular intervals. It is requested that a chart be made of the temperature of this iron at regular intervals as to the temperature at one minute, two minutes, etc., until the iron attains its maximum heat and the point at which it would be sufficient to burn the flesh of an individual."[21] The detailed instructions of the investigating agent, R. G. Danner, to the FBI laboratory convey the self-image honed by the FBI as a technologically advanced and efficient national investigative agency using state-of-the-art forensic methods—an image that was largely the brainchild of J. Edgar Hoover, the longtime director of the agency, and was bolstered by the media and popular culture.[22] The authority of the FBI (which went by the name of the Bureau of Investigation until 1935) massively increased during the 1920s and 1930s. In addition to its scope of action in the areas of intelligence and espionage, during the so-called war on crime in the 1930s it was granted sweeping powers to combat crime and corruption.[23] This development went hand in hand with an ever-growing professionalization of its investigative activities, which was reflected in the introduction of a standard dress code, a training program for FBI agents, and a cutting-edge forensic lab, known as the FBI Technical Laboratory, which was established in 1932.[24] Likewise, the first investigative manual for FBI agents was issued in 1927.[25] This regularly updated manual contained detailed instructions on standard procedures during investigations, along with precise information on the content and formal structure of investigative reports.[26] Among other things, it urged FBI agents to strictly observe formal procedures and maintain a clear and concise language style. For instance, with respect to the summary information at the beginning of every FBI report, it contained the following instructions: "Reports shall contain a clear, brief, grammatical comprehensive statement of all essential pertinent facts in proper relative sequence."[27] The instructions aimed to ensure the intelligibility and consistency of the investigative results and substantiate their objectivity. These aspirations also bore fruit in the FBI investigations against Sutherland launched in March 1940.

On March 16, 1940, Hoover forwarded the first report, written by Ronald R. Hassig, to the Department of Justice. This thirty-five page, typewritten report reflects the professionalized approach of the FBI and its efforts to produce an unbiased and standardized documentation of the results of the investigation.[28]

The report was preceded by a standardized cover page that included the location where the case originated, the FBI case number, where, when, and for which period the report was made, its author, the name of the suspect, and the criminal charges. Furthermore, under the heading "details," it provided a concise summary of the basic information about the case and the results of the initial investigative steps. The report itself contained all statements made by the persons interviewed during the course of the investigation.[29] Every transcript followed the same pattern: In an introductory declaration, the witnesses affirmed that they were speaking freely and voluntarily and without any "threats, promises or inducements." The statements all closed with the following declaration: "I have read this statement . . . and it is true to the best of my knowledge and belief. I have initialed the . . . pages of this statement below the last line of each page and place my signature to this a true statement."[30] In addition, every witness statement was signed by the investigating agents. This procedure was intended to ensure that the statement was legally binding and could be used as evidence in a court of law.

The report on the Sutherland investigation shows that numerous individuals were interviewed who were directly or indirectly involved in the case. It contains statements by Quintar South and a number of members of his family; declarations by people whom South had seen after he had been transferred to the juvenile detention center in Atlanta; the signed statement of the defendant, W. F. Sutherland; and testimony by numerous other police officers and employees of the Atlanta Police Department.[31]

The report documents that every single police officer who was questioned by the FBI denied that Quintar South had been tortured at Atlanta police headquarters. The defendant, William F. Sutherland, solemnly declared in the presence of his lawyer and FBI agents Ronald R. Hassig and Frank Angell that he "at no time . . . in any way abuse[d]" South.[32] These statements were diametrically opposed to those made by South and other witnesses. The FBI report noted that South had been questioned in the juvenile detention center of Fulton County on March 11, 1940, concerning his allegations of torture. During this interview, he stated that on February 26, 1940, he and four other African American youths were arrested by four police officers of the Atlanta Police Department on suspicion of committing a burglary. South said that two days later, he and two of the other detainees, eighteen-year-old John Biggs and sixteen-year-old Alphonso Jamieson, were brought by officers W. F. Sutherland and M. R. Dodd to the fingerprint room at police headquarters. South testified that Sutherland then brought him into a small adjacent room that was evidently used to develop photographs. Immediately thereafter, according to South, Sutherland slapped him in the face for the first time, punched him in the stomach, maintained that he was the one responsible for the burglary, and told him that he had better tell the truth.[33] Despite being slapped and punched, South said that he refused to make a confession and that Sutherland then took him out of the room again. He said that afterward, Sutherland first brought Alphonso Jamieson and then John Biggs into the adjacent room. In both cases, South said that he heard noises from the room that sounded like someone being beaten. Then he testified that Sutherland led him into the room again, where the following occurred:

> Mr. SUTHERLAND talked to me a while and then told me to put my fingers under a paper cutter, he then said that he had a better idea at which time he picked up an electric iron and put it in the socket, we then waited for what appeared to be five minutes for the iron to get hot. SUTHERLAND then placed a towel over the iron and tested its heat, he then removed the towel and stuck the iron toward me. I thought that he was going to burn me so I threw up my left iron [sic] and received a burn on the top of my arm, midway between my elbow and wrist. I do not know whether he meant to burn me on the arm where

he did but I do know that I thought he was going to burn me so I threw up my arm in self-defense.[34]

This quote clearly shows that the FBI agents had transformed the oral statements by Quintar South into a transcript that would be admissible in court and document legally relevant information about the alleged crime and the chronological sequence of events. This is also apparent in South's further account of the interrogation by Sutherland:

> After this burn he asked me if I was going to tell the truth to which I told him that I had told the truth when I said that I had not stolen any property nor had I broken into the Clark University Gym. He then jabbed the iron at me again and burned me in the elbow-joint, at which time he asked me if I was going to tell him the truth. He next placed the point of the iron on the base of the neck at the top of my chest, lightly[,] and again told me to tell the truth, to which I again told him that I had told the truth. SUTHERLAND then placed the iron in the same place on my neck and throat burning me more severely in the same place. This burning hurt so much I told him I would confess, since I did not want to be burned or slapped anymore.[35]

The strict rationality of the FBI's approach to gathering evidence is reflected by the virtual absence of any mention of physical pain or mental anguish, with the exception of the last passage of his statement, in which South recounted how he finally consented to make a confession: "This burning hurt so much I told him I would confess."[36] The experience of pain was presumably granted legal relevance here as the presumptive element that elicited the confession. These quotes show that the linguistic ductus of the signed statement had been molded with the aim of objectively establishing the truth.

The fact that the statement by Quintar South was included in the FBI report is important on another level, namely because it shows that the legal relevance of the torture allegations was recognized by the authority of the U.S. government and the FBI, and that the validity of the accusations was underpinned by the neutrality and objectivity of the investigative methods used. Indeed, the presumed African American victim of torture was elevated to the status of a full-fledged witness. This presented a challenge to the racial hierarchy of the justice system in the South, whereby—as we have already seen—witness statements by blacks were traditionally accorded less validity than testimony by whites.

This effect was amplified by the statements of numerous people who were questioned during the course of the investigation and confirmed the allegations of torture. For instance, Quintar South's mother, Rosa South, said in her statement that on the day of her son's arrest, she saw no wounds on his body, which implicitly meant that the injuries could only have been sustained at the police station.[37] Likewise, his two fellow prisoners, John Biggs and Alphonso Jamieson, confirmed the allegations and went on record as saying that they had also been physically abused during questioning by police.[38] Biggs told the FBI:

> While . . . SOUTH was in the room with Mr. SUTHERLAND, I heard noises that led me to believe that SUTHERLAND was slapping SOUTH. SOUTH stayed in this room with SUTHERLAND for about ten minutes and when he came out SUTHERLAND then took JAMIESON into the room. . . . While JAMIESON was in the room with Mr. SUTHERLAND, I heard SUTHERLAND slapping JAMIESON or at least the noises sounded like he was being slapped. JAMIESON stayed in the room for about ten minutes when SUTHERLAND brought him back into the main room. SUTHERLAND then took me back into the room and told me to confess; on my refusal he slapped me numerous times. At this time SUTHERLAND brought JAMIESON back into the room and it was at this time that we both confessed; after this confession SUTHERLAND hit me in the stomach two times with his fist.[39]

Afterward, Biggs said that South was called back into the room a second time and returned with burns on his skin: "He . . . then called QUINTER SOUTH back into the room. When QUINTER SOUTH was in the room this second time I heard someone hit up against the door twice and assumed that SUTHERLAND was hitting SOUTH as he hit me. SOUTH stayed in the room about 20 minutes this time and when he came back out I noticed that he was burned at the throat, which I assumed was a cigarette burn."[40] John Biggs's testimony confirmed the torture allegations leveled by South in a number of respects. He corroborated South's statements on the spatial and temporal sequence of events and drew a direct connection between the questioning of South behind closed doors and the wounds on his body. By confirming that the burns on South's body were only visible after the "questioning" session, Biggs fundamentally challenged the version of events presented by Sutherland. What's more, there was additional evidence in support of South's testimony. As Agent Hassig wrote in his report, during the course of the investigation he had prepared a number of photographs in which the wounds

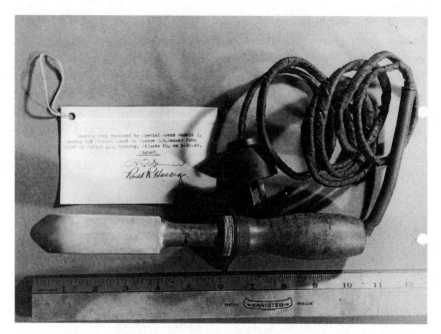

FIGURE 8 FBI photograph of the tacking iron. National Archives and Records Administration, RG 60/144, Box 17583, Fol. 144-19-5.

of the alleged torture victim were clearly recognizable.[41] Three of these eight-by-ten-inch black and white photos are included in the Justice Department's file on the Sutherland case. They were presumably taken with a Kodak Recomar or a Graflex Speed Graphic camera, which the FBI handbook prescribed as mandatory photographic equipment for official investigations.[42]

One FBI photograph showed the alleged weapon, the tacking iron (see figure 8). The photo shows the underside of the electric iron and the power cord. To determine the size of the weapon, the investigators placed it alongside a ruler. The image also included a note card with the signatures of Hassig and his superior, R. G. Danner, presumably to attest to the authenticity of the weapon and ensure that the photo could be used as evidence in court.[43]

Quintar South can be seen on the two other existing FBI photos from the investigation. One is reminiscent of a mug shot and shows South before a white background (see figure 9).[44] He is facing the camera. His left hand is resting on his right shoulder so that the wound on his forearm is recognizable. There is also a clearly visible burn scar at the base of the teenager's neck.

The FBI investigator used a light background and presumably a flash to ensure maximum recognition and visibility of the wounds sustained by

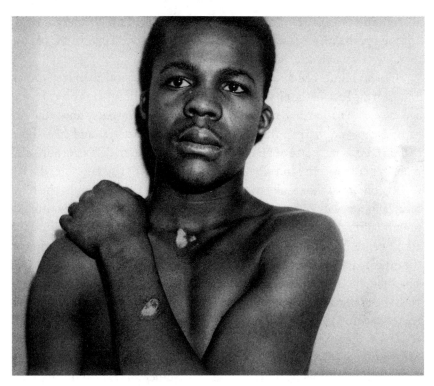

FIGURE 9 FBI photograph of Quintar South. National Archives and Records Administration, RG 60/144, Box 17583, Fol. 144-19-5.

South. He thus followed the directives contained in the FBI investigative manuals, which stipulated that photographic evidence of the subject of investigation and the crime scene were to be compiled that would "anticipate any questions which may later arise" during the course of the investigation.[45] The photograph exhibits unmistakable parallels to the image of South on the front page of the *Pittsburgh Courier*, as discussed in chapter 4. The handwritten comment "state 3 W. F. Sutherland"—short for "state exhibit no. 3 W. F. Sutherland"—on the back of the photo indicates that it was used as evidence in the subsequent trial of Sutherland.

These photographs played an important role in the investigation. By documenting the condition of South's body after the alleged torture, they corroborated the allegations in an apparently neutral and objective manner. According to Roland Barthes, a key characteristic of photography is its "certificate of presence."[46] He speaks in this context of the "evidential force" of the photographic image.[47] The FBI photos in the South case lay claim to such a corroborative impact. They forged an indexical connection between the allegations of torture made by Quintar South and the wounds on his body, and their probative value was enhanced by the widespread perception of photography as an objective and realistic medium.

This was reinforced by a detailed listing of the physical characteristics of South on the back of the photograph. In addition to information on eye color, age, race, and nationality, the list included the following entry under the category "scars and marks": "burn scar at base of neck 1 1/8" and small burn scar on base of neck size of pen; burn scar in elbow joint, left arm; burn scar midway between wrist and elbow 1½" × 1", left arm."[48] Furthermore, the FBI report contained the results of the examination of the weapon by the technical laboratory in Washington, D.C. This showed that the temperature of the iron after five minutes of heating was roughly 90 degrees Celsius, and after twenty-five minutes, it was approx. 300 degrees Celsius. According to the experts at the laboratory, a temperature between 55 and 65 degrees Celsius was sufficient to cause burns on a human body.[49] These findings matched with the statement by Quintar South, who declared that Sutherland had heated the iron for roughly five minutes before tormenting him with it.[50]

Hence, the investigative findings of the FBI corroborated the allegations of torture made by Quintar South on a number of levels and cast extensive doubt on the strict denials by the defendant, Sutherland. The probative value of the results was underpinned by the authority of the FBI as a professional investigative agency operating in accordance with the latest technical advances and firmly rooted in the prevailing discourse on modernity, rationality, and scientific standards.[51]

An examination of the further developments in the case, however, shows that the procedures for establishing the truth remained closely tied to local power structures. This became clear in the legal proceedings against Sutherland before the U.S. district court in Atlanta, which began in February 1941 after months of delays.

The Trial of Sutherland

Testifying before the U.S. district court in Atlanta, Quintar South repeated his allegations against William F. Sutherland. As the *Atlanta Daily World* reported, he was questioned by U.S. assistant attorney Raymond W. Martin for roughly an hour on the events that transpired at the headquarters of the Atlanta Police Department.[52] Afterward, the torture allegations were corroborated by the testimony of John Biggs, Alphonso Jamieson, and Rosa South.[53] Furthermore, several white witnesses, including probation officer

J. N. Starnes; the reporter from the *Atlanta Constitution*, Harold Martin; and South's former employer, Mrs. C. E. Harrison, testified that they had seen clearly visible wounds on South's body after his transfer to the juvenile detention center of Atlanta. Likewise, the photographs made during the course of the FBI investigation and additional photos by the press photographer of the *Atlanta Constitution* were entered as evidence in the case against Sutherland.[54]

As the *Atlanta Daily World* articles on the trial show, the case against Sutherland generated considerable interest among Atlanta's black community. At times there were more than fifty African Americans spectators in the courtroom, many of them pillars of the black community of Atlanta: "Among the large group of colored spectators were ministers, business men and civic leaders. Several women were present and among them were three or four school girls."[55] Already during the run-up to the trial, the local black newspaper had emphasized the symbolic importance of the indictment of a police officer by the local federal court, noting that the case was without a doubt one of the most important trials in recent years. The newspaper went on to say that the indictment of Sutherland was apparently intended to demonstrate the federal government's willingness to actively protect African American civil rights in the South.[56] As the trial began, the newspaper pointedly highlighted the fact that Sutherland was tried by an "all-white jury," despite the fact that two black jurors had been available for jury service in the court: Charles A. Crawford, who had been sworn in in October 1940, and Frank Wimberly, sworn in two days before the trial. "Neither of the men was chosen to try the Sutherland case," the *Atlanta Daily World* pointed out with thinly veiled criticism.[57]

The avid interest of the black community made it clear that the trial was of symbolic importance. It held out the prospect that rampant police brutality against blacks would finally result in legal consequences. A commentary in the *Atlanta Daily World* made the following observation: "There is a greater issue at stake in the Sutherland trial than the guilt or innocence of this white detective, whom the government charges stooped to torture practices reminiscent of the Middle Ages to wring a bogus confession from a Negro boy. The thoroughness with which U.S. Assistant Attorney Raymond W. Martin is delving into this 'confession' system used at Atlanta Police Headquarters is testimony to the government's apparent intention to break up an unconstitutional practice which for too long has prevailed in a free America."[58] The *Atlanta Daily World* went on to say that the trial shed light for the first time ever on the dark practice of forcing false confessions from prisoners, both "black and white," at the Atlanta Police Department. Furthermore, it stated that regardless of "the outcome of the present trial, there is no question that it will have a deterring effect on those policemen who in the past have been so quick to pounce upon and brutally beat and abuse helpless prisoners in their custody. For that we can all be thankful. And for that Quintar South will not have suffered his painful experience in vain."[59]

But the trial took a turn that dashed the hopes of the African American community. After hearing testimony from the witnesses for the prosecution, the defense called two high-ranking police officers, a probation officer, a banker, and a judge to the stand to call into question the credibility of the allegations made by Quintar South. Atlanta police chief M. A. Hornsby and police lieutenant M. B. Petty testified to Sutherland's "good reputation," while Sutherland declined to take the witness stand.[60] Moreover, several police witnesses expressed doubt that the electric iron could be used as a weapon because, in their opinion, it was not capable of causing burns.[61]

The trial reached a dramatic climax on the fifth day. After an agreement was reached between the district attorney and Sutherland's defense lawyers, the judge gave his assent for the alleged weapon to be tested in the courtroom. According to the *Atlanta Daily World*, the device was connected to a power source by an electrician and allowed to heat for ten minutes. Thereafter, Detective J. E. Helms, one of the witnesses for the defense, was granted an opportunity to test the apparatus before the eyes of the audience. Helms had earlier testified that, in his opinion, the iron was not capable of burning human skin.[62] The *Atlanta Daily World* described the test as follows: "City Detective J. E. Helms rubbed the instrument back and forth over his arm and close observers said the officer's arm turned red."[63] The *Atlanta Constitution* wrote, "City Detective J. E. Helms who said 'it would not burn' heated the iron 10 minutes then ran it across his forearm. A red mark appeared. Helms then touched the iron point to his arm and it made a red imprint."[64] According to the reports in local newspapers, the public test of the tacking iron actually tended to refute all previously raised doubts about Quintar South's testimony. The members of the jury were also given an opportunity to test the heating capacity of the apparatus and the result likewise called into question the position taken by the defense. As the *Atlanta Daily World* reported, "Several members [of the jury] who handled the iron indicated the iron was hot by snatching their hands from the instrument."[65]

Judging by the newspaper reports, the process of establishing the truth before the U.S. district court in Atlanta was fiercely contested. Although the prosecution had presented a wide range of evidence to support the allegations of torture, the defense invoked the statements of prominent police officials to refute the charges. The result of the trial indicates that this legal action had only a very limited ability to challenge the local position of power enjoyed by the police and the associated power structure of racial violence. Despite overwhelming evidence against Sutherland, the twelve members of the all-white jury could not agree on a verdict, even after long deliberation. When the jury was still deadlocked after one and a half days, Judge E. Marvin Underwood declared a mistrial.[66] As with Sutherland's prosecution before the Fulton Criminal Court in June 1940, the white jury shied away from pronouncing a guilty verdict. The African American press reacted with bitter resignation to this outcome. The *Atlanta Daily World* wrote that "the inability of a federal grand jury after thirty hours of deliberation to reach a verdict . . . cannot be anything but a sore disappointment to Atlantans of both races anxious to see justice in this case prevail."[67]

THE TRIAL OF William F. Sutherland illustrates that investigations of law enforcement authorities in the South had only very limited chances of success in the 1940s and early 1950s. Nevertheless, the court case made it possible to shed light on the pervasive use of torture by the police in Atlanta. This was primarily accomplished thanks to the efforts of FBI investigators, who meticulously examined and documented the evidence concerning the allegations made by the presumptive African American torture victim, thereby exposing the illegal treatment of police suspects. Hence, the FBI investigation presented a fundamental challenge to the system of police violence in the South, which was based on the interplay among the concealment of police torture, its official denial by law enforcement agencies, and its tolerance by local judicial authorities. The outcome of the trial reveals, however, how difficult it was to establish the truth in the courts of the South. Ultimately, truth and evidence were intricately intertwined with local power structures.[68] Furthermore, the case shows that the investigations into violent law enforcement officers themselves were a controversial issue within the federal agencies.

The Conflict Surrounding the FBI Investigation in the Sutherland Case

An analysis of the FBI file in the Sutherland case reveals that diverse interests influenced the investigation. Right from the start, there were substantial differences of opinion between the FBI agents and the leadership of the Atlanta Police Department. Several letters and reports written between

April and June 1940 show that officials such as Atlanta chief of police M. A. Hornsby raised objections to the FBI investigation. His criticism was sparked, among other things, by the fact that FBI agent Hassig had refused to recognize several previously prepared statements by the police officers who were implicated by the allegations. Instead, Hassig had insisted on personally questioning the police witnesses. Special Agent in Charge R. G. Danner wrote to J. Edgar Hoover that he had explained to Hornsby that the investigation had been ordered by the Department of Justice, and the investigating agent was merely following internal FBI procedures.[69] He had also told him that the goal was to conduct a "fair and impartial investigation" that would allow the bureau to get down "to the facts," adding that he wanted nothing done that would infuriate the chief of police.[70] Agent Hassig noted in an internal memo that Hornsby had told him that the Sutherland case would undoubtedly lead to "a racial flare-up" in Atlanta, and that the investigation was politically motivated and only instituted as a "vote-getter" to garner support from citizens in the North. Hornsby also refused to allow someone from the North to lecture him on how to deal with the African American population, since the "average Northerner" had no idea of "the negro problem and how it should be handled."[71]

These reservations and arguments by the police chief of Atlanta were later echoed by other southern officials in connection with other federal investigations. Investigations into police misconduct rekindled a deep-seated cultural resentment toward interventions by Washington. The activities of the Department of Justice were condemned by the officials in the South as an unjustified meddling in their sphere of influence.

Correspondence between the FBI leadership and the Department of Justice also reveals that the investigations led to considerable differences of opinion between the two agencies, not to mention within the Department of Justice itself. This internal conflict was sparked in part by a request submitted in August 1940 to the relevant authorities at the Department of Justice. In order to increase the chances of convicting Sutherland, the assistant U.S. attorney in Atlanta, Raymond W. Martin, called for additional FBI investigations to prove, among other things, that Sutherland had tortured prisoners earlier. It was argued that the trial could only be won if doubt were cast on Sutherland's reputation.[72]

When authorities at the CLU subsequently commissioned the FBI to conduct this type of investigation,[73] FBI director Hoover sent a letter to Assistant to the Attorney General Matthew McGuire to express his concerns over this development.[74] He wrote that the investigation conducted in March 1940 had already led to considerable frictions between the FBI and the Atlanta Police Department, although the inquiries were "conducted with as much tact and diplomacy as was possible under the circumstances."[75] According to Hoover, it was only after numerous meetings between FBI representatives and top officials at the police department that relations were "normalized" again. Hoover went on to say that further investigations would "undoubtedly" be misinterpreted and "rupture the friendly relationship which has been reestablished between this Bureau and the Atlanta Police Department."[76]

In a memo subsequently dispatched to the CLU, McGuire questioned both the legal basis for the Sutherland probe and the necessity of the further investigations that had been ordered, which he feared would probably put an end to the cooperation between the FBI and police authorities in Atlanta: "While I see no objection to your making a test case . . . , a serious practical situation arises if the Federal Bureau of Investigation is brought into the matter unduly. It is necessary for the Bureau to act in constant cooperation with local police departments. This cooperation will probably cease if the Federal Bureau of Investigation is required to investigate third-degree complaints adduced against local police departments, especially in view of the fact that Federal Jurisdiction in such matters is questionable, to say the least."[77]

After McGuire temporarily suspended the order to expand the probe, he held an internal conference with his aide, Alexander Holtzhoff, and Henry Schweinhaut, the head of the CLU, after which it was decided to call off any further investigations against Sutherland.[78] The civil rights initiative of the CLU thus did not enjoy the unconditional support of the Justice Department. Hoover's reaction illustrates that he was not willing to jeopardize the working relationship between the FBI and local police departments, and that he used his influence within the Department of Justice to prevent further investigations.[79]

In November 1941, Sutherland was put on trial again. In the meantime, despite renewed objections by Hoover, officials at the Department of Justice ordered the FBI to conduct further investigations of Sutherland.[80] But despite these efforts, the second trial before the U.S. federal court in Atlanta also ended in a mistrial. Once again, the members of the jury deliberated for several hours but were unable to reach a verdict.[81]

After subsequent efforts were made to take the case to court a third time, in June 1944 the Department of Justice decided at the request of M. Neil Andrews, Lawrence Camp's successor as the chief federal prosecutor in

Atlanta, to drop the investigation of Sutherland.[82] Meanwhile, Quintar South had been drafted into the military.[83] Andrews justified his decision by pointing out that the witnesses in the case had dispersed to various parts of the globe due to the war. He added that "since every effort was made" to retry the case before the war, in the opinion of his office "it would not be conducive to good race relations" to try it now.[84]

The failure to reach a verdict in the case of W. F. Sutherland proved to be the rule rather than the exception for other federal trials of police officers and sheriffs that followed in the 1940s and early 1950s. In many of these cases, lawmen accused of torturing black suspects were acquitted despite overwhelming evidence against them. One of the main reasons for this was that jurors were concerned that a conviction could undermine the local racial power structure and compromise the system of segregation. An examination of individual cases shows that it took merely a federal investigation and an indictment of local law enforcement officials to arouse strong opposition from segments of the white population. This is particularly illustrated by an investigation that was launched by the Department of Justice in 1942.

White Opposition: The Trial of Edwin E. Evans and Henry F. Faucett

In October 1942, the U.S. Department of Justice ordered FBI investigations of the sheriff of Macon County, Alabama, Edwin E. Evans, and his deputy sheriff, Henry F. Faucett. These men were accused of killing an African American man named Walter Gunn as well as physically abusing numerous black prisoners and forcing them to make confessions. There were also allegations that they had abused several white suspects.[85]

The investigation was sparked by a report filed by the FBI field office in Birmingham, Alabama. One of the local FBI agents wrote that he had been informed by a white individual of possible civil rights violations committed by Sheriff Evans and Deputy Sheriff Faucett. Two weeks after J. Edgar Hoover forwarded the report to the Department of Justice, the bureau was officially instructed to launch a probe into Evans and Faucett.[86]

During the course of the investigation, which began in late October 1942, numerous witnesses confirmed the allegations of physical abuse by Evans and Faucett. Eugene Brown, one of the alleged black victims of torture, told investigators how he had been arrested in March 1942 on suspicion of stealing car tires. Brown said that Evans and Faucett took him to a wooded area off the highway between Tuskegee and Auburn; handcuffed him to a tree; and beat him with heavy sticks, branches, and a blackjack to coerce him into making a confession. Despite his protestations of innocence, he said that he was then taken to the jail in Tuskegee. Brown said that the next evening, Evans and Faucett drove him to some forested land along the highway to Shorter, Alabama, where they beat him until he was unconscious.[87]

An African American woman named Lillie Mae Hendon also leveled massive allegations against the two men. Hendon was arrested in July 1942 after an African American man had accused her of stealing $154 from him. She told the FBI that Evans and Faucett had beaten her severely with a blackjack and a walking cane to force her to make a confession. Shortly after her release, Hendon was interviewed on the events at the law office of Henry Neill Segrest, a local white lawyer and member of the Alabama House of Representatives. Several white officials were present to confirm the physical abuse.[88]

Hendon's meeting at the law firm shows that there were segments of the local white population that had reservations about violent police practices, which belies the image of an apparently united white community in the South.[89] Indeed, the Evans-Faucett case indicates a certain amount of overlapping between diverse racial and social factions within the local population. Federal investigations of law enforcement officials could consequently lead to temporary coalitions among various segments of the local population who joined forces to oppose police brutality.

As historian Robert J. Norrell has shown in his seminal work on the civil rights movement in Tuskegee, Alabama, the local African American community launched an initiative against Sheriff Evans and Deputy Sheriff Faucett immediately after the murder of Walter Gunn in June 1942.[90] According to concurring witness statements, previous to his death, Evans had beaten Gunn over the head with handcuffs, a blackjack, and a pistol grip. When Gunn then tried to flee, he was shot and wounded by Faucett and pursued by Evans and Faucett to his home. Shortly thereafter, Gunn was found dead in his backyard. An autopsy conducted by three white doctors appeared unable to unequivocally ascertain the direct cause of Gunn's death. The doctors stated that while trying to escape from the sheriff, Gunn had presumably died when he fell on an engine block that was lying behind his house.[91] But the members of the black community were convinced that the two lawmen had killed Gunn.

In reaction to the incident, Tuskegee University professor and civil rights activist Charles C. Gomillion joined with members of the Tuskegee Civic Association in establishing a legal fund in August 1942 and urged the local African American community to make donations to finance a court case against

Evans and Faucett. Many members of the Civic Association were associated with Tuskegee University, which had been established in the late nineteenth century by Booker T. Washington, enjoyed an outstanding reputation in Macon County as a nationwide renowned institution of higher education, and was the largest black university in the South.[92] This show of protest against Evans and Faucett was supported by representatives of the local white community who expressed grave concerns about the manner in which Sheriff Evans exercised his duties. For instance, attorney Henry Neill Segrest and Tuskegee mayor Frank Carr urged the governor of Alabama to consider dismissing Evans from his position as sheriff.[93]

During the course of the FBI investigations, a number of white witnesses confirmed the allegations against Evans and Faucett. This included statements corroborating that Lillie Mae Hendon's body had clearly suffered violent trauma. For example, Dr. Murray Smith, a white physician working for the Macon County Health Department, told the FBI that he had examined a black woman in Henry Neill Segrest's office who had obviously been severely beaten: "[She] appeared sitting in a peculiar way, apparently being unable to sit up straight. She removed her clothes above her hips & I saw [that] her hips and backs of her legs above her knees were bruised, & there was considerable discoloration. No talking was done there & I did not know what happened to her, although it looked as if she had been whipped."[94] Smith's observations were confirmed by Henry Asa Vaughan, a white member of the Tuskegee City Council who had also been invited to Segrest's office to see the alleged victim. "She was afraid of me, I suppose, as she didn't know whether I would turn her over to the officers, or just why I came there. After Mr. SEGREST insisted[,] she pulled up her clothes & I saw that both buttocks & the back of both legs above her knees were bloodshot. Her eyes were bloodshot one worse than the other. . . . I saw her on the day she was released from jail which was several days after she was supposed to have been beaten."[95] Moreover, Hendon's allegations were confirmed by several African American witnesses. Mary Elza Lundy, an acquaintance of Hendon, also testified that she saw the alleged torture victim shortly after she was released from custody: "When she came home I could see that she was all bruised, her face and eyes were still swollen, her hip was bruised and her eyes ached so bad that I gave her [a] pair of sun glasses to wear."[96]

The FBI investigations also supported the allegations of torture made by Eugene Brown. Several of his fellow prisoners said that Brown's body had clearly visible signs of physical abuse when he was brought to the jail in Tuskegee. Willie Jenkins recalled: "When they brought him . . . his head was swollen, his eye was red & he couldn't stand for anyone hardly touching him. He had blood on his clothes & cap and he was bleeding. He couldn't walk. EUGENE said they had tied him to a tree while they took turns whipping him & would like to have whipped him to death. He also had mud on his clothes. He said they tried to make out he took some tires, but he said he didn't know anything about the tires."[97] In addition to Hendon and Brown, FBI investigators found numerous other African American victims of torture and violence. By all appearances, Evans and Faucett used the threat of physical abuse and arbitrary acts of violence as a means of disciplining alleged offenders and maintaining the authority of the sheriff's department. This violent treatment was not limited exclusively to the black population. A white man named Readie Glenn Huguley, for instance, told FBI agents that when Faucett had arrested him for an alleged traffic violation, the deputy had punched him in the stomach and in the face several times for no reason. Huguley would later testify in the trial of Evans and Faucett.[98]

The investigations by the FBI corroborated in every respect the allegations against Evans and Faucett. At the same time, they were opposed by certain segments of the local white population. At the outset of the investigations, local U.S. district attorney E. Burns Parker surmised that it would be extremely difficult to convict the two lawmen:

> On account of local conditions, and prejudices of which you are
> familiar, a conviction, to put it mildly, will certainly not be easy.
> In addition to other factors, the defendants will have tremendous
> advantage in that the hub of this matter is, and has been, a sheriff.
> The sheriffs of Alabama have a very close-knit organization and
> understanding, and every influence that they can assert will probably
> be used in favor of the subjects. It is well to remember that our jurors
> come from this area, and that this sheriff will know all about every one
> of them.[99]

Indeed, the investigations of Evans and Faucett prompted sheriffs and police officers throughout the state to rise to the defense of the two defendants. Three weeks before the trial of the two men was due to commence, U.S. district attorney Parker wrote that several members of the Alabama Sheriffs' and Peace Officers' Association had called for donations to support the two defendants in the upcoming court case. Parker also noted that it could be expected that the sheriffs in the districts surrounding Macon County would influence the selection of jury members for the trial of Evans and Faucett.[100]

Local white residents also sought to undercut the investigation by massively threatening and intimidating several African American witnesses who had given statements to the FBI.[101] Furthermore, it was rumored in the region that if Evans and Faucett were convicted, the white population would have to leave all counties in Alabama with a majority black population. As in many other districts of the so-called Black Belt, the majority of the inhabitants of Macon County were African American, but due to prevailing discriminatory voting laws, the white population had a greater number of eligible voters. The rumor reflected the fear that a conviction of the sheriff could shift the balance of political power in favor of the black population.[102] In short, many members of the local white community saw the trial of Evans and Faucett as a threat to local power structures.

The Trial of Evans and Faucett

The tension was palpable when the trial of Evans and Faucett opened before the federal court in Opelika, Alabama, on June 20, 1943. The importance of the case was underscored by the acute public interest that—in the words of the *Montgomery Advertiser*—had already risen to "an intense pitch" over the weekend before the trial.[103] More than three hundred police officers and sheriffs from several districts in Alabama attended the trial.[104] According to the indictment, Evans and Faucett were charged with thirteen counts of police brutality spanning a period of three years. If convicted, the defendants faced up to one year in prison and a fine of $1,000.[105]

Reports in the local press pointed to the symbolic importance of the proceedings. The African American witnesses were expected to use the trial as an opportunity to draw attention to civil rights violations and demand legal consequences for the physical abuse that they had suffered at the hands of law enforcement officials. These witnesses took considerable risks in coming forward, however, because they were the ones who had to fear reprisals for their courtroom testimony after the trial. By contrast, the defendants and their attorneys instrumentalized the trial to restore the racial hierarchies and power structures that had been challenged by the indictment.

These conflicting agendas came to a head when Lillie Mae Hendon took the stand as a witness for the prosecution. She gave detailed information on the physical abuse that Evans and Faucett had inflicted on her after her arrest.[106] But, as the *Montgomery Advertiser* reported, she was interrupted by one of the lawyers for the defense, who exhorted her to adjust her dress: "Lilly [sic] Mae, it must be admitted, excited some comment about her demeanor on the witness stand when Atty. Jake Walker for the defense told her to lower her dress. She was sitting in front of the jury in what might be called a movie pose by some. Somebody started to laugh at Mr. Walker's admonition and Judge Kennamer warned that the matter of the trial was serious and that if anybody took it any other way he would jail him or her."[107] The degrading comment by the defending attorney evidently aimed to denigrate the African American witness and reassert the racial and patriarchal hierarchies that had been called into question by her allegations against the two lawmen.

After Hendon's testimony, Henry Neill Segrest and Tuskegee mayor Frank Carr took the stand and corroborated Hendon's allegations of torture. Both witnesses testified that after she was released from the Tuskegee jail, Hendon's body was covered with severe bruises that extended from her back all the way down to her knees.[108] The police chief went on record as saying that Evans had bragged to him about the beating: "Chief of Police Trasher, of Tuskegee, testified that some time after Lilly [sic] Mae Hendon was released, Sheriff Evans told him 'he had slapped [the] hell out of [her],'" according to the *Montgomery Advertiser*.[109] Leading members of the local white community thus supported the case against Evans and Faucett.[110]

Eugene Brown also testified against the sheriff and his deputy. He stated under oath that he had suffered permanent damage from the abuse. As with the charges made by Hendon, the testimony of a number of witnesses supported his allegations of torture, including statements by Dr. Harry Winters, a white physician from Tuskegee, who confirmed the multiple wounds that Brown had sustained while in custody at the jail. Likewise, several African American former fellow prisoners took the stand to testify on his physical state during detention.[111] Throughout the course of the trial, eleven additional alleged victims of violence testified against Evans and Faucett, including the white Readie Glenn Huguley, who corroborated the allegations that came to light during the FBI investigation.[112]

After the witnesses for the prosecution had completed their testimony, the attorneys defending Evans and Faucett called dozens of individuals to the stand to refute the charges. Sheriff Evans testified that neither he nor his staff had ever beaten prisoners.[113] One strategy of the defense was to cast doubt on the reputation and credibility of the witnesses for the prosecution. This approach was wholeheartedly supported by the local press, which made no effort to disguise its blatant bias in favor of the witnesses testifying on behalf of the two indicted lawmen. For instance, the *Montgomery Advertiser* wrote that "prominent white citizens of Macon County began to appear in the witness chair in an effort to discredit the criminals and others who had gone before."[114]

The witnesses for the defense all testified that several of the alleged victims of police brutality had a criminal past and that either the "character" of the witnesses for the prosecution was "bad" or they had a "bad reputation."[115] The counsel for the defense thus strove to shift the focus to the question of the credibility and respectability of the alleged victims of violence. Likewise, a number of "reputable citizens" cast doubt on the credibility of Lillie Mae Hendon, as the *Montgomery Advertiser* reported with unmistakable bias against the witness for the prosecution: "It developed that Lilli [sic] Mae did not bear a good reputation in Macon County, either for veracity or character generally[,] as several reputable citizens swore her reputation was bad and that they would not believe her on oath."[116] In a bid to undermine the allegations by Lillie Mae Hendon even further, the defense called to the stand a black woman who testified that Hendon had been beaten several times in the past by her jealous "negro lover." Hence, the defense sought to suggest that the alleged signs of torture on Hendon's body were not the result of being beaten by the two defendants but had actually been inflicted by Hendon's partner. In doing so, the defense explicitly invoked the racist stereotype of the lying and licentious African American woman—a strategy that would later emerge in other trials of law enforcement officials.[117]

The credibility of Readie Glenn Huguley was also called into question. Huguley and a man named Willie Griggs were the only alleged white victims who had testified against the two defendants. The *Montgomery Advertiser* stated that "several prominent Macon County citizens" questioned Huguley's credibility by testifying that they "had known Reedie [sic] for a long time, that he had a bad reputation and that they would not believe him on oath."[118] Likewise, the testimony of Willie Griggs was derided. Griggs, who had been arrested for assaulting Evans, was accused of being a drunk, whereupon the presiding judge, C. D. Kennamer, ruled that his testimony was invalid and quashed the count on the indictment pertaining to him.[119] While the lawyers for the defense appealed to racial prejudice in the case of Lillie Mae Hendon, in the cases of Griggs and Huguley they invoked class-specific resentments to undermine the men's credibility and reliability.

After three days of legal proceedings, Evans and Faucett were acquitted on all counts.[120] According to reports in the local press, spectators in the courtroom were visibly relieved to hear the verdict by the jury: "The verdict was read in the presence of more than 200 friends of the two officers, including many sheriffs and peace officers from different sections of the State.

There was no demonstration in the courtroom but the evidence of satisfaction could be seen on every face."[121] The reaction of the audience to the outcome of the trial shows that the case against Evans and Faucett was deemed to be of key importance to local power structures. Accordingly, the *Montgomery Advertiser* suggested that a guilty verdict would have undermined the authority of local law enforcement officials: "[It was] feared that if Sheriff Evans was convicted it would mean that the federal government had laid its heavy hand upon local law enforcement in the counties and cities and that every peace officer would be at the mercy of the word of convicted criminals."[122] Another topic of the local press was the intervention of the federal government in the judicial spheres of individual states and districts, which was perceived as unlawful meddling. In the opinion of the *Montgomery Advertiser*, the trial had addressed the fundamental question of the "rights of counties and cities and the State to maintain their own local self government."[123]

The trial of Evans and Faucett was interpreted as more than just a threat to the local racial power structures. As with the case against Sutherland that was tried earlier, these court proceedings brought to light the historical conflict over the sovereignty rights of individual states versus the authority and jurisdiction of the federal government—a conflict that had characterized the relationship between the South and the states of the North during the nineteenth century, and had flared up with renewed intensity after the end of the Civil War.[124] The deep-seated resentment of southerners toward perceived federal meddling in the legal affairs of the South is illustrated by the investigation of Sheriff Erskine in 1943.

"It's None of Washington's Business": The Case against William J. Erskine

The case against Sheriff William J. Erskine in Anderson County, South Carolina, was one of the few federal investigations in the 1940s and early 1950s that ended with a conviction. Erskine was accused in 1943 of having tortured numerous black suspects to extract confessions for alleged thefts and other offenses. He was also accused of detaining several African American youths convicted on trumped-up charges in involuntary debt bondage on his farm and physically abusing them.

The case was opened when local U.S. district attorney Oscar Henry Doyle wrote a letter to the Department of Justice in December 1942 detailing the allegations against the sheriff.[125] During the FBI investigation that was launched shortly thereafter, numerous individuals testified that they had been physically abused by Erskine and other members of the local sheriff's department. For instance, several black youths accused Erskine of beating them in an effort to find out who had stolen his watch. One of the alleged victims, seventeen-year-old Lucis Cowan, made the following statement to investigators: "I had been in jail for about five minutes when three officers came down [the] stairs. . . . One of the tall slender officers sat on my head and the other used a strap on my back and buttox [sic]. The man beat me with the strap and it hurt so bad I yelled and screamed. When I would raise my head up off the floor the Sheriff would hit me in the face with his fist. All of them kept asking me what I did with the watch."[126] Another witness, Theodore Benson, gave a particularly descriptive account of the physical abuse that he endured while in custody on suspicion of stealing the watch:

> The first night I was in jail I was taken down in the basement of the jail. I was questioned about the watch. I told them I did not know where the watch was. They told me to pull my pants off and get down on my knees. I think the Sheriff was the one that did the talking. One of the officers beat me with a leather strap about eighteen inches long with a little handle on it. They beat my nude body till blood ran out. I was hurting so bad I told them stories or anything they wanted to know, although they were all lies. . . . They checked up and found out I was telling lies, so they beat me again. They beat me with a blackjack until my head was swollen so my eyes were closed.[127]

The investigation by the FBI corroborated the allegations of torture made by Cowan, Benson, and other alleged victims. Likewise, a court transcript was revealed in which Sheriff Erskine admitted to having "slapped" Cowan and other suspects.[128] In addition to numerous African Americans who were interviewed, several white witnesses substantiated the accusations of the victims, including a lawyer named Sanford Eugene Haley from Anderson, South Carolina. Haley said that Cowan's body showed clear signs of suffering violent trauma after his release from police custody. "At the time I interviewed LUCIS COWAN . . . his eyes were swollen and his left eye was red and inflamed and almost closed. LUCIS had several knots on his head and a cut somewhere on the front of his face. He also had several large welts on his back and his general appearance indicated he had been beaten severely."[129] Nellie S. Brewer, an elderly white woman from Cowan's neighborhood, told investigators that Lucis Cowan's mother had asked her to look at her son's physical state after his release from custody: "I went to see Lucis that afternoon and his face had a lot of bruises and skinned places on it. His eyes were swollen and bloodshot, and he had what looked like a blister on his shoulder."[130]

The FBI investigation brought to light a multitude of other allegations of mistreatment by African American prisoners and former prisoners.[131] A number of white former prisoners also leveled allegations against the sheriff and several deputy sheriffs.[132] Charlie Denny, a twenty-seven-year-old man who at the time of his interview was serving a sentence on the Anderson County chain gang, told investigators that after his arrest, he was repeatedly punched in the stomach and kicked by a member of Erskine's staff. Denny testified that it was primarily black prisoners who were subjected to floggings at the Anderson County jail. He also said that while serving his sentence, he often heard the sounds of screams and beatings.[133]

Denny's statement is yet another example of the racially motivated cultural traditions of violence that pervaded jails and prisons in the South. Particularly extreme and humiliating forms of abuse — such as whippings — were evidently reserved for African American prisoners. Law enforcement officials apparently saw no need to conceal the mistreatment of black prisoners.

Denny's story was corroborated by several other white former prisoners who said that they had also heard African American prisoners being whipped in the Anderson County jail. Corine McCoy, a woman who had been jailed on suspicion of adultery, testified that one night she had heard screams and the sound of lashes with a strap. The next morning, she said, Sheriff Erskine openly told her that he had beaten an African American prisoner.[134]

During the subsequent trial, the jury in the U.S. district court in Anderson, South Carolina, returned a guilty verdict against Erskine on December 1, 1943. Although the prosecution was seeking a sentence of three years behind bars and a fine of $1,000, the presiding judge, C. C. Wyche, reduced the sentence to sixty days' imprisonment and a fine of $500. As the judge explained in his statement, he had granted a more lenient sentence in view of the sheriff's "reputation."[135] According to an article in the *Anderson Independent*, before the verdict was announced, Sheriff Erskine made a personal plea to voice his objections to the looming conviction: "'Judge,' he said, 'all in the world I did was to slap that Negro.' 'You have no right to slap,' corrected Judge Wyche. 'A prisoner may call you a liar, your wife a liar and all your deputies liars — call you even worse — and you have no right to hit him when he is in your jail.'"[136]

Erskine's objection that he had merely slapped the black suspect clearly illustrates how brazenly law enforcement officials attempted to justify — to themselves and to others — the physical abuse of African Americans in their custody, as if it were a perfectly natural thing to do. The federal judge, however, used this as an opportunity to publicly inform the sheriff of the legal rights of prisoners and admonish him not to run roughshod over their civil liberties.

In a letter written after the trial and sent to the heads of the Civil Rights Section, U.S. district attorney Doyle underscored the positive reactions of some members of the local population concerning the outcome of the trial: "The good people of Anderson County, where I live myself, are very happy over the outcome of this case."[137] But he expressed serious doubt that the conviction would result in Sheriff Erskine being removed from office: "Frankly . . . I do not think anything will be done. In the first place the Attorney General of this State has no opinion and doesn't know how to make one, and in the second place I doubt if the Governor would have the courage to take any steps."[138]

While U.S. attorney general Francis Biddle and the representatives of the CRS celebrated the verdict as a "success," despite the relatively light sentence,[139] the sheriff's fine was paid by local citizens. An article in the *Anderson Independent* had this to say about the initiative: "Although Sheriff W. J. Erskine was fined $500 and sentenced to sixty days imprisonment . . . he did not have to dig down into his own pockets for one cent of the fine, it was learned yesterday. 'Citizens of Anderson County gladly payed [sic] Sheriff Erskine's fine,' Jack G. Kraft, manager of the Calhoun Hotel said last night. . . . 'It was easy,' he declared. . . . 'If the fine had been $10,000, the people of Anderson County would have paid it, too.'"[140] As the organizers of the initiative publicly proclaimed, the fund-raising drive was organized to express solidarity with the convicted sheriff and protest against the intervention by federal authorities in states' rights: "The issue involved is states [sic] rights. Are we Southerners going to sit idly by while the federal government arrests, prosecutes, fines and sends to jail our high sheriff? If the sheriff is guilty of any wrong, the Anderson County grand jury is capable of handling the matter. It's none of Washington's business."[141] Statements like this reveal the deep-seated aversion toward interference by the federal government in the political and legal sovereignty of southern states—an aversion that had already emerged in the case against Evans and Faucett. In the eyes of many commentators in the South, the federal investigations into law enforcement officials called into question the right to local and state-level self-determination and self-government. Moreover, the trials evoked memories of the Reconstruction era, in which the white southern elite was stripped of power and the political fortunes of the South were dictated by the Union states. Accordingly, during the civil rights trials that targeted violent and abusive law enforcement officials, the image of the "carpetbaggers" was repeatedly evoked—that is, the stereotype of the Republican politicians from the North who moved to the South after the Civil War and joined forces with newly elected black Republican members of Congress to exploit the chaotic political and economic situation and enrich themselves.[142]

This long-standing sense of resentment boiled to the surface again during the course of another federal investigation, the case of *United States v. Dailey*, from 1943. The probe focused on the police chief of DeKalb, Georgia, Joseph T. Dailey, and three of his staff members, who were indicted on charges of physically abusing several black suspects and prosecuted before the U.S. district court in Atlanta. During the trial, the defense repeatedly raised the objection that the charges against the police were reminiscent of the methods of the "carpetbag government" after the end of the Civil War.[143] The members of the jury clearly had similar reservations concerning the federal investigation and, despite overwhelming evidence against the defendants, acquitted them on all counts.[144]

These examples demonstrate that federal investigations of police violence in the South were permeated by a cultural conflict over racist concepts of law and order. While federal authorities justified their legal initiatives by pointing to the goal of implementing fundamental legal rights, officials in the South rejected the investigations as interference in the legal sovereignty of the southern states. Some newspaper reports explicitly referred to the American Civil War, which was being "fought over again."[145] The African American *Atlanta Daily World* countered such arguments with the following pithy commentary on the Erskine case: "The men who raise this bogus issue [of states' rights] know fully well that no one threatens state government. . . . When the federal government steps in to safeguard those of its citizens whose rights have been violated, the bogus yelp of states' rights is invariably raised by the very men who with blunt impunity have been trampling into dust the rights of the individual."[146]

The reaction of the white population was an expression of its aspiration to solve the so-called race problem in its own way—in other words, without the interference of the North. Hence, the initiatives against the civil rights investigations of federal authorities heralded the massive opposition of large segments of the white population of the South to the broad and rapid expansion of the civil rights movement in the mid-1950s. In view of these and other difficulties, the civil rights initiative of the federal government in the South was confined to narrow limits, as reflected in the cases from the early

1940s that have been presented here, and had only a very limited ability to dismantle local structures of racial power and subjugation.

After 1945: The Committee on Civil Rights and the Civil Rights Section

From the mid-1940s onward, African American civil rights activists increasingly criticized the highly selective policy of the U.S. Department of Justice in pursuing cases of police brutality in the South. As early as 1944, Thurgood Marshall, in his function as the head of the legal department of the NAACP, pointed to the limited impact of the federal government's civil rights initiative. In a speech at the NAACP Wartime Conference, he said that the initiative of the Civil Rights Section had achieved impressive results in a number of cases but pointed out that only a very few of these cases had resulted in indictments of southern officials. He went on to say that if the CRS continued to restrict its efforts to prosecuting individual, selected cases of racial violence, it could not effectively combat the racist structures of the South: "Our civil rights as guaranteed by the federal statutes will never become a reality until the U.S. Department of Justice decides that it represents the entire United States and is not required to fear offending any section of the country which believes it has the God-given right to be above the laws of the United States and the United States Supreme Court."[147] Beginning in the mid-1940s, the NAACP increasingly insisted on the sweeping prosecution of the pervasive use of racial police violence in the South instead of focusing on a limited number of individual test cases. This is clearly illustrated by a case from 1946 in which the NAACP urged the Justice Department to launch investigations into the death of Willie P. M. Lockwood.

In May 1946, Lockwood was shot in a public place by a deputy sheriff in Macon County, Alabama. Mary Lockwood, who witnessed the killing, wrote to the NAACP with a request to take the case to court. She said that her son, a World War II veteran, had been arrested by the local sheriff's department because he had resisted an assault by a white neighbor. Her husband, she wrote, had demanded that the sheriff justify the arrest of their son, and during the subsequent altercation, he was shot dead right in front of her eyes by one of the deputy sheriffs.[148]

Upon receiving the letter, Thurgood Marshall urged the CRS to investigate the case.[149] One year later, in June 1947, NAACP officials were informed that the Justice Department had decided against filing charges in the Lockwood case. The letter cited major discrepancies in witness testimony. In contrast to the version of events presented by Lockwood's wife, the sheriff and his deputies went on record as saying that he had violently resisted his arrest and was killed during the ensuing dispute. In view of the contradictory testimony, the Justice Department did not "believe that successful prosecution could be maintained," and the case had, accordingly, been closed.

The Lockwood case is an example of the considerable limitations placed on the CRS in the 1940s and early 1950s. Due to insufficient personnel, limited authority, and a lack of political support, it was only able to prosecute relatively few civil rights violations until the mid-1950s. To make matters worse, its activities were hindered by a Supreme Court decision in *Screws et al. v. United States* in 1945.

On January 30, 1943, the sheriff of Baker County, Georgia, M. Claude Screws, and two of his staff members arrested a thirty-year-old African American man, Robert Hall, on suspicion of stealing a car tire and beat him to death. During the subsequent trial before the U.S. district court, Screws was found guilty by the local jury. After reviewing the verdict, however, the U.S. Supreme Court decided in May 1945 to reverse the decision of the local federal court on the argument that the judge had not properly instructed the members of the jury. The Supreme Court said that officials could only be convicted of civil rights violations if they—in accordance with the relevant sections of the United States Code—had "willfully" violated someone's civil liberties. In doing so, the court instituted the requirement that defendants must be proven to have acted with willful intent.[150] Shortly thereafter, in a second trial before the local U.S. district court in Georgia, Screws was acquitted by the jury. The decision by the U.S. Supreme Court had far-reaching consequences that are of continuing relevance today, as it severely limited the chances of convicting law enforcement officials of civil rights violations. In 1945, it meant even further limitations to the already shaky legal foundation for the prosecution activities of the CRS.[151]

The limited scope and effectiveness of the CRS was also criticized in the 1947 report of the Committee on Civil Rights, a body that had been established by Democratic president Harry S. Truman (1945–53) to investigate the persistent violations of civil rights in the United States and develop proposals for political initiatives by the federal government.[152] Truman's move was partly in reaction to the fact that racism in the South was increasingly viewed as a burden for American foreign policy,[153] and partly in reaction to the growing criticism of a lack of assertiveness and effectiveness in the civil rights policy of the U.S. government. This criticism was spearheaded by the civil rights activists of the NAACP, who alleged that the government was not investigating the ongoing lynchings in the South with the requisite follow-through. For instance, the Justice Department and the FBI were accused of a lack of determination in their investigation of the Monroe lynching in Georgia, in which four African Americans were murdered by a lynch mob in 1946. Despite a large-scale FBI investigation into the case, which attracted both national and international attention, none of the alleged members or supporters of the lynch mob were charged.[154] Furthermore, in 1946 the NAACP openly criticized the inability of the Department of Justice to achieve a conviction in the case of Sheriff Lynwood Shull from South Carolina, who, as shown earlier, had brutally beaten Isaac Woodard, leaving him permanently blind.

After several months of research, the Committee on Civil Rights published its report on October 29, 1947. The report, titled "To Secure These Rights," referred to "widespread and varied forms of official misconduct" by law enforcement authorities, including "violent physical attacks by police officers on members of minority groups, the use of third degree methods to extort confessions, and brutality against prisoners."[155] The committee noted that the majority of civil rights violations occurred in the South and that it was "convinced" that "the incidence of police brutality against Negroes is disturbingly high."[156]

The report also included a comprehensive examination of the prosecution activities of the CRS, whose work, according to the authors, suffered from a number of structural shortcomings, despite its "remarkable" record. Criticism was levied, for example, at the ineffective legal basis for the civil rights activities of the department; its lack of personnel, with only seven full-time staff members; and its subordinate position within the Department of Justice.[157]

To strengthen the protection of civil rights, the committee suggested that the CRS be elevated to the rank of an independent division within the Justice Department. It also called for increases in funding and personnel, and the establishment of regional offices throughout the country, where complaints of civil rights violations were to be registered on location and forwarded to the Department of Justice. Furthermore, the committee proposed the passing of a federal law by the U.S. Congress that would explicitly make it a punishable offense for law enforcement officers to engage in discriminatory actions, the idea being to place the prosecution activities of the federal government in this area on a secure legal foundation.[158]

After the report was published, the Truman administration attempted on a number of occasions to implement the proposals of the committee. In February 1948, Truman called on Congress to pass several of the legislative amendments recommended by the Committee on Civil Rights. "The position of the United States in the world today makes it especially urgent that we adopt these measures to secure for all our people their essential rights," Truman said in his statement.[159] In addition to passing an anti-lynching law and other legal initiatives, Truman proposed improvements to the legal foundation for prosecuting civil rights violations by law enforcement officials.[160] He stressed that these laws were necessary to strengthen the leadership role of the United States and the world: "If we wish to inspire the peoples of the world whose freedom is in jeopardy, if we wish to restore hope to those who have already lost their civil liberties, if we wish to fulfill the promise that is ours, we must correct the remaining imperfections in our practice of democracy."[161] Legal historian Mary L. Dudziak contextualizes Truman's speech as follows: Amid the ensuing ideological tensions with the Soviet Union, the concerns over the external perception of ongoing violations of civil liberties in the United States had developed to become a key point of reference in American civil rights policies.[162]

Moreover, civil rights violations in the United States were increasingly being debated against the background of a growing international awareness of human rights. The United Nations Commission on Human Rights was established in February 1946, and the NAACP submitted a petition to the organization in October 1947 to protest the discriminatory treatment of blacks in the United States. The petition, under the title "An Appeal to the World," generated a huge response in the domestic and international press. U.S. government representatives and newspaper commentators expressed concern over its impact on American foreign policy. In a speech before the National Association of Attorneys General, U.S. attorney general Tom C. Clark (1945–49) said that he was "humiliated" that the African American population in the United States should have to turn to the United Nations to improve its civil rights situation. He urged the federal attorneys to use the existing legal possibilities to prosecute civil rights violations.[163] Although the United Nations Commission on Human Rights refused to transmit the petition to the United Nations General Assembly and declined to investigate the allegations, the reactions to the NAACP initiative revealed that from the late 1940s onward, the problem of racial discrimination in the United States was approached to a greater degree against the backdrop of the international political context.[164]

Despite Truman's efforts, none of the substantial recommendations of the Committee on Civil Rights were implemented during his presidency, which ended in 1953. Legislative proposals in Congress failed again and again in the face of opposition from senators representing southern states. During the presidential election of 1948, Truman's civil rights policies sparked a political backlash that led to a short-lived breakaway faction of the Democratic Party called the States' Rights Democratic Party, which was under the leadership of Strom Thurmond from South Carolina. Capitalizing on the groundswell of white opposition toward the federal investigations of law enforcement officials in the South, the "Dixiecrats," as they were called, built their party platform around the principle of the legal sovereignty of individual states, which they saw as threatened by the civil rights initiative of the federal government under President Truman.[165] It was not until the presidency of Dwight D. Eisenhower (1953–61) that both houses of Congress finally approved the Civil Rights Act of 1957, which implemented several recommendations by Truman's Committee on Civil Rights.[166]

The halting initiatives of the U.S. government in the 1940s and early 1950s meant that the efforts of the CRS had only a limited influence on the widespread discrimination against blacks in the South. As the following examination of two cases from Alabama shows, sheriffs and police officers continued to torture and physically abuse African Americans between 1945 and 1955, yet the CRS was still unable to achieve convictions.

African American Women as Plaintiffs: The Trials of Joseph L. Pickett and Curvin M. Covington

In September 1946, the CRS launched investigations into Joseph L. Pickett, the sheriff of Bullock County, Alabama—located southeast of the capital, Montgomery—and two other members of the local white community. The case was sparked by allegations of theft against Martha K. McMillan, a mother of eight who worked at the bus station in the county seat, Union Springs. A white woman named Margaret Green Cook suspected that McMillan had stolen several gold rings from her home.

As Martha McMillan testified in an affidavit, Sheriff Pickett and Margaret Green Cook's husband and brother, Reynold G. Cook and Rell (Verell) Green, forced their way into her home on the evening of September 5, 1946, asked where the rings were, and then searched her house in vain. Afterward, she said that Rell Green kicked her in the face and threatened to kill her if she did not divulge where the jewelry was hidden. Despite her protestations of innocence, she was brought to the jail at Union Springs, where she said that Rell Green whipped her with a roughly four-foot piece of hose and severely threatened her in a bid to force her to disclose the rings' hiding place. When she continued to assert her innocence, Rell Green and a second man whom she did not know—but who was identified as Margaret Green Cook's husband during the course of the FBI investigation—continued to whip her. She testified that Mr. Green pointed a pistol at her to keep her from screaming and then continued flogging her: "[He] put his pistol back in his pocket, put both hands on the hose and said, 'God damn you, negro, I'll kill you if you don't tell me where my sister's rings are.' I still told Mr. GREEN I didn't know anything about it. Mr. GREEN whipped again and kept whipping until he wore that rubber hose so short he could not strike with it."[167] McMillan said that throughout the entire ordeal, Sheriff Pickett made no attempt to keep the men from tormenting her: "I asked the sheriff, 'Would you let the two men whip a poor woman to death like this?' Sheriff Pickett said, 'Tell them what they want to know and they will leave you off.'"[168]

After being whipped and beaten, she said that she was driven back home by Sheriff Pickett and members of Margaret Green Cook's family. McMillan testified that another brother of Margaret Green Cook, Comer F. Green, threatened to kill her if she continued to refuse to confess to the theft: "[He] said, 'We're going to take you out and hang you up to a limb and kill you and let the buzzards get you.' I said, 'Well if you do that I'll just have to take it. There is nothing I can do, but I still don't know anything about the rings.'"[169] A week after the incident, Martha K. McMillan and her husband took the train to Montgomery to consult a white lawyer who advised them, in view of the extreme circumstances of the case, to contact the local government authorities. The McMillans then went to the Alabama Department of Public Safety, where, in the presence of the head of the Enforcement Division, Captain N. W. Kimbrough, Martha McMillan signed an affidavit detailing the events. To document the allegations, Kimbrough summoned a photographer who took several shots of the bruises on Martha McMillan's body.[170] Afterward, he brought the couple to the local federal prosecutor's office to inform U.S. district attorney E. Burns Parker of the case. It was Parker who only three years earlier had led the prosecutions of Sheriff Evans and Deputy Sheriff Faucett. The very same day, a member of Parker's staff named Hartwell Davis sent a letter to the CRS with a request to investigate the case.[171] Finally, Kimbrough and other staff members at the Department of Public Safety accompanied the McMillans back to Union Springs to protect them from further attacks. It was only after none of the suspects had appeared at the McMillan residence by midnight that the government officials headed back to Montgomery.[172]

The spontaneous initiative of the officials in Montgomery shows that they condemned the actions of the sheriff and his accomplices. By spontaneously seizing the initiative against the practice of vigilante justice in this case, they stood out from the predominately passive attitude of officials in the South.[173] Davis reported in a letter to the CRS: "It is my pleasure to inform you that Captain Kimbrough is most eager in this matter, and I believe in all matters, to see that any mistreatment by whites to the colored race is properly punished. . . . If we had more officers of Captain Kimbrough's caliber, there would be much better relations not only here but all over the country."[174] The FBI investigations launched in Union Springs shortly thereafter corroborated the allegations made by Martha McMillan. Although Rell Green, Reynold G. Cook, and Sheriff Joseph L. Pickett gave statements in which they denied inflicting any physical pain on Martha McMillan, several witnesses corroborated the accusations.[175] McMillan's children in particular confirmed to the FBI that their mother had been threatened and physically abused before she was arrested. Fourteen-year-old Arthurene McMillan testified as follows: "On the night of September 5, 1946, I was at home with my mother and six brothers and sisters. . . . Mr. Pickett came in and went to the kitchen of the house with his flashlight. . . . Two men who had been on the outside came in and one of them who Mama called Mr. Green kicked my mother in the face. She fell back on the bed and when she got back up her mouth was bleeding."[176] After her mother returned from the sheriff's office, Arthurene McMillan said that she had been badly beaten: "The next morning I saw her bruises. The left eye was completely closed and the right eye partly closed. I saw that she had bruises on both sides of her arms. She said the men that had carried her off put the bruises on her. She told us not to tell anybody about this."[177] Furthermore, McMillan's allegations were supported by several African American witnesses who were detained at the jail in Union Springs at the time. Junior Reed, for example, a twenty-eight-year-old man who had been arrested on vagrancy charges, said that he heard the sounds of blows, screams, and verbal exchanges between Sheriff Pickett and Martha McMillan.[178]

Local opposition to the federal investigation began to form already in the run-up to the trial. As a staff member at the local U.S. district attorney's office noted in a letter to the Department of Justice, Sheriff Pickett and a number of "his friends" in the local white community, along with the sheriffs of Alabama, had actively appealed for support in the upcoming trial before the federal court.[179] Relatives of Martha McMillan expressed concern that she could be the target of reprisals due to the upcoming trial.[180] In fact, out of fear for her own safety, McMillan had left Bullock County during the FBI investigation.[181]

After the investigations were completed in June 1947, the trial of Sheriff Joseph L. Pickett, Verell (Rell) Green, Reynold G. Cook, Margaret Green Cook, and Comer F. Green took place in Opelika, Alabama. With reference to Sections 52, 88, and 51 of the United States Code, the indictment charged the defendants with conspiracy to deprive Martha McMillan of her civil rights.[182]

In addition to the local newspapers, the trial was covered by two major national African American weekly newspapers: the *Pittsburgh Courier* and the *Chicago Defender*. On the front page of the *Defender*, the case was characterized as another example of the "Bourbon South's feudalism."[183] Meanwhile, the *Courier* compared the events in Union Springs with the horrors of a Nazi concentration camp: "The sordid story of a night of terror in a Union Springs jail cell, reminiscent of the torture of Hitler's concentration camp victims will be unfolded in the U.S. District Court . . . when five white defendants go on trial for the brutal hose-flogging of Mrs. Martha K. McMillan, a thirty-five-year-old colored bus station attendant."[184] This article is an example of how, even after the end of World War II, the black press and African American civil rights activists used comparisons with Hitler and Nazi Germany to denounce violations of African American civil rights.[185]

In the federal court, Martha McMillan repeated her allegations against Pickett and the other defendants. The two FBI agents investigating the case, Henry Slate and Pierce A. Pratt, and the Alabama civil servant Kimbrough testified in her favor, and the prosecution presented as evidence the previously mentioned photographs of the wounds suffered by Martha McMillan.[186]

Then the defense called several witnesses to the stand who denigrated the character and reputation of Martha McMillan. According to the report in the *Montgomery Advertiser*, a number of witnesses testified that they "would not believe her on oath."[187] As with the case of Evans and Faucett, the defense endeavored to undermine the credibility of the victim by accusing her of lying under oath and claiming that her injuries had not been caused by the defendants. The defense called an African American witness to the stand, Marie Pendleton, who testified that Martha McMillan had told her that her wounds had been inflicted by a white business owner to whom she owed money.[188]

In his summation, Assistant District Attorney Hartwell Davis urged the jury "not to let prejudice write your verdict" and confronted them with the question of how they would treat the case of the brutal beating of a white woman: "If . . . a white woman should be beat up like that, what would we do about it? . . . If this could happen to an almost friendless Negro woman, it might happen to a white person."[189]

Despite the emphatic appeals of the prosecution, the jury acquitted the five defendants on all counts. In a letter to the CRS, prosecuting attorney Davis expressed his disappointment at the outcome of the trial: "I regret to inform you that after a two-day trial, the Jury found the defendants not guilty. The Jury remained out 50 minutes." Nevertheless, Davis said that he was convinced that the trial would have a long-term positive impact: "The defendants are at liberty, but it is my humble opinion that the prosecution will do good for years to come. None of these state officers like to be hauled into the Federal court."[190]

The acquittals are but one example of the extreme difficulties faced by African American women who sought to have their allegations of torture heard in court. The categorical identification of African American witnesses and victims as "black" and "female" was often enough to cast a heavy shadow of doubt over their credibility.

Another example of this is a case that took place in Alabama in the early 1950s. In April 1953, forty-nine-year-old Mallie Pearson from Halsell accused the sheriff of Choctaw County, Curvin M. Covington, and the two deputy sheriffs, Harry Leon Clark Jr. and Ottis G. Wainright, of beating her for over an hour with a stick and a leather belt. She said the three men were trying to force her to confess to stealing a bale of cotton that had been removed from a local business.[191]

The investigation into the case was launched after a white pastor reported the incident to the FBI office in Mobile on April 15, 1953.[192] When Mallie Pearson was questioned by FBI agents on the events, she gave the following statement:

> They drove me to a point . . . in the swamp and made me get out of the car. One of the men made me lie on the floor and one of the other men went out to cut a stick. One man pulled off his belt and started whipping around my thighs and buttocks and the big man came back with a stick and whipped me on my back side with it. The third man squatted in front of me and told me to tell where the cotton was. He told me not to holler or he would run a stick down my throat or cram it full of dirt. After whipping me with my dress down one of the men took his stick and pulled my dress up exposing the flesh of my buttocks and both continued whipping.[193]

Since she had steadfastly maintained her innocence, she said that the men eventually released her, but first threatened to kill her if she were to mention the events to anyone else.[194]

Pearson was treated for four days at a local hospital. The doctors questioned by the FBI confirmed that she had severe bruises, which were also documented photographically. Dr. Columbus A. Jackson, a white physician, gave the following statement: "I examined her as she knelt, so weak she couldn't stand, and observed that her buttocks and hips were badly bruised. I observed that this area was very red, swollen and hard with the tissue thick and hard caused by the injury. I observed that it appeared that a flat surface instrument as well as a round instrument had been used to inflict the injury."[195] During the course of the FBI investigation, Pearson identified Sheriff Curvin M. Covington and the two deputy sheriffs, Harry Leon Clark Jr. and Ottis G. Wainright, as the perpetrators, but the two deputies denied having anything to do with the assault. Covington refused to make a statement on the allegations.[196]

Before the beginning of the trial, Mallie Pearson was subjected to massive intimidation. She told the FBI investigators that several whites pressured her to retract her accusations. She said that they had even threatened to burn down her house if she continued to maintain her allegations against the three defendants.[197]

After more than a year of delays, the trial of Covington, Clark, and Wainright commenced before the federal court in Mobile, Alabama, on September 15, 1954. On the witness stand, Mallie Pearson repeated her allegations against the three defendants. Her testimony was corroborated by the statements of two white physicians. Both Dr. Columbus A. Jackson and Dr. J. P. Tatum, who worked in the hospital in Meridian, confirmed the severe bruising that they had observed on Pearson's body. Likewise, FBI agent Robert L. Crongeyer testified that Pearson had not hesitated when she identified the three defendants as the perpetrators when she was shown a number of different suspects.[198]

This trial constituted yet another example of a typical strategy by the defense that sought to call into question the victim's credibility. Defense Attorney D. R. Coley Jr. claimed that the charges brought by Pearson were "based on an identification [of the presumed perpetrators] which was wholly unsatisfactory," and raised the accusation that the charges had been trumped up by a former candidate who had run against Covington in the election for sheriff.[199]

Despite the overwhelming evidence against the three defendants, the all-white jury pronounced them not guilty on all counts.[200] This may have had something to do with the landmark decision by the U.S. Supreme Court in *Brown v. Board of Education*. On May 17, 1954, the Supreme Court ruled that the segregation of public schools was unconstitutional, effectively overturning *Plessy v. Ferguson* and removing the legal foundation of the principle of "separate but equal" in the United States.[201] In a letter to the Civil Rights Section, U.S. district attorney Percy C. Fountain made the following observation: "The case was proven beyond any reasonable doubt. The judge felt certain of a conviction, and rumors have been heard that some of the jurors felt the defendants were guilty but did not wish to punish white men for this type of violation, particularly after the Supreme Court decision on segregation. The verdict was very discouraging."[202] Hence, the acquittal of Covington and his codefendants was at least in part a backlash reaction to the *Brown v. Board of Education* decision, which was perceived by large segments of the white population of the South as a harbinger of the end of segregated social structures in the region. Moreover, the acquittals in the Covington case illustrate the enormous power that racist mind-sets still exerted in the South during the 1950s. Despite unequivocal evidence against the defendants, the members of the jury refrained from condemning law enforcement officials for their assault of Mallie Pearson.

Also noteworthy are further comments by prosecuting attorney Fountain, in which he placed part of the blame for the negative verdict on the principal witness: "It might be noted that the victim, although implicitly and repeatedly advised to remain calm, truthful and humble while on the witness stand, was very smart-alecky and overbearing. She also tried to make a much better case than she actually had by greatly exaggerating her injuries. Both doctors testified that she suffered no permanent injuries and stated that all x-rays taken were negative. The victim claimed she was permanently injured and dramatically limped on the witness stand."[203] Historian Danielle McGuire has shown that the courtroom conduct of African American women in the South was linked to a specific, historical "politics of respectability."[204] In her studies on the few cases from the 1940s and 1950s in which white men from the South were charged for raping black women, she shows that the court appearances of rape victims were framed within racist and patriarchally coded modes of perception. They only had a chance of being heard in court if they assumed a self-effacing demeanor.[205] Fountain's comments on Pearson's behavior in the courtroom are an example of these discriminatory conceptual patterns.

This case illustrates once again the difficulties that African American women faced in making their allegations of torture heard before federal courts in the South as well as the indifference of jury members toward black women who had been subjected to extreme torment. Even during the early 1950s, federal authorities were confronted with massive obstacles when they attempted to protect the civil rights of African Americans in the South. As Arthur B. Caldwell, a leading attorney in the CRS, commented after the trial: "We can only hope . . . that indictments and public trials in those cases will discourage similar violations of the civil rights statues in the future."[206]

Conclusion

Nearly a year after the trial of Sheriff Curvin M. Covington and his two deputy sheriffs in Alabama ended with acquittals on all charges, a fourteen-year-old African American boy named Emmett Till was murdered in the small town of Money, Mississippi, in August 1955. In contrast to the brutal beating of Mallie Pearson by police, which had been ignored by the national and international press, this murder received an unprecedented degree of attention.

Till had grown up in Chicago and was spending a few weeks with his uncle's family in Mississippi during the summer of 1955. The youth had allegedly made a suggestive comment to a white woman, Carolyn Bryant, who owned a local store together with her husband, Roy. A few days later, in the early hours of the morning, Roy Bryant and his half brother, J. W. Milam, abducted Till with a pickup truck and drove him to a remote location, where he was beaten with pistol grips and punched. Afterward, the men brought him to the nearby Tallahatchie River, where they shot him in the head, tied a heavy piece of metal to his neck with barbed wire, and threw his body into the river.

The abduction and murder of Emmett Till shocked the American public and made international headlines. Newspapers as well as radio and TV stations worldwide reported on the circumstances of the case and the subsequent trial of the two men in Sumner, Mississippi, which ended in an acquittal.[1] The case engendered instantaneous sympathy, in large part because the victim was just a teenager and was the only child of a single mother. The incident was also particularly explosive against the background of the Cold War. As in the case of the Groveland Four in 1949, the murder of Emmett Till fueled a worldwide debate on the aspirations and grisly underside of American democracy.[2] Finally, the public reaction to Till's death was prompted by the unprecedented media coverage of the case. To alert the world to her son's horrific murder, Till's mother, Mamie Till Bradley, decided to have an open-casket funeral and agreed to the publication of several photographs of the young victim's bloated, mutilated body. These images exposed the naked brutality of racism in the South.

The immense public shock and outcry over the case galvanized the civil rights movement and became a rallying cry for the protests that followed.[3]

Rosa Parks, who refused a few months later to give up her seat on a public bus to a white man and thus triggered the Montgomery Bus Boycott, said her act of resistance was motivated by Till's murder: "I thought of Emmett Till and I just couldn't go back."[4]

The murder of Emmett Till and the increasing mobilization of the African American civil rights movement constitute the closing events of the present study, which began with the nine Scottsboro Boys from Alabama in the early 1930s. As has been shown, police torture of African Americans was of constitutive importance to the racist power structure of the South between 1930 and 1955. Court documents, federal investigative files, newspaper articles, and the archives of the NAACP reveal that the white majority society was by and large unwilling to curb this extreme form of racial violence. Nevertheless, African American victims of torture, civil rights activists, and federal authorities began to expose the widespread use of police torture and demand legal consequences for the perpetrators.

A central finding of *The Color of the Third Degree* is that there was a connection between the torture of African Americans to coerce confessions and both the decline in lynching violence and the growing capacity of state and local authorities to enforce their monopoly on the use of force in the South during the 1930s and 1940s. Torture was used to ensure the swift conviction of African American defendants and satisfy the local white population's need for retribution against African American offenders. The events that followed the murder of a white farmer in Kemper County, Mississippi, illustrate this in an exemplary manner, as analyzed in chapter 1. Immediately following the arrest of the black defendants Brown, Ellington, and Shields, local officials promised an expedited trial with speedy convictions and executions. Although the police took several precautions to prevent the men from being lynched by the enraged white community, they resorted to torture to coerce confessions that would seal the defendants' fate as quickly as possible. As many similar cases from the period under study show, this primarily occurred in cases where crimes had been committed that appeared to fundamentally challenge the racist power structure of the South—that is, charges brought against African Americans suspected of raping or murdering whites.

The rise in the use of torture by law enforcement officials points to a dark side of the decline in lynchings in the South that has been largely ignored by researchers. During the 1930s and 1940s, racial violence was increasingly concealed, generally behind the walls of state institutions and, at any rate, outside the public eye. The case of Brown, Ellington, and Shields shows, however, that the practice of torture was essentially an open secret. This made it possible to keep the white population abreast of the swift and ruthless approach taken by the police and, at the same time, intimidated the black population and warned of the harsh consequences of any infraction of the system of segregation. Hence, police torture of African American suspects represented a form of racial violence that perpetuated the claim of white supremacy under a new guise. It was an exceedingly violent and symbolic form of segregation that aimed to demonstrate the unequivocal assertion of white superiority over black suspects. At the same time, this case—and many others—bears witness to the virtually unlimited position of power enjoyed by law enforcement officers in the communities of the South.

When African American defendants attempted to make heard their allegations of torture in the justice system of the South, they usually failed. The position of inferiority assigned to black defendants meant that their accusations of torture had little or no impact on the verdict.

At the same time, the analyzed cases show that by providing detailed courtroom testimony of the allegations of torture, black defendants and witnesses called into question, however briefly, their prescribed subordinate role within the criminal justice system. Their demands of a fair trial and respect for their physical integrity can be interpreted against this background as a significant political practice that they pursued in a bid to resist their discrimination and disenfranchisement by southern courts. In that sense, these trials offered African Americans a forum in which they could publicly articulate their civil rights and demand equal treatment before the law.

The trial of Dave Canty and the case brought against Curtis Robinson and Henry Daniels clearly illustrate that the process of establishing the truth in the legal institutions of the South was a hotly contested battleground. Legal proceedings against alleged African American offenders were symbolically laden events in which racial hierarchies and the patriarchal order were proclaimed and reconstituted. Nevertheless, it was the act of speaking by black defendants that unlocked the potential for change.

From the mid-1930s, the allegations of torture leveled by black defendants elicited a growing response from people across the country. A key role in this development was played by the legal department of the NAACP, which from this point onward gradually endeavored to combat the use of forced confessions in the South by documenting individual cases and petitioning the U.S. Supreme Court to review them. The legal activities of the organization did more than just ensure that individual defendants did not suffer miscarriages of justice. They also resulted in Supreme Court decisions that further regulated the admissibility of forced confessions in U.S. courts and contributed to the development of a legal doctrine against the use of statements made under duress, which eventually led to the landmark 1966 Supreme Court decision of *Miranda v. Arizona*, which guarantees suspects the right to remain silent.[5]

The NAACP activities also helped raise awareness among the local black population of the importance of fighting for civil rights, and the organization's endeavors forged and reinforced the institutional base for future activities. In the case of Brown, Ellington, and Shields, the savage whippings and abuse of the three defendants sparked a quiet grassroots legal defense campaign by members of the local white and black communities. Eventually, local resistance to the brutal mistreatment of Brown, Ellington, and Shields led to the founding of a small NAACP chapter in one of the most racist parts of the country at the time.

Similarly, the campaign for Dave Canty enhanced the civil rights consciousness of Montgomery's black community. It created the local organizational structures that five years later would serve as the base of actions on behalf of Recy Taylor, who was brutally raped by six white men in Abbeville, Alabama. Eleven years later, the same NAACP chapter would buttress a further groundbreaking event in the African American struggle for civil rights: the Montgomery Bus Boycott of 1955 and 1956.[6]

The strategies of NAACP activists were in many ways similar to those pursued by subsequently established human rights organizations, such as Amnesty International. Like these institutions, the NAACP pursued the goal of documenting and exposing the use of torture to increase the pressure on potential perpetrators and express black people's demand that their fundamental rights be respected. Likewise, the local activities of the NAACP strengthened the position of African American defendants in the justice system of the South—for example, in the case of W. D. Lyons in Oklahoma, in which it was unmistakably demonstrated that blacks also had a right to fair and equal treatment in court.

The trial of Lyons also shows that the legal activities of the NAACP—at least temporarily and selectively—challenged the hierarchical power structures in the communities of the South and had an emancipatory effect. An outstanding example of this was the self-confident courtroom manner of NAACP lawyer Thurgood Marshall, which belied all expectations of how a black man was to act in court. But the fact that the U.S. Supreme Court upheld the prison sentence handed down to W. D. Lyons in Hugo, Oklahoma, is an indication of the limits of legal action by the NAACP.

Last but not least, the NAACP campaign against forced confessions helped shift public awareness in America and abroad to the ongoing endemic racism in the South. Against the background of World War II and the subsequent Cold War, it was argued that the practice of torture and other forms of racial violence stood in direct contradiction to the professed American values of civilization, democracy, and freedom. In large part thanks to this campaign, racial violence in the South was increasingly viewed as a national problem that required a permanent solution.

Despite these accomplishments, and despite the landmark decisions of the Supreme Court in *Brown v. Mississippi* (1936) and *Chambers v. Florida* (1940) that prohibited the use of forced confessions as evidence in state courts, up until 1955 the NAACP received scores of complaints about violent interrogation techniques to extract confessions. A probable indirect consequence of the NAACP legal campaign may have also been that law enforcement authorities tended to deny under oath that they had tortured African American defendants, making it more difficult for the defense to convince judges and juries of the veracity of the defendants' allegations of torture.[7] Furthermore, the legal initiative of the NAACP had virtually no impact on the pervasive physical abuse of black prisoners and suspects, because the organization primarily focused on cases in which allegations of torture had been raised in murder and rape trials. Hence, the campaign excluded all cases in which African Americans were arrested for minor offenses and subjected to violence and discriminatory treatment by police. According to the NAACP, these cases had to be challenged on the ground through continuous protest and legal action. As the present study shows, up until the mid-1950s police in the South generally did not have to fear any legal consequences for their torture practices and, due to the largely indifferent attitude of the white population toward cases of racial violence by police, the issue was very rarely a subject of public debate.

One exception was the case of sixteen-year-old Quintar South, which was presented in chapter 4. The media uproar over this case in Atlanta during the early 1940s provides insights into different contemporary perceptions of the ubiquitous police violence against blacks in the South. Whereas the local African American press used the case to underscore the pervasive nature of police violence and torture in Atlanta, and emphatically demanded that it come to an end, the national African American press focused on the scourge of racism throughout the American South. In the white newspapers of Atlanta, however, the incident was characterized as a regrettable, isolated case of police violence in which the local white community had neglected its duties to protect the "weaker elements" of the city's population.

The South case offered Atlanta's white middle class a safe opportunity to take the moral high ground without fundamentally questioning the prevailing structures of racial violence and discrimination. Since South had merely been accused of burglary, and not a violent crime like rape or murder, it was much easier to criticize his torture as a disproportionate use of force. Despite the indignant reactions of the white community, though, the case was not seized on as an opportunity to come to terms with the routine discrimination of African American citizens. Instead, the acquittal of William F. Sutherland by the criminal court in Atlanta in June 1940 suggests that the selective public outrage over individual cases of torture was unable to ruffle the general indifference of the white population of Atlanta toward the widespread racist brutality of law enforcement officials. In fact, it appears that this short-lived outcry actually made it that much easier for whites to continue to turn a blind eye to the ongoing prevalent problem of police violence against blacks in their city.

These findings are confirmed by the results of the civil rights investigations against police officers conducted by the U.S. Department of Justice and the FBI in the American South from 1940 onward. The cases examined here show for the first time that the investigations launched by the federal government subjected the denials of torture by local police officials, and their tolerance by local justice authorities, to a detailed and thorough examination. FBI agents carefully recorded the testimonies of witnesses, alleged victims, and defendants, and they verified the allegations of torture by collecting vast amounts of evidence and using state-of-the-art forensic methods. Of particular importance here was the medium of photography, which played a key role in the investigative efforts of the FBI. Some of the investigations described in this book were perceived by the white communities as a threat to the local racist structures of power and subjugation. But coalitions also occasionally formed between segments of the local white community, federal investigators, and the black population, who joined forces to speak out against local violent police practices.

At the same time, the federal investigations incited the opposition of law enforcement officials and many members of the local white community. As we can see from the cases against Sheriff Edwin E. Evans and Deputy Sheriff Henry F. Faucett in Georgia, and against William J. Erskine in South Carolina, federal efforts to curb physical abuse and torture came into conflict with local racist mind-sets. Likewise, they rekindled long-standing historical resentments of interventions by Washington in the legal and political sovereignty of the South.

All in all, the civil rights initiative by the federal government in the American South achieved mixed results. Although the federal government's efforts made local communities more aware of the extent of clandestine police torture and gave African American victims of violence an opportunity to draw the public's attention to violations of their civil rights—and demand that these rights be respected—the cases presented here show that the court proceedings were used to reaffirm and restore local racial hierarchies. As the cases of Lillie Mae Hendon, Martha Kendrick McMillan, and Mallie Pearson illustrate, African American women in particular were denied recognition as credible witnesses and as victims of violence within the southern racial and patriarchal social order. The many acquittals in the trials examined in this book document that federal investigations barely made a dent in the violent power structures of the segregated South.

THE RESULTS OF THIS examination of the diverse initiatives against police torture in the South between 1930 and 1955 thus paint a contradictory picture. By exposing torture, African American defendants, civil rights institutions, and federal authorities issued a clear challenge to the social order of the Jim Crow South. However, the cases examined here bear witness to the limited impact of these initiatives. The case of Mallie Pearson from 1953 is a paragon example of how, even during the early 1950s, police forces could still resort to methods of torture without being held legally accountable for their actions. The issue of police torture serves as a focal point to study the conflict between those who clung to a deeply racist social order and those who strove to change this system. It was not until the civil rights movement picked up steam and militant black resistance groups formed in the 1960s and 1970s that the racist power structure of the South was seriously called into question.

In 1954, the Supreme Court issued its landmark decision in *Brown v. Board of Education*, which stipulated that the practice of racial segregation in public schools was unconstitutional. As previously mentioned, this put an end to the doctrine of "separate but equal" that had been established by the Supreme Court with its *Plessy v. Ferguson* decision sixty years earlier. The *Brown* ruling ordered the authorities in the South to proceed with the integration of the school system, which resulted in the formation of a broad reactionary resistance movement. The often violent protests of the southern white population against the integration of public schools were, in many ways, a continuation of the opposition to the torture investigations of the federal government in the region during the 1940s and early 1950s.

At the same time, the *Brown* verdict and the murder of Emmett Till intensified the civil rights protests of the black population in the South. In the early 1960s, the struggle against segregation and racial oppression culminated in a wide range of direct protests. Black and white students organized sit-ins and protest marches in scores of cities. With the support of the Congress of Racial Equality, black and white freedom riders traveled on public buses throughout the South to put an end to the segregation of public transport. The Student Nonviolent Coordinating Committee initiated projects to register African American voters in the South.[8]

In May 1963, Martin Luther King Jr. organized a rally in Birmingham, Alabama, that attracted several thousand people to protest against the continuing disregard for African American civil rights in the South. Shortly thereafter, photos and TV images circulated around the globe showing white police officers attacking black demonstrators with police dogs, fire hoses, and nightsticks. These iconic images became a symbol of the racial discrimination by the white population of the South, whose representatives used every means at their disposal to prevent African Americans from laying claim to their constitutional civil rights.[9]

During the 1960s and 1970s, the struggle against repressive police violence became one of the main rallying cries of the emerging Black Power movement. Groups such as the Deacons for Defense and Justice formed in the South to protect their communities and families by force of arms from attacks by the police and the Ku Klux Klan. The Deacons were an armed self-defense group that was founded primarily to protect civil rights activists and their families against violent attacks.[10] Rampant police violence in large American cities was a main reason for the foundation of the Black Panther Party in 1966. Active black resistance to police repression and discrimination led in a number of American cities to violent confrontations between police and members of the Black Panther Party. For the activists of the Black Power movement, the notorious use of police violence symbolized the ongoing racial oppression of African Americans in American society.[11]

This rough overview clearly indicates that even after 1955, police violence remained an essential element of the African American civil rights struggle. The protests and initiatives of the civil rights movement helped curb police brutality in the South, however. Of particular importance was the successful defense of African American voting rights in the late 1960s and 1970s.[12] This meant that African Americans—particularly in the Deep South, where they often represented the majority of the population—began to occupy important offices, such as sheriff, and leading police positions. This was a development that partially—although certainly not generally—led to a destabilization of the racist culture of violence within the law enforcement institutions of the South.[13]

American history of the late twentieth and early twenty-first centuries nevertheless points to a continuity of torture. Numerous scandals reveal that police torture practices, despite their moral rejection by large segments of society, persisted even after 1955. For instance, in 1983 James C. Parker—the former sheriff of San Jacinto County, Texas—and three of his deputy sheriffs were sentenced to several years' imprisonment for waterboarding a number of white prisoners. They had handcuffed the suspects to chairs, placed towels over their heads, and poured water over them until, overwhelmed by the sensation of being suffocated, the suspects broke down and made a confession. One victim recalled: "I thought I was going to be strangled to death. . . . I couldn't breathe."[14]

The ongoing use of torture practices against people of color bears witness to the continued existence of racist structures of discrimination and oppression. In 1985, for example, five New York City police officers were accused of beating several black suspects and tormenting them with stun guns to extort confessions. In contrast to many other cases of police brutality, the investigations, which lasted for several years, culminated with the conviction of four of the five defendants.[15]

One decade later, a wide-ranging torture scandal shook the city of Chicago. As years of investigations revealed, members of the Chicago Police Department had been torturing primarily black suspects since the 1970s. Dozens of cases came to light in which groups of white police officers had violently coerced confessions from prisoners. Some had been tormented with a homemade electric device, while others had been burned with electric heaters and nearly suffocated with plastic bags. The police officers were also accused of terrorizing suspects with mock executions. Several of the more than one hundred victims had received death sentences. In January 2003, Illinois governor George Ryan commuted the sentences of all prisoners on death row in the state of Illinois to life imprisonment after a number of them testified that they had been tortured into making confessions. Since many of the cases exceeded the statute of limitations, and members of the police department categorically refused to comment on the allegations, none of the accused police officers could be brought to justice for many years. It was not until June 2010 that the man who was mainly responsible for this systematic torture, former commander Jon Burge, was convicted of perjury and obstruction of justice and sentenced to four-and-a-half-years of imprisonment.[16]

The history of torture against black suspects in the United States is closely tied with other forms of police misconduct—including illegal arrests, arbitrary abuse, and unlawful shootings—that have increasingly been the focus of public attention in recent years. This debate is driven by new means of exposing police violence in the age of digitalization. Private smartphone footage and dashboard camera images of police shootings—usually released by court order over the objections of law enforcement agencies—are posted on online platforms, shared on social media, and watched and commented on by millions of people.

What is groundbreaking about these recordings is that they expose the killings of black people by American police officers to a worldwide audience. In addition to providing a harrowing insight into the apparently unlimited position of power enjoyed by police officers in the United States and their all too frequent contempt for black lives, this footage has fueled nationwide protests and initiatives under the Black Lives Matter banner that confront the criminalization and dehumanization of black people by the police and other state institutions.[17] Moreover, video images provide crucial evidence for the prosecution of incidents that would otherwise, in all probability, remain without legal consequences. There can be no doubt that the trial of Michael T. Slager—a white police officer—for the shooting of Walter Scott in North Charleston, South Carolina, would not have resulted in a guilty plea and conviction by the U.S. district court in Charleston if Feidin Santana had not filmed the crime with his cell phone.[18]

The vast majority of cases show, however, that law enforcement's position of power over the black population and other minorities in the United States remains intact despite this new visibility of police violence. The exoneration of police officer Darren Wilson for the death of Michael Brown in Ferguson, Missouri, and the acquittal of Jeronimo Yanez, who shot Philando Castile in his car before the eyes of his girlfriend and her daughter in a suburb of St. Paul, Minnesota, underscore the continuing inability of the American justice system to convict police officers for the unjustified shootings of African Americans. This reinforces the impression of many African American citizens that the police serve as a bastion of white interests and are thereby protected by the justice system. *The Color of the Third Degree* clearly shows that there is a long history to the African American community's intense frustration with this state of affairs. It draws attention to the deep historical roots of the feelings of powerlessness and disenfranchisement experienced by many segments of the African American population that has come to light during the current protests. This book also shows that the current initiatives of the Black Lives Matter movement against racially biased police violence — and for the recognition of black humanity — are the continuation of a struggle that began during the first half of the twentieth century. It is encouraging to see the vehemence and urgency with which the activists of the Black Lives Matter movement pursue this struggle against police violence while expanding both the scope and methods of their campaign. The history of torture in the American South reveals the importance of these interventions. It challenges us to ask which voices are heard and which are ignored within a specific historical context. Moreover, it highlights the necessity of confronting and challenging the practices and structures of disenfranchisement and dehumanization in both word and deed.

Acknowledgments

First and foremost, I would like to express my deepest thanks to Jürgen Martschukat. He has inspired this project with his avenues of research and encouraged me time and again to pursue my own paths and ask new questions. I am also very grateful to Norbert Finzsch, who served as the project's second dissertation adviser and whose works on U.S. history were essential to this study.

A number of institutions provided financial support for the creation of this work. I would like to thank the German Academic Scholarship Foundation, the Max Weber Center for Advanced Cultural and Social Studies at the University of Erfurt, the DFG graduate school on human dignity and human rights of the Universities of Erfurt and Jena, and the Gerda Henkel Foundation. The University of Erfurt also supported the project by providing a workplace and, for the final phase of my dissertation, a scholarship.

I would also like to thank the many archivists at the Library of Congress in Washington, D.C.; the National Archives in College Park, Maryland, and Morrow, Georgia; and the Alabama Department of Archives and History in Montgomery, Alabama, for helping me gain access to the material basis of this work.

The North American History Colloquium at the University of Erfurt served as the key point of reference for discussions of the project. Many individuals have contributed to this book with their questions, comments, and readings of the text. I would like to express my lasting thanks to all of them. Furthermore, I would like to thank my colleagues in Germany and the United States who encouraged me to publish an English version of my book as well. I am grateful to Amy Wood for spurring me to approach UNC Press. My thanks to Brandon Proia at UNC Press for his interest in my work and his assistance during the review process.

Many thanks also to Paula Bradish from my German publisher, Hamburger Edition, for procuring translation funding from the Geisteswissenschaften International program. I am deeply grateful to my friend and colleague Christine Knauer for her encouragement and support during the work on the English edition. Finally, I would like to convey my heartfelt thanks to Paul Cohen for his tireless and meticulous work on the English translation of this book.

Erfurt, Germany, May 2018

Notes

Introduction

1. Anonymous drawing, "A Negro 'Confesses' to 'Rape,' Tavares, Fla.—July, 1949," LOC, NAACP Papers, Group II, Box B-117, Fol. T [1941–1949].

2. See the description of the Groveland Four case in chapter 3 of this text.

3. "Race" is understood here as a socially and discursively constructed concept that continues to be of far-reaching influence in American society, *not* as a biological, objective fact. As scholars like Eileen O'Brien have established, there is "more genetic and physiological variation within the members of a given race than between individuals of different races." The terms "black," "white," "race," and "racial" are used in this book in line with this understanding. O'Brien, "Race," 7.

4. It is only in recent years that several studies have pointed to the critical importance of the phase between 1930 and 1955 with respect to the social, economic, political, and cultural history of the South. For instance, historian J. William Harris and the authors of the anthology that he edited in 2008, *The New South: New Histories*, have emphasized the necessity of intensively studying the history of the American South during the interwar period. Special attention here has been devoted to the 1930s, which, according to these studies, constitutes a decisive phase in this transition. See Harris, introduction; Sullivan, *Southern Seeds*.

5. On the phenomenon of lynching in the South and other regions of the United States, see, for example, Pfeifer, "At the Hands of Parties Unknown?," Berg, *Popular Justice*; Brundage, *Lynching in the New South*; Goldsby, *Spectacular Secret*; Nevels, *Lynching to Belong*; Pfeifer, *Rough Justice*; Wood, *Lynching and Spectacle*. For an international perspective on the phenomenon of lynching, see the essays in Berg and Wendt, *Globalizing Lynching History*; Pfeifer, *Global Lynching and Collective Violence*.

6. Hall, "Long Civil Rights Movement," 1235. See also Sullivan, *Lift Every Voice*, 190–236; John Egerton, *Speak Now against the Day*.

7. For critical perspectives on "the long civil rights movement" concept, see Cha-Jua and Lang, "The 'Long Movement' as Vampire"; Eric Arnesen, "Reconsidering the 'Long Civil Rights Movement.'"

8. McGuire, "'It Was Like All of Us Had Been Raped,'"; McGuire, *At the Dark End of the Street*.

9. McMahon, *Reconsidering Roosevelt*, 167–75; Carr, *Federal Protection of Civil Rights*, 151–62; Elliff, *United States Department of Justice*.

10. Waldrep, "National Policing," 589–90, here 589. For more on the covert operations and surveillance activities of the FBI against African American members of the civil rights movement during the 1960s, see, for example, O'Reilly, *FBI's Secret File on Black America*. For more on the investigations of the U.S. Department of Justice and

the FBI into lynching cases during the 1940s, see Capeci, *Lynching of Cleo Wright*; Capeci, "Lynching of Cleo Wright"; Wexler, *Fire in a Canebrake*.

11. Hunt, *Inventing Human Rights*, 70–112, 176–214.

12. Lindenberger and Lüdtke, "Physische Gewalt," 19.

13. Scarry, *Body in Pain*, 27–59; Reemtsma, "'Wir sind alles für dich!'"

14. Amnesty International, *Amnesty International Report 2016/17*.

15. Greenberg, *Torture Debate*; Levinson, *Torture*.

16. Article 1 of the United Nations Convention against Torture, adopted by General Assembly resolution 39/46 of December 10, 1984.

17. Chafee, Pollak, and Stern, *Report on Lawlessness in Law Enforcement*, 29, 213–24.

18. Hopkins, *Our Lawless Police*, 288–313; Johnson, *Street Justice*, 143–44.

19. In a presentation from the year 1910, the president of the International Association of Chiefs of Police, Richard Sylvester, traced the origins of the term "third degree" to the process of detaining and questioning suspects. He said that while arrest and detention were the "first" and "second degrees," the term "third degree" stood for the phase of questioning and checking the veracity of the statements made. Chafee, Pollak, and Stern, *Report on Lawlessness in Law Enforcement*, 20. For other possible origins of the term, see Leo, *Police Interrogation and American Justice*, 68–69.

20. The term "third degree" was also used by the Nazis during World War II to describe torture practices used by state authorities. See Peters, *Torture*, 124–25. Furthermore, during the Middle Ages and the early modern period, a distinction was made between the first, second, and third degree of judicial torture. The first degree usually referred to the application of thumbscrews, the second degree to stretching a victim on the rack, and the third degree to even harsher procedures, such as scorching the skin with torches. See Zagolla, *Im Namen der Wahrheit*, 70–77.

21. Chafee, Pollak, and Stern, *Report on Lawlessness in Law Enforcement*, 21.

22. Hopkins, *Our Lawless Police*; Lavine, *Third Degree*.

23. Chafee, Pollak, and Stern, *Report on Lawlessness in Law Enforcement*, 153. The Wickersham Commission was charged with investigating the abuses by law enforcement authorities that had emerged during prohibition. The commission's report listed twenty-nine cities with widespread evidence of the use of the third degree. The four southern cities listed were Birmingham, New Orleans, Waco, and Wichita Falls. Chafee, Pollak, Stern, *Report on Lawlessness in Law Enforcement*, 152–72. See also Walker, introduction.

24. Johnson, *Street Justice*, 122–48; Dale, *Robert Nixon*, 21–27, 83–101.

25. Johnson, *Street Justice*, 142–48; Dale, *Robert Nixon*, 102–23.

26. Chafee, Pollak, and Stern, *Report on Lawlessness in Law Enforcement*, 99–101, 225–32.

27. Johnson, *Street Justice*, 135–36. See also the statistical information in Chafee, Pollak, and Stern, *Report on Lawlessness in Law Enforcement*, 99–101, 225–32.

28. Chafee, Pollak, and Stern, *Report on Lawlessness in Law Enforcement*, 55–68. On the use of the water cure during the Philippine-American War, see Schumacher, "'Marked Severities'"; Kramer, "Water Cure."

29. Chafee, Pollak, and Stern, *Report on Lawlessness in Law Enforcement*, 239; "Judge Orders Destruction of Electric Chair Used by Arkansas Sheriff for Confessions," *New*

York Times, November 23, 1929, 12. According to another article, that very same year allegations were leveled against officers in Alabama who had allegedly used the electric chair in Kilby Prison, Montgomery, to coerce confessions from a suspect. "Says Electric Chair Forced Confession," *New York Times*, December 29, 1929, 24.

30. Chafee, Pollak, and Stern, *Report on Lawlessness in Law Enforcement*, 71–72.

31. Chafee, Pollak, and Stern, *Report on Lawlessness*, 55, 70–71.

32. Waldrep, *Roots of Disorder*, 37–58; Flanigan, "Criminal Procedure."

33. Chafee, Pollak, and Stern, *Report on Lawlessness in Law Enforcement*, 152. "These police Courts of Pre-Trial Inquisition are held in the 'third-degree rooms' of police headquarters, at outlying station houses, in cells, in basements, in police garages, in patrol wagons or department sedans, at the place of arrest—anywhere that is fairly secret." Hopkins, *Our Lawless Police*, 21.

34. Foucault, "Of Other Spaces"; Krasmann, "Andere Orte."

35. In his encyclopedic 1944 study *An American Dilemma*, Gunnar Myrdal wrote that torture was "routinely" used on African American suspects in many police stations in the South. Myrdal, *An American Dilemma*, 541.

36. Martschukat and Niedermeier, "Violence and Visibility"; Foucault, *Discipline and Punish*; Rejali, *Torture and Democracy*; Sofsky, *Traktat über die Gewalt*.

37. Foucault, *Discipline and Punish*, 11.

38. Martschukat, *Inszeniertes Töten*; Martschukat, "'Art of Killing by Electricity.'"

39. Asad, *Formations of the Secular*, 105.

40. Asad, *Formations*, 104–5; Asad, "On Torture"; Reemtsma, "'Wir sind alles für dich!'" Building on this notion, political scientist Darius Rejali has shown that public monitoring of police, military, and intelligence services in democratic countries has led to the development of "stealth torture," which leaves no physical trace. Rejali, *Torture and Democracy*.

41. See, for example, Dube, Leacock, and Ardener, *Visibility and Power*; Mason, *Spectacle of Violence*; Samuels, "My Body, My Closet"; Casper and Moore, introduction; Kozol, "Marginalized Bodies."

42. According to literary and cultural studies scholar Doris Bachmann-Medick, this concept of visibility "refers not only to opportunities of social self-portrayal and the new sensibilities regarding social staging and forms of surveillance, but also to strategies of social power and exclusion that are aimed at concealment and invisibility (of poverty, inequality, disease, etc.). However, any attempt to render visible such concealed phenomena presupposes a complex context of visualization." Bachmann-Medick, *Cultural Turns*, 270.

43. Maasen, Mayerhauser, and Renggli, "Bild-Diskurs-Analyse," 18. For more on Foucault's concept of visibility, see Certeau, "Laugh of Michel Foucault"; Deleuze, *Foucault*, 47–69.

44. Butler, *Precarious Life*; Butler, *Frames of War*.

45. Butler, *Precarious Life*, 20 (emphasis in the original); Butler, *Frames of War*, 6.

46. This is also particularly clear in the current forms of violence and repression against so-called illegal immigrants, refugees, and asylum seekers. See Bauman, *Wasted Lives*. A similar perspective is also found in cultural science studies on racial, sexual, and domestic violence that highlight the links between violence and marginalized

positions in society. See, for example, Finzsch, "Conditions of Intolerance"; Mason, *Spectacle of Violence*.

47. Spivak, "Can the Subaltern Speak?"

48. For a similar perspective on African American testimony of racial violence, see the groundbreaking study by Kidada E. Williams, *They Left Great Marks on Me*.

49. Cuntz et al., *Die Listen der Evidenz*, 9.

50. Tagg, *Burden of Representation*, 3.

51. Hodes, "Power of Indifference."

52. On the transition between close-ups and long-distance shots as a methodical approach to historical analyses, see Pomata, "Close-Ups and Long-Shots."

Chapter One

1. Goodman, *Stories of Scottsboro*, 1–23.

2. Goodman, *Stories of Scottsboro*, 1–23.

3. Goodman, *Stories of Scottsboro*, 1–23.

4. For more on the national and international implications of the Scottsboro case, see Pennybacker, *From Scottsboro to Munich*; Rosenhaft, Miller, and Pennybacker, "Mother Ada Wright." For more on the case's influence on U.S. American culture of the twentieth century, see Miller, *Remembering Scottsboro*. Although over the following years the U.S. Supreme Court overturned the death sentences against the Scottsboro Boys in two decisions, the nine defendants were sentenced to long prison terms during follow-up trials. It was not until the 1950s that the last of them was released from prison.

5. Miller, *Remembering Scottsboro*, 7–51.

6. Kinshasa, *Man from Scottsboro*, 41.

7. "Negro Lad Tells Scottsboro Story," *New York Times*, March 10, 1933, 32.

8. See, for example, Litwack, *Trouble in Mind*; Horton and Horton, *Slavery and the Making of America*, 120–61.

9. For a seminal overview of the Reconstruction era, see Foner, *Reconstruction*.

10. The term "Jim Crow" originally referred to a stereotypical black character in a minstrel show. Like "Sambo" and "coon," the term was used to denigrate African American people and highlight their purported inferior status with respect to the Euro-American population of the South. For more on the contemporary connotations and ambivalent adoption of the term, see Lhamon, introduction.

11. By "Jim Crow signs," Kelley is referring to plates proclaiming "For whites only" and "For colored only" that aimed to enforce separate use of toilets, drinking fountains, bus stops, and so on. Kelley, *Race Rebels*, 56.

12. Finkelman, "Racial Desegregation (U.S.)." The *Plessy v. Ferguson* decision legitimized the system of racial segregation in the South until the mid-twentieth century and established the principle of "separate but equal," which officially condoned the establishment of separate areas for blacks and whites.

13. Hale, *Making Whiteness*, 284.

14. Brundage, "Roar on the Other Side of Silence."

15. For more on the violence of the Ku Klux Klan, see Foner, *Reconstruction*, 425–43.

16. Niedermeier, "Police Brutality." After the end of the Civil War, the police system of the South continued in many respects with the tradition of the slave patrols, which were dispatched during the age of slavery to thwart impending slave revolts and pursue fugitive slaves. See, for example, Hadden, *Slave Patrols*.

17. Myrdal, *American Dilemma*, 535.

18. Myrdal, *American Dilemma*, 541.

19. Du Bois, *Dusk of Dawn*, 182.

20. See, for example, Bolton, "Police"; Dulaney, *Black Police in America*, 1–7; Kelley, "'Slangin' . . . Rocks Palestinian Style,'" 25–32.

21. Myrdal, *American Dilemma*, 536; Dollard, *Caste and Class*, 315–63. On the tradition of vigilantism, see Brown, *Strain of Violence*. On the ties between the tradition of vigilante justice and the phenomenon of lynching violence in the diverse regions of the United States, see Pfeifer, *Rough Justice*.

22. Arthur Franklin Raper, "Race and Class Pressures," Atlanta: 1940, NYPL, SC, CMSNA, microfilm no. F 13, 242, reels 10, 11, 3–63; Myrdal, *American Dilemma*, 535–46.

23. The term "Black Belt" denotes a region in the South ranging from southwestern Tennessee to Mississippi and as far as Alabama's border with Georgia. According to Booker T. Washington, the term was initially used to describe the dark color of the soil in a region of the South where the soil was primarily tilled by slaves. Particularly after the American Civil War, the meaning of the term changed to become primarily a descriptive of the region in the southern United States in which blacks represented the majority of the population. Washington, *Up from Slavery*, 108.

24. Arthur Franklin Raper, "Race and Class Pressures," Atlanta: 1940, NYPL, SC, CMSNA, microfilm no. F 13, 242, reels 10, 11, 3–63; Myrdal, *American Dilemma*, 535–46; Berg, *Popular Justice*, 155.

25. For more on these figures, see Smith and Horton, *Historical Statistics of Black America*, 495. The figures used in that source are primarily based on the records of the *Chicago Tribune*, which began compiling data on lynchings in 1882 as part of its annual crime statistics in America. Starting in 1908, these figures were supplemented by data collected by the Tuskegee Institute in Alabama. Both institutions relied primarily on newspaper articles on lynchings. The problematic implications of this type of survey are discussed by W. Fitzhugh Brundage, who, while conducting his study of Georgia and Virginia, came across a number of lynchings that had not yet been entered into the statistics. See Brundage, *Lynching in the New South*, 291–96.

26. Hale, *Making Whiteness*, 203.

27. Not every lynching in the southern states followed this elaborate ritual course of events. Most lynchings were carried out by small groups of individuals, not large mobs. Brundage, *Lynching in the New South*, 17–48.

28. Hall, "'Mind That Burns in Each Body,'" 331. For more on the term "spectacle lynching" and the connections between consumer culture and lynching rituals, see Hale, *Making Whiteness*, 199–240. On the role of lynching photography in the American South of the late nineteenth and early twentieth centuries, see Wood, *Lynching and Spectacle*.

29. Hale, *Making Whiteness*, 203.

30. See also Hodes, *White Women, Black Men*; Williamson, *Crucible of Race*, 111–19.

31. See, in particular, Hall, "'Mind That Burns in Each Body'"; Harris, *Exorcising Blackness*; Sielke, *Reading Rape*; Wood, "Lynching Photography."

32. Hall, "'Mind That Burns in Each Body,'" 130–36.

33. Brundage, *Lynching in the New South*, 51.

34. Zangrando, *NAACP Crusade against Lynching*.

35. For more on this, see Berg, *Popular Justice*, 144–64; Brundage, *Lynching in the New South*, 234–59. The term "New South" had been used in the southern states since the late nineteenth century in a bid to differentiate contemporary southern culture from the antebellum social order of the Old South.

36. Berg, *Popular Justice*, 144–64; Hall, "'Mind That Burns in Each Body,'" 127–41; Hall, *Revolt against Chivalry*.

37. Berg, *Popular Justice*, 144–64; Hall, "'Mind That Burns in Each Body,'" 136–41; Hall, *Revolt against Chivalry*.

38. Berg, "Das Ende der Lynchjustiz," 613–16; Berg, *Popular Justice*, 144–64.

39. For a comprehensive interpretation of this data, see Berg, "Das Ende der Lynchjustiz," 602–7; Berg, *Popular Justice*, 156. See also the figures in Smith and Horton, *Historical Statistics of Black America*, 491. The data there show a continual decline in the number of lynchings that were carried out compared to the number that were prevented between 1914 and 1936. While the statistics show fifty-two lynching deaths and twenty-four averted lynchings in 1914, the number of lynching victims had fallen to eight in 1936, whereas seventy-nine had been prevented.

40. See the tabular listing in Smith and Horton, *Historical Statistics of Black America*, 493–95; Berg, *Popular Justice*, 144.

41. In his study of twenty-one lynchings that were perpetrated in the South in 1930, sociologist Arthur Raper notes that local police and justice officials often had a passive, if not supportive, attitude toward lynch mobs. Raper, *Tragedy of Lynching*, 13–19.

42. Berg, "Das Ende der Lynchjustiz," 603–7; Berg, *Popular Justice*, 156–59; Brundage, *Lynching in the New South*, 239–42.

43. See also Berg, "Das Ende der Lynchjustiz," 607–15; Berg, *Popular Justice*, 159–61.

44. Clarke, "Without Fear or Shame," 285; Vandiver, *Lethal Punishment*; Wright, *Racial Violence in Kentucky*, 215–50; Smith and Horton, *Historical Statistics of Black America*, 473; Berg, "Das Ende der Lynchjustiz," 610; Berg, *Popular Justice*, 159–64.

45. Tolnay and Beck, *Festival of Violence*.

46. Historian Lisa Lindquist Dorr summarizes this process as follows: "White men remained civilized because the court enacted their primitive desires for revenge, and indeed folded the threat and desire for violence into the legal process." Dorr, *White Women, Rape, and the Power of Race in Virginia*, 20; Berg, *Popular Justice*, 159–64.

47. Raper, *Tragedy of Lynching*, 19.

48. Pfeifer, *Rough Justice*, 139–47; Berg, "Das Ende der Lynchjustiz," 608–11; Berg, *Popular Justice*, 144–64.

49. Martschukat, "Lynching und Todesstrafe."

50. Dorr, *White Women, Rape, and the Power of Race in Virginia*, 20.

51. Blue, "'A Dark Cloud Will Go Over.'" For more on the continuities between mob law and the death penalty in the United States, see the essays in Ogletree and Sarat, *From Lynch Mobs to the Killing State*.

52. Baker, review, 665.

53. See the entries relating to the term "forced confession" in Bracey and Meier, *Papers of the NAACP*.

54. Bracey and Meier, *Papers*. These were followed by Tennessee with three cases, North Carolina with two cases, and Oklahoma and Virginia with one case each.

55. Bracey and Meier, *Papers*. In two cases, the charges were burglary, and in one case theft. In the remaining ten cases, the charges cannot be clearly determined because either the statements on file are inconclusive or more detailed information on the cases is missing.

56. Brundage, *Lynching in the New South*, 51.

57. Raper, *Tragedy of Lynching*, 92.

58. Raper, *Tragedy of Lynching*, 74–84, 91–93.

59. Raper, *Tragedy of Lynching*, 93; Smith and Horton, *Historical Statistics of Black America*, 489.

60. Raper, *Tragedy of Lynching*, 85–88.

61. Local newspapers used both the names Raymond Steward and Raymond Stuart. The present account uses the name Stuart. The original spelling is maintained in the quoted source material.

62. "Kemperite Dies from Axe Blows," *Daily Clarion-Ledger*, March 31, 1934, 1.

63. "Kemperite Dies," *Daily Clarion-Ledger*, 1.

64. "Kemperite Dies," *Daily Clarion-Ledger*, 1.

65. "Two Negroes Held Here in Giles Murder," *Meridian Star*, April 1, 1934, 1.

66. "Officers Say Two Admit Kemper Murder," *Meridian Star*, April 2, 1934, 1, 9.

67. "Officers Say," *Meridian Star*, 1, 9.

68. "Jail Is Armed Fort as Report Mob," *Meridian Star*, April 3, 1934, 1, 9.

69. "Jail Is Armed Fort," *Meridian Star*, 1, 9.

70. "Jail Is Armed Fort," *Meridian Star*, 1, 9.

71. "3 Negroes on Trial in Stuart Case at DeKalb," *Meridian Star*, April 5, 1934, 1.

72. "Order 3 Kemper Negroes to Hang May 11," *Meridian Star*, April 7, 1934, 1.

73. "Order 3 Kemper Negroes," *Meridian Star*, 1.

74. "Order 3 Kemper Negroes," *Meridian Star*, 1.

75. "Kemper Proves Itself," *Meridian Star*, April 8, 1934, 4.

76. Transcript of Record, MoML/USSCRB, *Brown v. Mississippi*, 297 U.S. 278, 1936. Richard C. Cortner has also examined the transcript of the proceedings against Brown, Ellington, and Shields in his work on the case of *Brown v. Mississippi*, focusing largely on a chronological account of the testimony before the court. See Cortner, *"Scottsboro" Case in Mississippi*, 15–32.

77. On the use of the concept of performativity in cultural and historical studies, see Bachmann-Medick, *Cultural Turns*, 73–101; Martschukat and Patzold, *Geschichtswissenschaft und "performative turn."* For more on the performative dimensions of torture, see Scarry, *Body in Pain*, 27–59.

78. Transcript of Record, MoML/USSCRB, *Brown v. Mississippi*, 297 U.S. 278 (1936), 5–20.

79. *Brown*, 24.

80. *Brown*, 24.

81. *Brown*, 41.

82. For a discussion of the prominent position occupied by confessions in American culture and U.S. criminal law, see P. Brooks, *Troubling Confessions*.

83. Transcript of Record, MoML/USSCRB, *Brown v. Mississippi*, 297 U.S. 278 (1936), 25–34.

84. *Brown*, 32.

85. *Brown*, 35.

86. *Brown*, 39–40.

87. *Brown*, 39–40.

88. *Brown*, 43.

89. *Brown*, 43.

90. *Brown*, 48.

91. *Brown*, 51.

92. *Brown*, 59.

93. *Brown*, 69.

94. *Brown*, 69.

95. *Brown*, 69.

96. *Brown*, 70.

97. Brown, 70.

98. As researchers like legal scholar and sociologist David Garland have shown, the violent public "interrogation" of suspects was often a key element of lynching rituals. See Garland, "Penal Excess and Surplus Meaning."

99. Transcript of Record, MoML/USSCRB, *Brown v. Mississippi*, 297 U.S. 278 (1936), 59.

100. *Brown*, 56, 59.

101. See, for example, the case of Dave Canty, which is examined in chapters 2 and 3.

102. Reemtsma, "'Wir sind alles für dich!,'" 14.

103. Transcript of Record, MoML/USSCRB, *Brown v. Mississippi*, 297 U.S. 278 (1936), 43.

104. *Brown*, 45.

105. As English and American studies scholar Elaine Scarry points out, the interconnection between language and physical violence is of constitutive importance for the torture. She says that the questioning is part of the "inner structure" of the torture, in which it legitimizes the violence unleashed on the victim as part of the rational process of the search for truth. Both Scarry and sociologist Wolfgang Sofsky emphasize that the questioning goes hand in hand with the violence of the torture. According to Scarry, the continual questioning during the course of the torture is a specific "form of injury." Sofsky refers to the language of torture as a "tool of violence." See Scarry, *Body in Pain*, particularly 28–38, 45–51, here 46; Sofsky, *Traktat über die Gewalt*, 97.

106. Butler, *Excitable Speech*, 11.

107. Transcript of Record, MoML/USSCRB, *Brown v. Mississippi*, 297 U.S. 278 (1936), 57.

108. See also Burschel, Distelrath, and Lembke, "Eine historische Anthropologie der Folter"; Scarry, *Body in Pain*, 4; Sofsky, *Traktat über die Gewalt*, 87.

109. Wolfgang Sofsky calls the torture in this context a "total situation": "The violence," according to Sofsky, "encompasses the victim's body, self and world." Sofsky, *Traktat über die Gewalt*, 98.

110. By consistently addressing officials as "sir," the three suspects reacted to the white claim to superiority that was played out during the torture sessions. As various works on everyday life in the segregated South have shown, forms of address played a key role in the efforts of the white southern population to assert its supremacy over African Americans. The requirement that African Americans address all white adults with "sir" or "ma'am" was one of the many behavioral codices in the public sphere that were enforced in an attempt to maintain the fragile system of racial segregation. See Berrey, "Resistance Begins at Home"; Collins, *Black Feminist Thought*.

111. Transcript of Record, MoML/USSCRB, *Brown v. Mississippi*, 297 U.S. 278 (1936), 106.

112. *Brown*, 113.

113. *Brown*, 111.

114. *Brown*, 112.

115. See, for example, Clark, "'Sacred Rights of the Weak'"; M. Smith, "Getting in Touch with Slavery and Freedom."

116. Cooper and Terrill, *American South*, 236. For more on the role of violence in the system of slavery, see, for example, Horton and Horton, *Slavery and the Making of America*, 120–61.

117. Cortner, *"Scottsboro" Case in Mississippi*, 29–31.

Chapter Two

1. Letter from Curtis Robinson to Walter White, Mobile, AL, November 27, 1941, LOC, NAACP Papers, Group II, Box B-127, *Robinson and Daniels v. Alabama*, 1941–1943.

2. Letter from Curtis Robinson to Walter White.

3. Mangum, *Legal Status of the Negro*, 274.

4. West, "Opera in Greenville." See also Waldrep, *Many Faces of Judge Lynch*, 162.

5. G. Johnson, "Negro and Crime," 97.

6. Philologist Peter Schneck interprets court proceedings as an "intermedial situation" that "displays theatrical elements, i.e. visible dramatization and performance." Schneck notes that the "orchestration of evidence" in the form of a "strategic staging of linguistic acts in the service of establishing the truth" is an integral component of legal processes. Schneck, "Wort und Bild im Kreuzverhör," 44.

7. Dorr, *White Women, Rape, and the Power of Race in Virginia*, 5 (italics for emphasis in the original).

8. Myrdal, *American Dilemma*, 550.

9. "Two Nurses Slugged by Negro Thug," *Montgomery Advertiser*, March 21, 1938, 1, 3.

10. "Dogs Trail Negro in Ward Murder," *Montgomery Advertiser*, March 25, 1938, 1.

11. "Mobile Seizes Prime Suspect in Ward Case," *Montgomery Advertiser*, March 27, 1938, 1.

12. "Mobile Seizes Prime Suspect," *Montgomery Advertiser*, 1.

13. "Nurse Fails to Identify Dave Canty," *Montgomery Advertiser*, March 30, 1938, 1.

14. "Three Boys Pick Negro in Ward Case," *Montgomery Advertiser*, April 2, 1938, 1.

15. "Dave Canty Admits He Beat Nurses," *Montgomery Advertiser*, April 4, 1938, 1, 3.

16. "Dave Canty Admits," *Montgomery Advertiser*, 1, 3. (text in italics is emphasized in boldface in the original). See also the parallel publishing of the confession in the *Alabama Journal*: "Indictment of Canty Sought in Ward Case," *Alabama Journal*, April 4, 1938, 1, 3.

17. "Dave Canty Admits He Beat Nurses."

18. As will be shown in greater detail in chapter 3, before the trial the two lawyers had contacted the legal department of the NAACP in New York City. Furthermore, the local chapter of the NAACP had become active in the case immediately after Canty's arrest.

19. "'Soothsayer' Tells Jury of Cantey's Call," *Montgomery Advertiser*, June 3, 1938, 1, 3.

20. "Whip Drew Confession Says Cantey," *Montgomery Advertiser*, June 4, 1938, 1, 3. Author's note: Newspaper articles on the case vary between "Dave Canty" and "Dave Cantey." This text will use "Dave Canty," but the original spelling has been left in the quotes.

21. *Dave Canty v. State of Alabama*, ADAH, ASC/RoC, vol. 3697, 147.

22. *Dave Canty*, 147.

23. *Dave Canty*, 149.

24. *Dave Canty*, 147.

25. "The Solicitor" in the court transcript is the prosecuting district attorney.

26. *Dave Canty v. State of Alabama*, ADAH, ASC/RoC, vol. 3697, 151.

27. *Dave Canty*, 156.

28. "Whip Drew Confession Says Cantey."

29. "Whip Drew Confession Says Cantey."

30. *Dave Canty v. State of Alabama*, ADAH, ASC/RoC, vol. 3697, 168.

31. *Dave Canty*, 168.

32. *Dave Canty*, 177, 178.

33. "Dave Canty Guilty; Must Die in Chair," *Montgomery Advertiser*, June 5, 1938, 1–2. For more on these court proceedings, see the descriptions in chapter 3.

34. Conquergood, "Rethinking Elocution," 155. See also the articles in Ugwu, *Let's Get It On*, particularly Gilroy, "'. . . To Be Real'"; hooks, "Performance Practice." On performance and African American resistance in the South of the 1930s and 1940s, see Kelley, *Race Rebels*. On the connections between race, performativity, and African American identity, see D. Brooks, *Bodies in Dissent*.

35. On the "arts of resistance" under repressive structures of domination, see Scott, *Domination and the Arts of Resistance*; Lüdtke, "Einleitung. Herrschaft als soziale Praxis."

36. "Attack Suspects Taken to Kilby," *Mobile Register*, August 22, 1941, 2.

37. "Assault on Woman Will Bring Death," *Mobile Register*, November 27, 1941, 3.

38. *Henry Daniels Jr. v. State of Alabama*, ADAH, ASC/RoC, vol. 8346, 1 Div. 162; *Curtis Robinson v. State of Alabama*, ADAH, ASC/RoC, vol. 8346, 1 Div. 163.

39. *Henry Daniels Jr. v. State of Alabama*, ADAH, ASC/RoC, vol. 8346, 1 Div. 162, 14–15.

40. Hodes, "Sexualization of Reconstruction Politics"; Hodes, *White Women, Black Men*.

41. *Henry Daniels Jr. v. State of Alabama*, ADAH, ASC/RoC, vol. 8346, 1 Div. 162, 14–21.

42. *Henry Daniels Jr.*, 17.

43. *Henry Daniels Jr.*, 31–35.

44. *Henry Daniels Jr.*, 38.

45. *Henry Daniels Jr.*, 37.

46. *Henry Daniels Jr.*, 38.

47. *Henry Daniels Jr.*, 53.

48. *Henry Daniels Jr.*, 53.

49. *Curtis Robinson v. State of Alabama*, ADAH, ASC/RoC, vol. 8346, 1 Div. 163, 70.

50. *Henry Daniels Jr. v. State of Alabama*, ADAH, ASC/RoC, vol. 8346, 1 Div. 162, 53.

51. *Henry Daniels Jr.*, 55.

52. *Curtis Robinson v. State of Alabama*, Alabama Supreme Court, Record of Cases, 1824–1974, vol. 8346, ADAH, 1 Div. 163, 74.

53. *Curtis Robinson*, 74.

54. "Youth Sentenced to Electrocution," *Mobile Register*, November 29, 1941, 3.

55. "Sparks Delays 2 Executions; Orders Inquiry," *Montgomery Advertiser*, July 16, 1943, 1.

56. "Sparks Delays 2 Executions," *Montgomery Advertiser*, 1.

57. "Ala. Governor Blasts Police Third Degree," *Chicago Defender*, July 24, 1943, 8.

58. Anonymous letter (1) to Gov. Chauncey Sparks, Birmingham, AL, July 19, 1943, ADAH, AG, 1943–1947: Sparks, CHCF, Henry Daniels Jr.

59. Anonymous letter (2) to Gov. Chauncey Sparks, Birmingham, AL, July 19, 1943, ADAH, AG, 1943–1947: Sparks, CHCF, Henry Daniels Jr.

60. Letter from Hon. Bart B. Chamberlain to Hon. A. M. McDowell, Mobile, AL, March 11, 1943, ADAH, AG, 1943–1947: Sparks, CHCF, Henry Daniels Jr.

61. Letter from Hon. Bart Chamberlain to Hon. A. M. McDowell, Mobile, AL, August 2, 1943, ADAH, AG, 1943–1947: Sparks, CHCF, Henry Daniels Jr.

62. Letter from Judge David H. Edington to Gov. Chauncey Sparks, Mobile, AL, July 20, 1943, ADAH, AG, 1943–1947: Sparks, CHCF, Curtis Robinson.

63. Letter from W. T. Holcombe to H. W. Nixon, Mobile AL, July 22, 1943, ADAH, AG, 1943–1947: Sparks, CHCF, Curtis Robinson.

64. Letter from W. T. Holcombe to H. W. Nixon, Mobile AL, July 22, 1943, ADAH, AG, 1943–1947: Sparks, CHCF, Curtis Robinson. A blackjack is a type of leather bludgeon, roughly 8 to 12 inches long, that consists of a flexible handle and a weighted head with a piece of lead sewn into it. Blackjacks are still used by some police departments in the United States today. See Roth, "Blackjack."

65. Letter from W. T. Holcombe to H. W. Nixon, Mobile, AL, July 22, 1943, ADAH, AG, 1943–1947: Sparks, CHCF, Curtis Robinson.

66. Affidavit by J. J. Hyde in the report by H. W. Nixon to A. M. McDowell, Legal Advisor, Office of the Governor, Auburn, AL, August 2, 1943, ADAH, AG, 1943–1947: Sparks, CHCF, Curtis Robinson.

67. Barthes, *Camera Lucida*, 89.

68. Affidavit by Nelson E. Grubbs in the report by H. W. Nixon to A. M. McDowell, Legal Advisor, Office of the Governor, Auburn, AL, August 2, 1943, ADAH, AG, 1943–1947: Sparks, CHCF, Curtis Robinson.

69. Letter from E. R. Wilson to Carl Williams, Senior Assistant Warden, Kilby Prison, Montgomery, AL, July 26, 1943, ADAH, AG, 1943–1947: Sparks, CHCF, Curtis Robinson.

70. Letter from E. R. Wilson to Carl Williams.

71. Letter from Edgar M. Parkman to Gov. Sparks, Montgomery, AL, August 7, 1943, ADAH, AG, 1943–1947: Sparks, CHCF, Curtis Robinson.

72. Letter from Edgar M. Parkman to Gov. Sparks.

73. Affidavit by Mattie Williams, no location information, undated, ADAH, AG, 1943–1947: Sparks, CHCF, Curtis Robinson.

74. Report by W. T. Kemp, Mobile State Parole Officer, to Gov. Chauncey Sparks, Mobile, AL, August 9, 1943, ADAH, AG, 1943–1947: Sparks, CHCF, Curtis Robinson.

75. The term "Cajan" most likely derives from "Cajun"—the French-speaking settlers who were expelled from Acadia by the British and settled in Louisiana during the eighteenth century. Gilbert, *Memorandum*, 439.

76. Report by W. T. Kemp.

77. Report by W. T. Kemp.

78. Report by W. T. Kemp.

79. Dorr, *White Women, Rape, and the Power of Race in Virginia*, 112–40.

80. Dorr, 112–40.

81. Executive Order No. 37, Gov. Chauncey Sparks, August 12, 1943, ADAH, AG, 1943–1947: Sparks, CHCF, Curtis Robinson.

82. Letter from E. M. Parkman to Gov. Chauncey Sparks, Montgomery, AL, August 13, 1943, ADAH, AG, 1943–1947: Sparks, CHCF, Curtis Robinson.

Chapter Three

1. "Escapes Noose; Near Death from Torture," *Crisis*, April 1935, 119.

2. "Escapes Noose," *Crisis*, 119.

3. In 1908, a riot erupted in Springfield, Illinois, after two black men accused of raping white women were arrested and transferred for their own protection to the jail in Bloomington, roughly sixty miles away. A mob of more than ten thousand whites destroyed numerous homes and businesses in black neighborhoods, and thousands of black residents fled the city. See Senechal de la Roche, *Sociogenesis of a Race Riot*.

4. For more on the history of the NAACP, see Berg, *Ticket to Freedom*; Sullivan, *Lift Every Voice*.

5. Zangrando, *NAACP Crusade against Lynching*; Wood, *Lynching and Spectacle*, 179–221.

6. Sullivan, *Lift Every Voice*, 249; Sullivan, "Prelude to Brown."

7. Houston's appointment was part of a restructuring process within the NAACP, whose leadership positions were increasingly occupied by African Americans during the 1930s. Berg, *Ticket to Freedom*, 174; Meier and Rudwick, "Attorneys Black and White."

8. In 1940, Marshall became the executive director of the Legal Defense and Education Fund, which was founded that same year as a financially independent legal arm of the NAACP. See Tushnet, *Making Civil Rights Law*; Tushnet, *Making Constitutional Law*.

9. Thurgood Marshall, "Equal Justice under Law," *Crisis*, July 1939, 199–201.

10. Masrhall, "Equal Justice," *Crisis*, 199–201.

11. See, for example, Benjamin Kaplan, "The Legal Front: Some Highlights of the Past Year," *Crisis*, July 1940, 206–7, 210; Marshall, "Equal Justice under Law"; Berg, *Ticket to Freedom*, 151–82.

12. See the index entries in Bracey and Meier, *Papers of the NAACP*.

13. Cortner, *"Scottsboro" Case*, 46.

14. Cortner, 46.

15. Cortner, 49.

16. Cortner, 56.

17. Cortner, 57.

18. Cortner, 59.

19. Cortner, 60.

20. Cortner, 64–77.

21. Cortner, 72.

22. Cortner, 73.

23. Cortner, 81.

24. Cortner, 89–108.

25. See table in Cortner, 95.

26. Cortner, 94.

27. Cortner, 94.

28. Klarman, *From Jim Crow to Civil Rights*, 117–21.

29. Klarman, 117–35, 152–58.

30. Brown v. State of Mississippi, 297 U.S. 278 (1936), https://www.law.cornell.edu/supremecourt/text/297/278.

31. The cases in question were *Brown v. Mississippi* (1936), *Chambers v. Florida* (1940), *Canty v. Alabama* (1940), *White v. Texas* (1940), *Vernon v. Alabama* (1941), *Lomax v. Texas* (1941), *Ward v. Texas* (1942), and *Lyons v. Oklahoma* (1944). The only case in which the NAACP was not involved was *Lomax v. Texas* (1941). See Blevins, "*Lyons v. Oklahoma*."

32. See note 31.

33. See note 31.

34. "Trio Is Saved from Legal Lynching," *Chicago Daily Tribune*, March 15, 1936, D5.

35. "A Strike for Human Rights," *Washington Post*, February 19, 1936, 8; "What the Court Obstructs," *New York Times*, February 21, 1936, 16.

36. Quoted by "Press Favors Judgment in Cropper Case," *Chicago Defender*, February 29, 1936, 4.

37. "Take Torture Case before U.S. High Court," *Chicago Defender*, November 2, 1935, 2.

38. "Supreme Court Reverses Mississippi Mock Trial," *Chicago Defender*, February 2, 1936, 16.

39. "U.S. Supreme Court Hears Their Case," *Crisis*, February 1936, 42.

40. Wood, *Lynching and Spectacle*, 179–221; see also Zangrando, *NAACP Crusade against Lynching*; Bederman, *Manliness and Civilization*, 23–76.

41. "No Torture," *Crisis*, April 1936, 113; see also "U.S. Supreme Court Reverses Torture Case," *Crisis*, April 1936, 118–19.

42. Cortner, *"Scottsboro" Case*, 153, 159.

43. See, for example, the cases of Dave Canty and W. D. Lyons, described in this chapter.

44. Letter from Thurgood Marshall to E. Norman Lancey, New York, NY, July 2, 1942, LOC, NAACP Papers, Group II, Box-123, *Flowers v. Florida*, Correspondence, 1942–43.

45. The cases were *Chambers v. Florida* (1940), *Canty v. Alabama* (1940), and *White v. Texas* (1940).

46. Transcript of Record, MoML/USSCRB, *Chambers v. State of Florida*, 309 U.S. 227 (1940); *Chambers v. State of Florida*, 309 U.S. 227 (1940), https://www.law.cornell.edu /supremecourt/text/309/227.

47. "Florida's 'Scottsboro Case' Goes before Supreme Court," *Atlanta Daily World*, January 11, 1940, 6.

48. *Chambers v. State of Florida*, 309 U.S. 227 (1940), https://www.law.cornell.edu /supremecourt/text/309/227.

49. *Chambers v. Florida*.

50. *Chambers v. Florida*.

51. "Justice Has No Politics," *New York Times*, February 13, 1940, 21; "Shield of Liberty," *Washington Post*, February 13, 1940, 12.

52. "Outlaw 'Torture Confession,'" *Pittsburgh Courier*, February 17, 1940, 1.

53. "Outlaw 'Torture Confession,'" *Pittsburgh Courier*, 1.

54. "High Court Denounces Fla. Justice," *Chicago Defender*, February 17, 1940, 1–2.

55. Arthur Spingarn, *NAACP Daily Letter*, February 13, 1940, LOC, NAACP Papers, Group II, Box B-28, *Chambers v. Florida*, Correspondence 1940–1942.

56. "Rebuke to Torture," *Crisis*, March 1940, 81.

57. "Rebuke to Torture," *Crisis*, 81.

58. Letter from Charles H. Houston to Hubert T. Faulk, Esq., New York, NY, September 29, 1937, LOC, NAACP Papers, Group I, Box D-99, Young, Roscoe and Henderson, 1937–1938; letter from Thurgood Marshall to P. Waite Stennett, New York, NY, August 7, 1940, LOC, NAACP Papers, Group II, Box B-26, Bryant, Willie, 1940–1944.

59. Tushnet, *Making Civil Rights Law*, 28–29.

60. See, for example, the case of Roscoe and Henderson Young and the case of Willie Bryant: LOC, NAACP Papers, Group I, Box D-99, Young, Roscoe and Henderson, 1937–1938; LOC, NAACP Papers, Group II, Box B-26, Bryant, Willie, 1940–1944. See also Klarman, *From Jim Crow to Civil Rights*, 109–10, 155.

61. Letter from George Edwards Jr. to William Henry Huff, De Ridder, LA, March 24, 1946; letter from George Edwards Jr. to William Henry Huff, De Ridder, LA, April 4, 1946, both in: LOC, NAACP Papers, Group II, Box B-31, Edwards, George Jr., 1946.

62. King, *Execution of Willie Francis*, 137.

63. Letter from Robert L. Carter, NAACP-Assistant Special Counsel, to Frederick E. Robin, Assistant to the Director, American Civil Liberties Union, May 14, 1940, LOC, NAACP Papers, Group II, Box B-31, Edwards, George Jr., 1946.

64. "Execution of Ala. Torture Victim Halted," *Chicago Defender*, March 23, 1940, 8; "High Court Saves Another Negro," *New York Times*, March 12, 1940, 22.

65. Letter from William G. Porter to Walter White, Montgomery, AL, April 7, 1938, LOC, NAACP Papers, Group II, Box B-27, *Canty v. Alabama*, 1940–1942.

66. Letter from Charles H. Houston to William G. Porter, New York, NY, April 14, 1938, LOC, NAACP Papers, Group II, Box B-27, *Canty v. Alabama*, 1940–1942.

67. Letter from Thurgood Marshall to Dr. E. W. Taggart, New York, NY, May 12, 1938, LOC, NAACP Papers, Group II, Box B-27, *Canty v. Alabama*, 1940–1942.

68. Letter from Thurgood Marshall to Dr. E. W. Taggart.

69. E. W. Taggart, Facts in the Case of Dave Canty, Birmingham, AL, May 31, 1938, LOC, NAACP Papers, Group II, Box B-27, *Canty v. Alabama*, 1940–1942.

70. Taggart, Facts in the Case of Dave Canty.

71. Taggart, Facts in the Case of Dave Canty.

72. "Canty Confession Not Gained by Beating, Says Col. Screws," *Montgomery Advertiser*, no date, no page number, filed in: LOC, NAACP Papers, Group II, Box B-27, *Canty v. Alabama*, 1940–1942.

73. "Canty Confession Not Gained," *Montgomery Advertiser*.

74. Letter from Thurgood Marshall to E. W. Taggart, New York, NY, June 16, 1938, LOC, NAACP Papers, Group II, Box B-27, *Canty v. Alabama*, 1940–1942.

75. Letter from E. W. Taggart to E. G. Jackson, Birmingham, AL, June 8, 1938, LOC, NAACP Papers, Group II, Box B-27.

76. Letter from William G. Porter to Walter White, Montgomery, AL, May 31, 1938, LOC, NAACP Branch Files, Montgomery Branch, NAACP Papers, Group I, Box G-7.

77. Letter from William G. Porter to Walter White, Montgomery, AL, July 9, 1938, LOC, NAACP Papers, Group II, Box B-27, *Canty v. Alabama*, 1940–1942.

78. Letter from William G. Porter to Walter White, Montgomery, AL, November 14, 1938, LOC, NAACP Papers, Group II, Box B-27, *Canty v. Alabama*, 1940–1942.

79. See the membership lists of July 18, August 1, and August 4, 1938, LOC, NAACP Branch Files, Montgomery Branch, NAACP Papers, Group I, Box G-7.

80. Letter from T. M. Blair to Walter White, Montgomery, AL, June 24, 1939, LOC, NAACP Papers, Group II, Box B-27.

81. Letter from T. M. Blair to Walter White.

82. Letter from Thurgood Marshall to Alex C. Birch, New York, NY, Aug. 3, 1939; letter from Alex C. Birch to Thurgood Marshall, Montgomery, AL, October 14, 1939, LOC, NAACP Papers, Group II, Box B-27.

83. This number is given in a letter of W. G. Porter to Walter White, Montgomery, Oct. 29, 1939, LOC, NAACP Papers, Group I, Box G 7, NAACP Branch Files, Montgomery Branch. In March, April, and September 1939, the Montgomery branch gained about 350 new members. See LOC, NAACP Branch Files, Montgomery Branch, NAACP Papers, Group I, Box G-7.

84. Letter from William G. Porter to Walter White, Montgomery, AL, November 14, 1938, LOC, NAACP Papers, Group II, Box B-27, *Canty v. Alabama*, 1940–1942 (emphasis in original).

85. Letter from Alex C. Birch to Thurgood Marshall, Montgomery, AL, July 11, 1939, LOC, NAACP Papers, Group II, Box B-27, *Canty v. Alabama*, 1940–1942.

86. James, *Root and Branch*, 121.

87. "Farmhouse Fire Takes 3 Lives; Murder Hinted," *Tulsa Daily World*, January 1, 1940, 1; "Farmhouse Fire Deaths Probed," *Tulsa Daily World*, January 2, 1940, 1; Transcript of Record, MoML/USSCRB, *Lyons v. State of Oklahoma*, 322 U.S. 596 (1944).

88. See Klarman, *From Jim Crow to Civil Rights*, 171; "Tortured with Charred Bones!," *Crisis*, March 1941, 85.

89. "Negro Confesses in Triple Slaying," *Tulsa Daily World*, January 24, 1940, 2.

90. Letter from Roscoe Dunjee to Walter White, Oklahoma City, OK, March 26, 1940, LOC, NAACP Papers, Group II, Box B-39, *Lyons v. Oklahoma*, Correspondence, 1940–1941.

91. Letter from Roscoe Dunjee to Thurgood Marshall, December 26, 1940, Oklahoma City, OK, LOC, NAACP Papers, Group II, Box B-39, *Lyons v. Oklahoma*, Correspondence, 1940–1941.

92. Letter from Roscoe Dunjee to Thurgood Marshall, January 13, 1941, Oklahoma City, OK, LOC, NAACP Papers, Group II, Box B-39, *Lyons v. Oklahoma*, Correspondence, 1940–1941.

93. NAACP press release, New York, NY, January 24, 1941, LOC, NAACP Papers, Group II, Box B-39, *Lyons v. Oklahoma*, Correspondence, 1940–1941.

94. Letter from Thurgood Marshall to Walter White, Hugo, OK, January 29, 1941, LOC, NAACP Papers, Group II, Box B-39, *Lyons v. Oklahoma*, Correspondence, 1940–1941.

95. Letter from Thurgood Marshall to Walter White, Hugo, OK, February 2, 1941, LOC, NAACP Papers, Group II, Box B-39, *Lyons v. Oklahoma*, Correspondence, 1940–1941.

96. Letter from Thurgood Marshall to Walter White.

97. Transcript of Record, MoML/USSCRB, *Lyons v. State of Oklahoma*, 322 U.S. 596 (1944), 212.

98. *Lyons*, 213.

99. *Lyons*, 212–22.

100. *Lyons*, 73.

101. Letter from Thurgood Marshall to Walter White, Hugo, OK, February 2, 1941, LOC, NAACP Papers, Group II, Box B-39, *Lyons v. Oklahoma*, Correspondence, 1940–1941.

102. Letter from Thurgood Marshall to Walter White.

103. Letter from Thurgood Marshall to Walter White.

104. "Negro's Statement Ruled Out at Hugo," *Daily Oklahoman*, February 1, 1941, 1.

105. Letter from Thurgood Marshall to Walter White, Hugo, OK, February 2, 1941, LOC, NAACP Papers, Group II, Box B-39, *Lyons v. Oklahoma*, Correspondence, 1940–1941.

106. Letter from Thurgood Marshall to Walter White.

107. Letter from Thurgood Marshall to Walter White.

108. Klarman, "Is the Supreme Court Sometimes Irrelevant?," 120, 147.

109. Klarman, 120, 147.

110. Letter from Thurgood Marshall to Walter White, Hugo, OK, February 2, 1941, LOC, NAACP Papers, Group II, Box B-39, *Lyons v. Oklahoma*, Correspondence, 1940–1941.

111. Wood, *Lynching and Spectacle*, 179–221; Apel and Smith, *Lynching Photographs*; Hale, *Making Whiteness*; Wood, *Lynching and Spectacle*; Wood, "Lynching Photography." See also the collection of lynching photographs in Allen, *Without Sanctuary*.

112. "Tortured with Charred Bones!," *Crisis*, March 1941, 85 (emphasis in original). There are inconsistencies in the archival sources with regard to Lyons's age. According to local newspapers, Lyons was twenty-one years old when the crime was committed and twenty-two years old when he was put on trial. See, for example, "Negro Confesses in Triple Slaying," *Tulsa Daily World*, January 24, 1940, 2; "Son of Victims Witness at Murder Trial of Negro," *Tulsa Daily World*, January 28, 1941, 7.

113. "Tortured with Charred Bones!," *Crisis*, 85.

114. McMahon, *Reconsidering Roosevelt*, 160–61.

115. Berg, *Ticket to Freedom*, 186–96; Sullivan, *Lift Every Voice*, 237–52.

116. "Oklahoma Murder Case Is Upheld, Appeal to U.S. Supreme Court," *New York Amsterdam News*, June 26, 1943, 5.

117. Dudziak, *Cold War Civil Rights*.

118. Lyons v. Oklahoma, 322 U.S. 596 (1944), https://www.law.cornell.edu/supremecourt/text/322/596; letter from Charles Elmore Cropley, Clerk of Supreme Court of the United States, to Thurgood Marshall, Washington D.C., October 9, 1944, LOC, NAACP Papers, Group II, Box B-39, *Lyons v. Oklahoma*, Correspondence, 1940–1941.

119. Letter of Thurgood Marshall to E. Frederic Morrow, August 28, 1943, LOC, NAACP Papers, Group II, Box A-593, cited by Sullivan, *Lift Every Voice*, 281.

120. Knauer, *Let Us Fight as Free Man*, 33–54; Parker, *Fighting for Democracy*.

121. Plummer, *Rising Wind*, 86; Dudziak, *Cold War Civil Rights*, 5–7.

122. Du Bois, "Negro since 1900," 57, 59.

123. See, for example, Dudziak, *Cold War Civil Rights*; Plummer, *Rising Wind*.

124. See the newspaper articles and comments on the Woodard case in LOC, NAACP Papers, Group II, Box B 219, Woodard Case, Press Clippings.

125. Knauer, *Let Us Fight as Free Men*, 38–43; Klarman, *From Jim Crow to Civil Rights*, 185; Myers, *Resonant Ripples in a Global Pond*.

126. See the anonymous drawing at the beginning of this book (figure 1).

127. Green, *Before His Time*, 83–86.

128. Green, 91–92.

129. Green, 92; Walter Irvin's statement, July 31, 1949, http://www.pbs.org/harrymoore/terror/irvin.html.

130. Green, 92.

131. Green, *Before His Time*, 92.

132. Green, 100–8.

133. The term "night riding" refers to nighttime attacks on blacks by members of the Ku Klux Klan.

134. NAACP brochure "GROVELAND U.S.A.," LOC, NAACP Papers, Group II, Series B, Box B-123, Groveland, Florida, 1949–1955.

135. "GROVELAND U.S.A." (emphasis in original).

136. Green, *Before His Time*, 107.

137. See Shepherd v. Florida, 341 U.S. 50 (1951), https://www.law.cornell.edu/supremecourt/text/341/50.

138. Klarman, *From Jim Crow to Civil Rights*, 275–77; Green, *Before His Time*, 81–108.

139. NAACP national office, "Legal Defense Materials: Part IV, Methods of Combating Police Brutality," New York, NY, June 1939, LOC, NAACP Papers, Group I, Series B, Box 16. I thank Brandon Jett for bringing this pamphlet to my attention.

Chapter Four

1. "Detective Burned Him with Iron, Says Negro Boy," *Atlanta Constitution*, March 8, 1940, 1–2; "Two Probes Sift Torture Story at City Jail," *Atlanta Journal*, March 8, 1940, 1, 12. In several instances, Quintar South's first name is given as Quinter. Quintar, however, is the most prevalent spelling used by local newspapers and in court records.

2. "Detective Burned Him with Iron, Says Negro Boy," 1–2.

3. "Detective Burned Him," 1–2.

4. "Alleged Torturing of Suspects Arouses Citizens, Authorities," *Atlanta Constitution*, March 9, 1940, 2; "Protests Mount in 'Torture Case,'" *Atlanta Constitution*, March 10, 1940, 1.

5. "Alleged Torturing of Suspects Arouses Citizens, Authorities," 2; "Police 'Torture' Must Go Says Hartsfield," *Atlanta Journal*, March 9, 1940, 1–2.

6. "Justice for the Weak," *Atlanta Constitution*, March 9, 1940, 4; "Abolish the 'Third Degree,'" *Atlanta Journal*, March 9, 1940, 3.

7. See the letters to the editor published in the *Atlanta Constitution* on March 11, 1940, under the headline "The Pulse of the Public," 5.

8. My findings on this case concur with the observations of Judith Butler, who has called the selective awareness of individual incidents of racial violence—and the concurrent ignorance of the structures of racism—the result of a "racially saturated field of visibility." Butler, "Endangered/Endangering," 205. Butler's analysis pertains to the Rodney King case from the year 1991. King was brutally beaten with batons by Los Angeles Police Department officers following a high-speed car chase. A private video of the beating was broadcast around the world. The officers involved were charged with assault with a deadly weapon and the use of excessive force but later acquitted, sparking massive protests and riots. According to Butler, the acquittals of the four defendants, despite comprehensive video evidence, are indicative of a "racist disposition of the visible" that prepares and achieves "its own inverted perceptions under the rubric of 'what is seen.'" Butler, 207.

9. "Detective Burned Him with Iron, Says Negro Boy," 1–2.

10. For more on the orientation of the *Atlanta Constitution* under the guidance of its longtime publisher Ralph McGill, see Lippman, "McGill and Patterson."

11. Lippman, "McGill and Patterson."

12. For more on paternalistic conceptions of race and gender in southern society and literature after the American Civil War, see McPherson, *Reconstructing Dixie*; Williamson; *Crucible of Race*.

13. "Officer Indicted as Chief Starts Brutality Probe," *Atlanta Constitution*, March 9, 1940, 1.

14. "Officer Indicted," 1; "Abolish the 'Third Degree,'" 3.

15. "Officer Indicted," 1; "Abolish the 'Third Degree,'" 3.

16. "Justice for the Weak," 4.

17. Mixon, "'Good Negro—Bad Negro.'"

18. "Justice for the Weak," 4.

19. "Justice for the Weak," 4.

20. Stockton Hume, "Dangerous Abdication of Fundamental Rights," letter to the editor, *Atlanta Constitution*, March 11, 1940, 5.

21. Ettianne Baldwin, "Editorial Inspired Pride and Interest," letter to the editor, *Atlanta Constitution*, March 11, 1940, 5.

22. Stuart R. Oglesby, "Expresses Sentiment of Atlanta People," letter to the editor, *Atlanta Constitution*, March 11, 1940, 5.

23. George W. Willingham, "Relieving Atlanta of a Curse," letter to the editor, *Atlanta Constitution*, March 11, 1940, 5.

24. "Federal Jury Told of Burns on Boy's Neck," *Atlanta Constitution*, February 13, 1941, 4.

25. "Federal Jury Told," *Atlanta Constitution*, 4.

26. Report by Ronald R. Hassig, FBI Special Agent, Atlanta, GA, March 16, 1940, NARA, RG 60/144, Box 17583, Fol. 144-19-5, 2.

27. "Youth Branded with Hot Iron," 1, 4; "White Atlantans Push Torture Case of Boy, 16," *Chicago Defender*, March 23, 1940, 6.

28. "Youth Branded with Hot Iron," 1; "Tells of Torture," *Chicago Defender*, March 16, 1940, 5. According to the caption, the *Chicago Defender* acquired its photo from the news agency Acme Newspictures.

29. On the cultural studies concept of the *gaze*, see Mulvey, "Visual Pleasure and Narrative Cinema"; Finzsch, "Male Gaze and Racism." To read about the use of the concept with regard to African American identity politics, see the works of bell hooks on the "white supremacist gaze" and "white gaze": hooks, *Black Looks*; hooks, "In Our Glory."

30. Carroll, *Word, Image, and the New Negro*, 1.

31. Quoted by Teel, "W. A. Scott and the Atlanta World," 160.

32. Teel, 160.

33. "Officer Indicted, Suspended in Burning-Beating of School Boy," *Atlanta Daily World*, March 9, 1940, 1.

34. "Sutherland Faces New Brutality Charge," *Atlanta Daily World*, March 10, 1940, 1.

35. "Let's End Police Brutality," *Atlanta Daily World*, March 10, 1940, 4.

36. "Let's End Police Brutality," *Atlanta Daily World*, 4.

37. "Let's End Police Brutality," *Atlanta Daily World*, 4.

38. J. P. Reynolds, "Hit While the Iron Is Hot: Right Now," *Atlanta Daily World*, March 10, 1940, 4.

39. For more details on these investigations, see chapter 5.

40. William A. Fowlkes, "Shall Brutalities Continue," *Atlanta Daily World*, March 31, 1940, 4 (emphasis in original).

41. "Tells of Torture," 5. "Youth Branded with Hot Iron," 1; "White Atlantans Push Torture Case of Boy, 16," 6.

42. "Youth Branded with Hot Iron," 1.

43. As will be shown in chapter 5, shortly after the news broke of the torture allegations of Quintar South, the U.S. Department of Justice launched FBI investigations against W. F. Sutherland. During the course of the investigations, FBI agents took a number of photographs of Quintar South as evidence. The surviving photographs have striking similarities with the photograph on the front page of the *Pittsburgh Courier* (see figure 7).

44. See note 43.

45. "White Atlantans Push Torture Case of Boy, 16," 6.

46. "Torture Victim Back from Sea," *Pittsburgh Courier*, September 11, 1943, 5; "'Torture' Victim Back from South Pacific," *Chicago Defender*, September 18, 1943, 9.

47. For more details on these cases, see chapter 5.

48. "Torture Victim Back from Sea," 5.

49. Jefferson, *Fighting for Hope*; Berg, "Soldiers and Citizens"; Jobs, *Welcome Home, Boys!*.

50. "Torture Victim Back from Sea," 5.

51. Jarvis, *Male Body at War*.

52. See hooks, *Black Looks*, 2, in which bell hooks describes the African American struggle for a liberating practice of self-representation as a "struggle to break with the hegemonic modes of seeing, thinking, and being that block our capacity to see ourselves oppositionally, to imagine, describe, and invent ourselves in ways that are liberatory."

53. Knauer, *Let Us Fight as Free Man*, 33–54; Parker, *Fighting for Democracy*.

54. S. Hall, "Spectacle of the 'Other,'" 251.

55. "Detective Found Not Guilty in Hot Iron Case," *Atlanta Daily World*, June 21, 1940, 1, 6; "Jury Clears Policeman in Torture Case," *Atlanta Constitution*, June 21, 1940, 2.

Chapter Five

1. Quoted by Elliff, *United States Department of Justice*, 151. For more on the case of Cleo Wright, see Capeci, *Lynching of Cleo Wright*; Capeci, "The Lynching of Cleo Wright."

2. Letter from O. John Rogge, Assistant Attorney General, to FBI Director J. Edgar Hoover, Washington D.C., March 8, 1940, NARA, RG 65/44, Box 42, File 44-330.

3. Zangrando, *NAACP Crusade against Lynching*.

4. Waldrep, "National Policing, Lynching, and Constitutional Change," 607–12.

5. Carr, *Federal Protection of Civil Rights*, 24–32. Frank Murphy was appointed to the U.S. Supreme Court by Franklin D. Roosevelt in 1940. His successors in office until the mid-1950s were Robert H. Jackson (1940–41), Francis Biddle (1941–45), Tom C.

Clark (1945–49), J. Howard McGrath (1949–52), James P. McGranery (1952–53), and Herbert Brownell Jr. (1953–57).

6. Carr, *Federal Protection of Civil Rights*; Elliff, *United States Department of Justice*; Capeci, *Lynching of Cleo Wright*; Capeci, "Lynching of Cleo Wright"; McMahon, *Reconsidering Roosevelt*; Waldrep, "National Policing, Lynching, and Constitutional Change."

7. Frank Murphy, "Civil Liberties: A Radio Address," March 27, 1939, 8 (transcript), NARA, Library, call number: J12C49/4.

8. McAdam, *Political Process*, 77–87; Waldrep, "National Policing, Lynching, and Constitutional Change," 611–12.

9. Waldrep, "National Policing, Lynching, and Constitutional Change," 607–12.

10. Walker, *In Defense of American Liberties*, 86–92; M. Johnson, *Street Justice*, 114–48.

11. Capeci, "Lynching of Cleo Wright," 859–60; Cover, "Origins of Judicial Activism."

12. Capeci, "Lynching of Cleo Wright," 871–73; Dudziak, *Cold War Civil Rights*, 8–11; Elliff, *United States Department of Justice*, 147–59; McMahon, *Reconsidering Roosevelt*, 159–76.

13. Coleman, "Freedom from Fear on the Home Front," 415.

14. The United States Code is the official compilation and codification of the general and permanent federal statutes of the United States.

15. Carr, *Federal Protection of Civil Rights*, 56–84.

16. Memorandum, Federal Criminal Jurisdiction Over Violations of Civil Liberties, Circular No. 3356 (Supplement 1), May 21, 1940, quoted by Elliff, *United States Department of Justice*, 98–100.

17. See the numbers in Lawson, *To Secure These Rights*, 145. See also the much higher numbers of complaints compiled by Robert Carr in Carr, *Federal Protection of Civil Rights*, 125, 129. Carr tallies eight thousand complaints in 1942, of which twenty-six resulted in indictments, and approx. twenty thousand complaints in 1944, sixty-four of which led to court cases. In his study on the letters of complaint to the CLU/CRS from the years 1939 to 1941, George Lovell notes that only 8 percent of the complaints had a specific connection to "race." Lovell, "Imagined Rights without Remedies," 113.

18. Wendell Berge, Assistant Attorney General, Memorandum to James Rowe Jr., Assistant to the Attorney General, Washington D.C., March 3, 1942, NARA, RG 60/144, Box 17583, Fol. 144-19-5.

19. Wendell Berge Memo to James Rowe Jr.

20. Letter from O. John Rogge, Assistant Attorney General, to FBI Director J. Edgar Hoover, Washington D.C., March 8, 1940, NARA, RG 60/144, Box 17583, Fol. 144-19-5; memo from E. A. Tamm to FBI Director J. Edgar Hoover, Washington D.C., March 8, 1940, and memo from O. John Rogge, Assistant Attorney General, to FBI Director J. Edgar Hoover, Washington D.C., March 8, 1940, NARA, RG 65/44, Box 42, File 44-330; letter from Lawrence C. Camp, U.S. Attorney, Northern District of Georgia, to Henry A. Schweinhaut, head of the Civil Liberties Unit, Atlanta, GA, March 12, 1940, NARA, RG 60/144, Box 17583, Fol. 144-19-5.

21. Letter from R. G. Danner, FBI Special Agent in Charge, to FBI Director J. Edgar Hoover, Atlanta, GA, March 11, 1940, NARA, RG 65/44, Box 42, File 44-330.

22. J. Edgar Hoover was the director of the Federal Bureau of Investigation from 1935 to 1972. He had previously directed the Bureau of Investigation from 1924 to

1935. For more on the image of the FBI in contemporary popular culture, see Potter, *War on Crime*.

23. Waldrep, "National Policing, Lynching, and Constitutional Change," 604–7, 609–10.

24. Jeffreys-Jones, *The FBI: A History*, 81–99.

25. Manual, Bureau of Investigation, Department of Justice, 1927, RWWL, FBI MoI, Microfilm 1473.

26. Manual, 134–35.

27. Manual, 137.

28. Report by Ronald R. Hassig, FBI Special Agent, Atlanta, GA, March 16, 1940, NARA, RG 60/144, Box 17583, Fol. 144-19-5.

29. Report by Ronald R. Hassig.

30. Report by Ronald R. Hassig, 4–6.

31. Report by Ronald R. Hassig, 4–6.

32. Statement by W. F. Sutherland, Atlanta, GA, March 15, 1940, report by Ronald R. Hassig, FBI Special Agent, Atlanta, GA, March 16, 1940, NARA, RG 60/144, Box 17583, Fol. 144-19-5, 31–32.

33. Statement by Quintar South, Atlanta, GA, March 11, 1940, report by Ronald R. Hassig, FBI Special Agent, Atlanta, GA, March 16, 1940, NARA, RG 60/144, Box 17583, Fol. 144-19-5, 4 (the names are written in capital letters here and in the following quotes just as they were in the original FBI report).

34. Statement by Quintar South, 5. Note: The word "iron" was erroneously transcribed instead of "arm." The error was spotted later and underlined by the FBI agents.

35. Statement by Quintar South, 5.

36. Statement by Quintar South, 5.

37. Statement by Rosa South, Atlanta, GA, March 14, 1940, report by Ronald R. Hassig, FBI Special Agent, Atlanta, GA, March 16, 1940, NARA, RG 60/144, Box 17583, Fol. 144-19-5, 17–18.

38. See also the statements by Biggs and Alfonso Jamieson (Alphonso Jamieson's first name is misspelled as Alfonso in the FBI reports), Atlanta, GA, March 11, 1940, report by Ronald R. Hassig, FBI Special Agent, Atlanta, GA, March 16, 1940, NARA, RG 60/144, Box 17583, Fol. 144-19-5, 8–11.

39. Statement by John Biggs, Atlanta, GA, March 11, 1940, report by Ronald R. Hassig, FBI Special Agent, Atlanta, GA, March 16, 1940, NARA, RG 60/144, Box 17583, Fol. 144-19-5, 11.

40. Statement by John Biggs. Quintar South's first name is presumably misspelled in the FBI records as Quinter.

41. Report by Ronald R. Hassig, FBI Special Agent, Atlanta, GA, March 16, 1940, NARA, RG 60/144, Box 17583, Fol. 144-19-5, 1.

42. Manual of Instruction, Federal Bureau of Investigation, 1936, Section 23: Scientific Aids in Criminal Investigations, RWWL, FBI MoI, Microfilm 1473, 5.

43. FBI photograph of the tacking iron, NARA, RG 60/144, Box 17583, Fol. 144-19-5.

44. FBI photograph of Quintar South, NARA, RG 60/144, Box 17583, Fol. 144-19-5.

45. Manual of Instruction, Federal Bureau of Investigation, 1936, Section 23: Scientific Aids in Criminal Investigations, RWWL, FBI MoI, Microfilm 1473, 5.

46. Barthes, *Camera Lucida*, 87.

47. Barthes, 89.

48. Reverse side of the FBI photograph of Quintar South, NARA, RG 60/144, Box 17583, Fol. 144-19-5.

49. Report by Ronald R. Hassig, FBI Special Agent, Atlanta, GA, March 16, 1940, NARA, RG 60/144, Box 17583, Fol. 144-19-5, 34–35.

50. Statement by Quintar South, Atlanta, GA, March 11, 1940, report by Ronald R. Hassig, FBI Special Agent, Atlanta, GA, March 16, 1940, NARA, RG 60/144, Box 17583, Fol. 144-19-5, 4–6.

51. On the "forensic gaze" and the construction of evidence, see Valverde, *Law's Dream of a Common Knowledge*, 54–85.

52. "Officer Sutherland on Trial in U.S. Court," *Atlanta Daily World*, February 11, 1941, 1, 6.

53. "South's Cell Mate Tells of Police Brutality," *Atlanta Daily World*, February 12, 1941, 1, 6; "Mother Denies Son Was Burned Before Police Took Him to Jail," *Atlanta Daily World*, February 13, 1941, 1, 6.

54. "South's Cell Mate," *Atlanta Daily World*, 1, 6.

55. "South's Cell Mate," *Atlanta Daily World*, 1, 6; "'Torture' Officer Expected to Testify Today," *Atlanta Daily World*, February 18, 1941, 1.

56. William A. Fowlkes, "Shall Brutalities Continue," *Atlanta Daily World*, March 31, 1940, 4.

57. "South's Cell Mate Tells of Police Brutality," Atlanta Daily World, February 12, 1941, 1.

58. Cliff Mackay, "The Issue at Stake," *Atlanta Daily World*, February 16, 1941, 8.

59. "The Issue at Stake," 8.

60. "'Torture' Officer Expected to Testify Today," 1; "Sutherland's Trial Resumed in U.S. Court," *Atlanta Constitution*, February 18, 1941, 9.

61. "'Torture' Officer," 1.

62. "Test Shows Iron Can Be Heated," *Atlanta Daily World*, February 16, 1941, 1.

63. "Test 'Torture Iron,'" *Atlanta Daily World*, February 15, 1941, 1.

64. "'Torture' Iron Tested in Court," *Atlanta Constitution*, February 15, 1941, 1.

65. "'Torture' Iron Tested," *Atlanta Constitution*, 1.

66. "Sutherland Jury Deadlocks," *Atlanta Daily World*, February 21, 1941, 1.

67. "A Disappointing Result," *Atlanta Daily World*, February 21, 1941, 4.

68. Tagg, *Burden of Representation*, 3; see also the remarks on evidence and power in the introduction.

69. Letter from R. G. Danner, FBI Special Agent, to FBI Director J. Edgar Hoover, Atlanta, GA, June 13, 1940, NARA, RG 65/44, Box 42, File 44-330, 3.

70. Letter from R. G. Danner, FBI Special Agent, to FBI Director J. Edgar Hoover, Atlanta, GA, April 30, 1940, NARA, RG 65/44, Box 42, File 44-330.

71. Report by Ronald R. Hassig, FBI Special Agent, to Robert G. Danner, FBI Special Agent in Charge, Atlanta, GA, April 29, 1940, NARA, RG 65/44, Box 42, File 44-330.

72. Letter from Raymond W. Martin, Assistant United States Attorney, Northern District of Georgia, to O. John Rogge, Assistant Attorney General, Atlanta, GA, August 12, 1940, and letter from Raymond W. Martin, Assistant United States Attorney,

to O. John Rogge, Assistant Attorney General, Atlanta, GA, September 4, 1940, NARA, RG 65/44, Box 42, File 44-330.

73. Memo from O. John Rogge, Assistant Attorney General, to FBI Director J. Edgar Hoover, Washington D.C., August 30, 1940, NARA, RG 65/44, Box 42, File 44-330.

74. Memo from FBI Director J. Edgar Hoover to Matthew F. McGuire, Assistant to the Attorney General, Washington D.C., September 25, 1940, NARA, RG 60/144, Box 17583, Fol. 144-19-5. As assistant to the attorney general, Matthew F. McGuire occupied the third-highest position in the Justice Department and was officially responsible for FBI oversight.

75. Memo from J. Edgar Hoover to Matthew F. McGuire.

76. Memo from J. Edgar Hoover to Matthew F. McGuire.

77. Memo from Matthew McGuire, Assistant to the Attorney General, to O. John Rogge, Assistant Attorney General, Washington D.C., September 30, 1940, NARA, RG 60/144, Box 17583, Fol. 144-19-5.

78. Memo from Matthew F. McGuire, Assistant to the Attorney General, to Wendell Berge, Assistant Attorney General, Washington D.C., January 29, 1941, NARA, RG 60/144, Box 17583, Fol. 144-19-5.

79. As late as the 1960s, the FBI leadership and segments of the U.S. Department of Justice maintained an ambivalent attitude toward the work of the Civil Rights Section, as described in Elliff, "Aspects of Federal Civil Rights Enforcement."

80. Memo from J. Edgar Hoover, FBI Director, to Matthew F. McGuire, Assistant to the Attorney General, Washington D.C., May 1, 1941, and memo from Matthew F. McGuire, Assistant to the Attorney General, to J. Edgar Hoover, FBI Director, Washington D.C., September 29, 1941, NARA, RG 60/144, Box 17583, Fol. 144-19-5.

81. "Officer Again on Trial in Torture Case," *Atlanta Daily World*, November 14, 1941, 4; "Police Torture Case Ends in 2nd Mistrial," *Atlanta Daily World*, November 20, 1941, 1, 4.

82. Memo from James Rowe Jr., Assistant to the Attorney General, to J. Edgar Hoover, FBI Director, Washington D.C., March 5, 1942, and letter from Tom C. Clark, Assistant Attorney General, to M. Neil Andrews, United States Attorney, Northern District of Georgia, Washington D.C., June 20, 1944, NARA, RG 60/144, Box 17583, Fol. 144-19-5.

83. Memo from Wendell Berge, Assistant Attorney General, to J. Edgar Hoover, FBI Director, Washington D.C., March 20, 1943, NARA, RG 60/144, Box 17583, Fol. 144-19-5.

84. Letter from M. Neil Andrews, United States Attorney, Northern District of Georgia, to Francis Biddle, Atlanta, GA, June 13, 1944, NARA, RG 60/144, Box 17583, Fol. 144-19-5. Regarding the violent race riots in Detroit and many other cities in the United States during World War II, see Sitkoff, "Racial Militancy and Interracial Violence."

85. "U.S. Attorney Ready to Try Macon Sheriff," *Montgomery Advertiser*, June 20, 1943, 1.

86. Memo from FBI agent Edwin D. Kuykendall, Birmingham, AL, 9.10.1942; letter from J. Edgar Hoover, FBI Director, to Wendell Berge, Assistant Attorney General, Washington D.C., October 15, 1942; memo from Wendell Berge to J. Edgar

Hoover, Washington D.C., October 24, 1942, NARA, RG 60/144, Box 17575, Fol. 144-2-3.

87. Memo from Edwin D. Kuykendall.

88. Report by FBI agent Edwin D. Kuykendall, Birmingham, AL, October 9, 1942, NARA, RG 60/144, Box 17575, Fol. 144-2-3.

89. Report by Edwin D. Kuykendall; report by Special Agent Hugh A. Page Jr., November 10, 1943, Charlotte, NC, NARA, RG 60/144, Box 17575, Fol. 144-2-3.

90. Norrell, *Reaping the Whirlwind*, 44–58.

91. Statement by Dr. H. W. Nixon, report by Special Agent Hugh A. Page Jr., November 10, 1943, Charlotte, NC, S. 24-25, NARA, RG 60/144, Box 17575, Fol. 144-2-3.

92. Norrell, *Reaping the Whirlwind*, 44–58.

93. Norrell, 54.

94. Statement by Dr. Murray Smith, report by FBI agent Edwin D. Kuykendall, Birmingham, AL, April 9, 1943, NARA, RG 60/144, Box 17575, Fol. 144-2-3.

95. Statement by Henry A. Vaughan, report by FBI agent Edwin D. Kuykendall, Birmingham, AL, April 9, 1943, NARA, RG 60/144, Box 17575, Fol. 144-2-3.

96. Statement by Mary Elza Lundy, report by FBI agent Edwin D. Kuykendall, Birmingham, AL, April 9, 1943, NARA, RG 60/144, Box 17575, Fol. 144-2-3.

97. Statement by Willie Jenkins, report by FBI agent Edwin D. Kuykendall, Birmingham, AL, April 9, 1943, NARA, RG 60/144, Box 17575, Fol. 144-2-3.

98. Report by FBI agent Edwin D. Kuykendall, Birmingham, AL, June 1, 1943, NARA, RG 60/144, Box 17575, Fol. 144-2-3, 7.

99. Letter from E. Burns Parker, U.S. Attorney, Middle District of Alabama, to Francis Biddle, Attorney General, Montgomery, AL, January 21, 1943, NARA, RG 60/144, Box 17575, Fol. 144-2-3.

100. Letter from E. Burns Parker, U.S. Attorney for the Middle District of Alabama, to Francis Biddle, Attorney General, Montgomery, AL, May 28, 1943, and memo from James Rowe Jr. to J. Edgar Hoover, Washington D.C., June 5, 1943, NARA, RG 60/144, Box 17575, Fol. 144-2-3.

101. Letter from D. K. Brown, FBI Special Agent in Charge, to J. Edgar Hoover, FBI Director, Birmingham, AL, May 20, 1943, NARA, RG 60/144, Box 17575, Fol. 144-2-3.

102. Letter from E. Burns Parker, U.S. Attorney for the Middle District of Alabama, to Wendell Berge, Assistant Attorney General, Montgomery, AL, May 20, 1943, and report by FBI Special Agent Edwin D. Kuykendall, Birmingham, AL, June 1, 1943, NARA, RG 60/144, Box 17575, Fol. 144-2-3.

103. "Trial of Macon Officials Stirs Fever Pitch Interest," *Montgomery Advertiser*, June 21, 1943, 1.

104. "Macon County Sheriff, Deputy Are Acquitted," *Montgomery Advertiser*, June 25, 1943, 1, 3.

105. "Trial of Macon Officials Stirs Fever Pitch Interest," 1.

106. "Negro Woman Tells U.S. Court Sheriff and Deputy Beat Her," *Birmingham News*, June 21, 1943, 1–2.

107. "Witness Parade against Macon Sheriff in U.S. Trial," *Montgomery Advertiser*, June 22, 1943, 1, 7.

108. "Witness Parade," *Montgomery Advertiser*, 1, 7.

109. "Witness Parade," *Montgomery Advertiser*, 1, 7.

110. See Norrell, *Reaping the Whirlwind*, 54.

111. "Witness Parade against Macon Sheriff in U.S. Trial," 1, 7.

112. "Witness Parade," *Montgomery Advertiser*, 1, 7.

113. "Sheriff Takes Stand during Brutality Case, Denies Beating Negro," *Birmingham News*, June 23, 1943, 1, 8.

114. "U.S. Witnesses under Fire by Evans Defense," *Montgomery Advertiser*, June 23, 1943, 1–2.

115. "U.S. Witnesses under Fire," 1–2.

116. "Jury Gets 'Brutality' Cases; U.S. Testimony Is Assailed," *Montgomery Advertiser*, June 24, 1943, 1–2.

117. "Jury Gets 'Brutality' Cases," 1–2.

118. "Witness Parade against Macon Sheriff in U.S. Trial," 1, 7.

119. "Witness Parade," 7.

120. "Macon County Sheriff, Deputy Are Acquitted," 1, 3.

121. "Macon County Sheriff," 1, 3.

122. "Macon County Sheriff," 1, 3.

123. "Macon County Sheriff," 1, 3.

124. Regarding the history of the conflict between states' rights and federalism in the United States, see Drake and Nelson, introduction.

125. Letter from O. H. Doyle, United States Attorney, Western District of Carolina, to Francis Biddle, Attorney General, Greenville, SC, December 15, 1942, NARA, RG 60/144, Box 17601, Fol. 144-68-9.

126. Statement by Lucis Cowan, report by T. D. Easterling, FBI Special Agent, Charlotte, NC, May 19, 1943, NARA, RG 60/144, Box 17601, Fol. 144-68-9, 6–7.

127. Statement by Theodore Benson, report by T. D. Easterling, FBI Special Agent, January 21, 1943, Charlotte, NC, NARA, RG 60/144, Box 17601, Fol. 144-68-9.

128. Report by T. D. Easterling, FBI Special Agent, Charlotte, NC, May 19, 1943, NARA, RG 60/144, Box 17601, Fol. 144-68-9, 20–21.

129. Statement by Sanford Eugene Haley, report by Gaston C. Thompson, FBI Special Agent, Atlanta, Georgia, July 8, 1943, NARA, RG 60/144, Box 17601, Fol. 144-68-9, 2.

130. Statement by Nellie S. Brewer, report by T. D. Easterling, FBI Special Agent, Charlotte, NC, May 19, 1943, NARA, RG 60/144, Box 17601, Fol. 144-68-9, 11.

131. See additional statements in the report by FBI Special Agent T. D. Easterling, Charlotte, NC, May 19, 1943, NARA, RG 60/144, Box 17601, Fol. 144-68-9.

132. See the statements in the report by Hugh A. Page, FBI Special Agent, Charlotte, NC, November 10, 1943, NARA, RG 60/144, Box 17601, Fol. 144-68-9.

133. Statement by Charlie Denny, report by Hugh A. Page, FBI Special Agent, Charlotte, NC, November 10, 1943, NARA, RG 60/144, Box 17601, Fol. 144-68-9, 3–4.

134. Statement by Corine McCoy, report by Hugh A. Page, FBI Special Agent, Charlotte, NC, November 10, 1943, NARA, RG 60/144, Box 17601, Fol. 144-68-9, 10–11.

135. "Sheriff Given 60 Days in Jail, and Fined $500," *Anderson Independent*, December 2, 1943, 1.

136. "Sheriff Given 60 Days," *Anderson Independent*, 1.

137. Letter from O. H. Doyle, U.S. Attorney, District of South Carolina, to Victor M. Rotnem, Assistant Attorney General, Head of the Civil Rights Section, Greenville, SC, December 3, 1943, NARA, RG 60/144, Box 17601, Fol. 144-68-9.

138. Letter from O. H. Doyle to Victor M. Rotnem.

139. Letter from Francis Biddle, Attorney General, to Oscar Henry Doyle, U.S. Attorney, District of South Carolina, Washington D.C., December 11, 1943, NARA, RG 60/144, Box 17601, Fol. 144-68-9.

140. "County Citizens Pay Erskine Fine," *Anderson Independent*, no date, no page number, NARA, RG 60/144, Box 17601, Fol. 144-68-9.

141. "County Citizens Pay," *Anderson Independent*.

142. Hume and Gough, *Blacks, Carpetbaggers, and Scalawags*, 1–10.

143. "Candler Blames U.S. Procedure," *Atlanta Constitution*, December 30, 1943, 1.

144. "Jury Acquits Defendants in Dailey Trial," *Atlanta Constitution*, April 8, 1944, 1.

145. Carr, *Federal Protection of Civil Rights*, 140.

146. "States' Rights vs. Human Rights," *Atlanta Daily World*, January 30, 1944, 8.

147. Quoted by Elliff, *United States Department of Justice*, 199. For more on the largely positive reactions of the African American press to the activities of the Civil Rights Section in the South during the early 1940s, see "U.S. Government Acts to Protect Civil Rights of Race Group," *Atlanta Daily World*, March 31, 1942, 1; "Justice Department Keeps Close Vigil on Civil Rights Violations in South," *Chicago Defender*, June 19, 1943, 7; "The FBI Can Halt Lynchings," *New York Amsterdam News*, July 31, 1943, 10.

148. Letter from Mary Lockwood to Mary White [Ovington], Tuskegee, AL, May 3, 1946, LOC, NAACP Papers, Group II, Box B-113, Lockwood, William P. 1946–1947.

149. Letter from Thurgood Marshall, NAACP Special Counsel, to Turner L. Smith, Civil Rights Section, New York City, May 8, 1946, LOC, NAACP Papers, Group II, Box B-113, Lockwood, William P. 1946–1947.

150. Screws et al. v. United States, 325 U. S. 91 (1945), https://www.law.cornell.edu/supremecourt/text/325/91.

151. Elliff, *United States Department of Justice*, 159–170; Lawson, *To Secure These Rights*, 143–44, 146; McMahon, *Reconsidering Roosevelt*, 167–75.

152. Lawson, introduction, 1–41.

153. Dudziak, *Cold War Civil Rights*.

154. Elliff, *United States Department of Justice*, 224–36; Wexler, *Fire in a Canebrake*.

155. Lawson, *To Secure These Rights*, 66.

156. Lawson, 66–68.

157. Lawson, 139–50.

158. Lawson, 172–73.

159. Truman, "Special Message," 126.

160. Truman, 123.

161. Truman, 126.

162. Dudziak, *Cold War Civil Rights*.

163. Quoted by Carol Anderson, *Eyes off the Prize*, 108.

164. Anderson, 58–113; Dudziak, *Cold War Civil Rights*, 43–45.

165. Frederickson, *Dixiecrat Revolt*.

166. The Civil Rights Act of 1957 significantly bolstered the authority of the U.S. Department of Justice in its efforts to combat violations of civil rights in the United States. One consequence of this was that the CRS was transformed into an independent division within the Department of Justice—that is, the Civil Rights Division (CRD), which still exists today. See Belknap, *Federal Law and Southern Order*, 33–38.

167. Affidavit by Martha Kendrick McMillan, Montgomery, AL, September 12, 1946, NARA, RG 60/144, Box 104, Fol. 144-2-20.

168. Affidavit by Martha Kendrick McMillan.

169. Affidavit by Martha Kendrick McMillan.

170. See the photographs in the court file for *U.S. v. Pickett*, NARA, SR, RG 21/ RDCUS, Middle District of Alabama, Northern Division, Criminal Case No. 9999, Box 147.

171. Letter from Hartwell Davis, Assistant United States Attorney, Middle District of Alabama, to Fred Folsom, Head of the Civil Rights Section, Montgomery, AL, September 13, 1946, NARA, RG 60/144, Box 104, Fol. 144-2-20.

172. Letter from Hartwell Davis to Fred Folsom.

173. Raper, *Tragedy of Lynching*, 13–19.

174. Letter from Hartwell Davis, Assistant United States Attorney, Middle District of Alabama, to Fred Folsom, Head of the Civil Rights Section, Montgomery, AL, September 13, 1946, NARA, RG 60/144, Box 104, Fol. 144-2-20.

175. See the statements by Sheriff Joseph L. Pickett, Rell (Verell) Green, and Reynold G. Cook, report by Pierce A. Pratt, FBI Special Agent, Birmingham, AL, October 15, 1946, NARA, RG 60/144, Box 104, Fol. 144-2-20.

176. Statement by Arthurene McMillan, report by Pierce A. Pratt, FBI Special Agent, Birmingham, AL, October 15, 1946, NARA, RG 60/144, Box 104, Fol. 144-2-20, 11–12.

177. Statement by Arthurene McMillan.

178. Statement by Junior Reed, report by Pierce A. Pratt, FBI Special Agent, Birmingham, AL, October 15, 1946, NARA, RG 60/144, Box 104, Fol. 144-2-20, 37–38.

179. Letter from Hartwell Davis, Assistant United States Attorney, Middle District of Alabama, to Tom C. Clark, United States Attorney General, Montgomery, AL, April 16, 1947, NARA, RG 60/144, Box 104, Fol. 144-2-20.

180. Letter from Theron L. Claude, Civil Rights Section, to E. Burns Parker, United States Attorney, Middle District of Alabama, Washington D.C., April 18, 1947, NARA, RG 60/144, Box 104, Fol. 144-2-20.

181. See the report by Pierce A. Pratt, FBI Special Agent, Birmingham, AL, October 15, 1946, NARA, RG 60/144, Box 104, Fol. 144-2-20, 45.

182. See the indictment "United States v. Joseph L. Pickett, Verell Green, alias Rell Green, Reynolds G. Cook, Margaret Green Cook, and Comer F. Green," NARA, RG 60/144, Box 104, Fol. 144-2-20.

183. "Sheriff, Four Others Indicted for Torturing Mother of Eight," *Chicago Defender*, February 22, 1947, 1.

184. "Flogging of Ala. Woman Aired in Federal Court," *Pittsburgh Courier*, May 17, 1947, 4.

185. See, for example, the reports in the NAACP magazine the *Crisis* on lynchings in the United States, including "Three for Hitler," *Crisis*, November 1942, 343; Hobbs, *Lynching in Florida*.

186. "Lash Trial Prosecution Rests; Woman's Recital Challenged," *Montgomery Advertiser*, June 17, 1947, 1–2.

187. "Lash Trial Prosecution Rests," *Montgomery Advertiser*, 1–2.

188. "Lash Trial Prosecution Rests," *Montgomery Advertiser*, 1–2.

189. "Jury Frees Bullock Sheriff, Four Others, of Abuse Charge," *Montgomery Advertiser*, June 18, 1947, 1, 9.

190. Letter from Hartwell Davis, Assistant United States Attorney, Middle District of Alabama, to Tom C. Clark, United States Attorney General, Montgomery, AL, June 19, 1947, NARA, RG 60/144, Box 104, Fol. 144-2-20.

191. Statement by Mallie Pearson, report by Pierce A. Pratt, FBI Special Agent, Birmingham, AL, May 12, 1953, NARA, RG 60/144, Box 104, 144-3-87, 4–6.

192. See report by Richard B. Lee, FBI Special Agent, Mobile, AL, April 24, 1953, NARA, RG 60/144, Box 104, 144-3-87, NA.

193. Statement by Mallie Pearson, report by Pierce A. Pratt, FBI Special Agent, Birmingham, AL, May 12, 1953, NARA, RG 60/144, Box 104, 144-3-87, 5.

194. Statement by Mallie Pearson.

195. Statement by Columbus A. Jackson, report by Thomas M. Hendricks Jr., FBI Special Agent, May 12, 1953, New Orleans, LA, NARA, RG 60/144, Box 104, 144-3-87, 2.

196. Statements by Harry Leon Clark Jr., Ottis G. Wainright, report by Robert L. Crongeyer Jr., FBI Special Agent, May 26, 1953, Mobile, AL, NARA, RG 60/144, Box 104, 144-3-87.

197. Report by Robert L. Crongeyer, FBI Special Agent, Mobile, AL, May 26, 1953, report by Robert L. Crongeyer, FBI Special Agent, Mobile, AL, June 17, 1953, report by Robert L. Crongeyer, FBI Special Agent, Mobile, AL, July 9, 1953, report by Robert L. Crongeyer, FBI Special Agent, Mobile, AL, July 28, 1953, NARA, RG 60/144, Box 104, 144-3-87.

198. "Woman Testifies She Was Beaten," *Mobile Register*, September 16, 1954, 1–2.

199. "3 Officers Acquitted in Civil Rights Case," *Mobile Register*, September 18, 1954, 1. See also "Sheriff Defense Motion Is Lost," *Mobile Press*, September 16, 1954, 10; "Jury to Get Case against Sheriff Today," *Mobile Register*, September 17, 1954, 1, 4.

200. "3 Officers Acquitted in Civil Rights Case," 1.

201. On the importance of *Brown v. Board of Education* for the African American civil rights movement, see Klarman, *From Jim Crow to Civil Rights*, 344–442. On the radicalization of white opposition to the civil rights movement in the wake of the Supreme Court decision, see Klarman, *From Jim Crow to Civil Rights*, 385–442; Belknap, *Federal Law and Southern Order*.

202. Letter from Percy C. Fountain, United States Attorney, Southern District of Alabama, to Arthur B. Caldwell, Chief, Civil Rights Section, Criminal Division, October 25, 1954, NARA, RG 60/144, Box 104, 144-3-87.

203. Letter from Percy C. Fountain to Arthur B. Caldwell.

204. McGuire, "Sexual Violence," 906–31.

205. McGuire, 913–14, 922–23. See also McGuire, *At the Dark End of the Street*; Napson-Williams, "Violating the Black Body."

206. Letter from Arthur B. Caldwell, Chief of Civil Rights Section, to Percy C. Fountain, United States Attorney, Southern District of Alabama, November 4, 1954, NARA, RG 60/144, Box 104, 144-3-87.

Conclusion

1. On the case of Emmet Till, see Metress, *Lynching of Emmett Till*; Goldsby, "High and Low Tech of It"; Tyson, *Blood of Emmett Till*.

2. Goldsby, *Spectacular Secret*, 294–305.

3. Goldsby, 294.

4. Quoted by Houck and Grindy, *Emmett Till*, x.

5. See G. Brown, "Coerced Confessions / Police Interrogations."

6. See McGuire, *At the Dark End of the Street*.

7. See also the findings in Klarman, "Is the Supreme Court Sometimes Irrelevant?," 138–40.

8. For a recent overview of the civil rights movement in the South and the wealth of research in this field, see Lawson, *Civil Rights Crossroads*; Klarman, *From Jim Crow to Civil Rights*, 344–442.

9. Klarman, 434.

10. See Wendt, *Spirit and the Shotgun*; Estes, *I am a Man!*, 78–79.

11. Austin, *Up against the Wall*; Finzsch, "Die Black Panther Party"; Rhodes, *Framing the Black Panthers*; Moore, *Black Rage in New Orleans*, 70–96.

12. Berg, *Ticket to Freedom*, 140–220.

13. Moore, *Black Rage in New Orleans*, 115–203; Dulaney, *Black Police*, 65–103.

14. "Ex-Deputy Tells Jury of Jail Water Torture," *New York Times*, September 1, 1983, A22; "Ex-Sheriff Guilty in Torture Case," *New York Times*, September 15, 1983, A16.

15. Ross, *Making News of Police Violence*; M. Johnson, *Street Justice*, 279–80.

16. Conroy, *Unspeakable Acts*, 21–26, 60–87, 158–168, 225–241; "Officer Accused of Torture Is Guilty of Perjury," *New York Times*, June 29, 2010, A20; "Former Chicago Police Officer Jon Burge Sentenced for Lying about Police Torture," press release by U.S. Department of Justice, January 21, 2011, https://www.justice.gov/opa/pr /former-chicago-police-officer-jon-burge-sentenced-lying-about-police-torture.

17. See Hill, *Nobody*; Taylor, *From #BlackLivesMatter to Black Liberation*; Camp and Heatherton, *Policing the Planet*.

18. See Hill, *Nobody*, 48–54; "Ex-Officer Who Shot Walter Scott Pleads Guilty in Charleston," *New York Times*, May 2, 2017, https://www.nytimes.com/2017/05/02/us /michael-slager-walter-scott-north-charleston-shooting.html; "Michael Slager, Officer in Walter Scott Shooting, Gets 20-Year Sentence," December 7, 2017, https:// www.nytimes.com/2017/12/07/us/michael-slager-sentence-walter-scott.html.

Bibliography

Archives and Manuscript Collections

Alabama Department of Archives and History, Montgomery, Alabama (ADAH)
    Alabama Governor (1943–1947: Sparks), Clemency Hearing Case Files
        (AG, 1943–1947: Sparks, CHCF)
    Alabama Supreme Court, Record of Cases, 1824–1974 (ASC/RoC)
Library of Congress, Washington, DC (LOC)
    Papers of the National Association for the Advancement of Colored People,
        1842–1999 (NAACP Papers)
National Archives and Records Administration, College Park, Maryland (NARA)
    General Records of the Department of Justice, Record Group 60, Classified
        Subject Files Correspondence, Class 144 (Civil Rights Litigation Case Files)
        (RG 60/144)
    Records of the Federal Bureau of Investigation, Record Group 65, Classified
        Subject Files, Class 44 (Civil Rights), 1920–1978 (RG 65/44)
National Archives and Records Administration, Southeast Region, Morrow, Georgia
    (NARA, SR)
    Records of District Courts of the United States, Record Group 21 (RG 21)
New York Public Library, Schomburg Center for Research in Black Culture,
    New York City (NYPL, SC)
    Carnegie-Myrdal Study of the Negro in America Research Memoranda
        Collection, 1935–1948 (microfilm) (CMSNA)
Robert W. Woodruff Library, Emory University, Atlanta, Georgia (RWWL)
    FBI Manuals of Instruction, Investigative Procedures and Guidelines, 1927–1978
        (microfilm) (FBI MoI)

Databases

The Making of Modern Law: U.S. Supreme Court Records and Briefs, 1832–1978
    (MoML/USSCRB)

Newspapers and Magazines

Alabama Journal
Anderson Independent
Atlanta Constitution
Atlanta Daily World
Atlanta Journal

Birmingham News
Chicago Daily Tribune
Chicago Defender
Crisis
Daily Clarion-Ledger
Daily Oklahoman
Meridian Star
Mobile Press
Mobile Register
Montgomery Advertiser
New York Amsterdam News
New York Times
Pittsburgh Courier
Tulsa Daily World
Washington Post

Books and Journals

Agamben, Giorgio. *State of Exception.* Translated by Kevin Attell. Chicago: University of Chicago Press, 2005.

Allen, James, ed. *Without Sanctuary: Lynching Photography in America.* Santa Fe: Twin Palms, 2000.

Amnesty International. *Amnesty International Report 2016/17: The State of the World's Human Rights.* London: Amnesty International, 2017.

Anderson, Carol. *Eyes off the Prize: The United Nations and the African American Struggle for Human Rights, 1944–1955.* Cambridge: Cambridge University Press, 2003.

Apel, Dora, and Shawn Michelle Smith. *Lynching Photographs.* Berkeley: University of California Press, 2007.

Arnesen, Eric. "Reconsidering the 'Long Civil Rights Movement.'" *Historically Speaking* 10, no. 2 (April 2009): 31–34.

Asad, Talal. *Formations of the Secular: Christianity, Islam, Modernity.* Stanford, CA: Stanford University Press, 2003.

———. "On Torture, or Cruel, Inhuman or Degrading Punishment." In *Social Suffering,* edited by Arthur Kleinman, Veena Das, and Margaret M. Lock, 285–308. Berkeley: University of California Press, 1997.

Austin, Curtis J. *Up against the Wall: Violence in the Making and Unmaking of the Black Panther Party.* Fayetteville: University of Arkansas Press, 2006.

Bachmann-Medick, Doris. *Cultural Turns: New Orientations in the Study of Culture.* Translated by Adam Blauhut. Berlin: De Gruyter, 2016.

Baker, Bruce E. Review of *The Many Faces of Judge Lynch: Extralegal Violence and Punishment in America,* by Christopher Waldrep. *Law and History Review* 22, no. 3 (2004): 664–66.

Barthes, Roland. *Camera Lucida: Reflections on Photography.* Translated by Richard Howard. Vintage: London, 2000.

Bauman, Zygmunt. *Wasted Lives: Modernity and Its Outcasts.* Cambridge: Polity Press, 2003.

Bederman, Gail. *Manliness and Civilization: A Cultural History of Gender and Race in the United States, 1880–1917.* Chicago: University of Chicago Press, 1995.

Belknap, Michal R. *Federal Law and Southern Order: Racial Violence and Constitutional Conflict in the Post-Brown South.* Athens: University of Georgia Press, 1995.

Berg, Manfred. *Popular Justice: A History of Lynching in America.* Chicago: Ivan R. Dee, 2011.

———. "Das Ende der Lynchjustiz im amerikanischen Süden." *Historische Zeitschrift* 283, no. 3 (2006): 583–616.

———. "Soldiers and Citizens: War and Voting Rights in American History." In *Reflections on American Exceptionalism*, edited by David K. Adams and Cornelis A. van Minnen, 188–225. Staffordshire: Ryburn, 1994.

———. *The Ticket to Freedom: The NAACP and the Struggle for Black Political Integration.* Gainesville: University Press of Florida, 2005.

Berg, Manfred, and Simon Wendt, eds. *Globalizing Lynching History: Vigilantism and Extralegal Punishment from an International Perspective.* New York: Palgrave Macmillan, 2011.

Berrey, Stephen A. "Resistance Begins at Home: The Black Family and Lessons in Survival and Subversion in Jim Crow Mississippi." *Black Women, Gender, and Families* 3, no. 1 (2009): 65–90.

———. *The Jim Crow Routine: Everyday Performances of Race, Civil Rights, and Segregation in Mississippi.* Chapel Hill: University of North Carolina Press, 2015.

Blevins, John F. "*Lyons v. Oklahoma*, the NAACP, and Coerced Confessions under the Hughes, Stone, and Vinson Courts, 1936–1949." *Virginia Law Review* 90, no. 1 (2004): 387–464.

Blue, Ethan. "'A Dark Cloud Will Go Over': Pain, Death, and Silence in Texas Prisons in the 1930s." *Humanities Research* 14, no. 2 (2007): 5–24. http://press-files.anu.edu .au/downloads/press/p14431/pdf/ch029.pdf.

Bolton, Kenneth, Jr. "Police." In *Encyclopedia of Race, Ethnicity, and Society*, vol. 2, edited by Richard T. Schaefer, 1053–55. Los Angeles: SAGE, 2008.

Bracey, John H., and August Meier, eds. *Papers of the NAACP. Part 8, Discrimination in the Criminal Justice System, 1910–1955. Series A & B: Legal Department and Central Office Records.* Bethesda: University Publications of America, 1988.

Brooks, Daphne. *Bodies in Dissent: Spectacular Performances of Race and Freedom, 1850–1910.* Durham, NC: Duke University Press, 2006.

Brooks, Peter. *Troubling Confessions: Speaking Guilt in Law and Literature.* Chicago: University of Chicago Press, 2000.

Brown, Geneva. "Coerced Confessions / Police Interrogations." In *Encyclopedia of American Civil Liberties*, vol. 1, edited by Paul Finkelman, 315–21. New York: Routledge, 2006.

Brown, Richard Maxwell. *Strain of Violence: Historical Studies of American Violence and Vigilantism.* Oxford: Oxford University Press, 1975.

Brundage, W. Fitzhugh. *Lynching in the New South: Georgia and Virginia, 1880–1930.* Urbana: University of Illinois Press, 1993.

———. "The Roar on the Other Side of Silence: Black Resistance and White Violence in the American South, 1880–1940." In *Under Sentence of Death: Lynching in the South*, edited by W. Fitzhugh Brundage, 271–91. Chapel Hill: University of North Carolina Press, 1997.

Burschel, Peter, Götz Distelrath, and Sven Lembke. "Eine historische Anthropologie der Folter: Thesen, Perspektiven, Befunde." In *Das Quälen des Körpers: eine historische Anthropologie der Folter*, edited by Peter Burschel, Götz Distelrath, and Sven Lembke, 1–26. Cologne: Böhlau, 2000.

Butler, Judith. "Endangered/Endangering: Schematic Racism and White Paranoia." In *The Judith Butler Reader*, edited by Sara Salih, 204–11. Malden: Wiley-Blackwell, 2003.

———. *Excitable Speech: A Politics of the Performative*. New York: Routledge, 1997.

———. *Frames of War: When Is Life Grievable?* London: Verso Books, 2009.

———. *Precarious Life: The Powers of Mourning and Violence*. London: Verso Books, 2004.

Camp, Jordan T., and Christina Heatherton, eds. *Policing the Planet: Why the Policing Crisis Led to Black Lives Matter*. London: Verso, 2016.

Capeci, Dominic J., Jr. *The Lynching of Cleo Wright*. Lexington: University Press of Kentucky, 1998.

———. "The Lynching of Cleo Wright: Federal Protection of Constitutional Rights during World War II." *Journal of American History* 72, no. 4 (1986): 859–87.

Carr, Robert Kenneth. *Federal Protection of Civil Rights: Quest for a Sword*. Ithaca, NY: Cornell University Press, 1947.

Carroll, Anne Elizabeth. *Word, Image, and the New Negro: Representation and Identity in the Harlem Renaissance*. Bloomington: Indiana University Press, 2005.

Casper, Monica J., and Lisa Jean Moore. Introduction to *Missing Bodies: The Politics of Visibility*, 1–24. New York: New York University Press, 2009.

Certeau, Michel de. "The Laugh of Michel Foucault." Chap. 14 in *Heterologies: Discourse on the Other*. Translated by Brian Massumi. Minneapolis: University of Minnesota Press, 2010.

Chafee, Zechariah, Walter H. Pollak, and Carl S. Stern. *Report on Lawlessness in Law Enforcement*. Washington, DC: Government Printing Office, 1931.

Cha-Jua, Sundiata Keita, and Clarence Lang. "The 'Long Movement' as Vampire: Temporal and Spatial Fallacies in Recent Black Freedom Studies." *Journal of African American History* 92, no. 2 (Spring 2007): 265–88.

Clark, Elizabeth B. "'The Sacred Rights of the Weak': Pain, Sympathy, and the Culture of Individual Rights in Antebellum America." *Journal of American History* 82, no. 2 (1995): 463–93.

Clarke, James W. "Without Fear or Shame: Lynching, Capital Punishment and the Subculture of Violence in the American South." *British Journal of Political Science* 28, no. 2 (1998): 269–89.

Coleman, Frank. "Freedom from Fear on the Home Front: Federal Prosecution of 'Village Tyrants' and Lynch-Mobs." *Iowa Law Review* 29, no. 3 (1944): 415–29.

Collins, Patricia Hill. *Black Feminist Thought: Knowledge, Consciousness, and the Politics of Empowerment*. New York: Routledge, 2000.

Conquergood, Dwight. "Rethinking Elocution: The Trope of the Talking Book and Other Figures of Speech." In *Opening Acts: Performance in/as Communication and Cultural Studies*, edited by Judith Hamera, 141–62. Thousand Oaks, CA: SAGE, 2006.

Conroy, John. *Unspeakable Acts, Ordinary People: The Dynamics of Torture*. New York: Alfred A. Knopf, 2000.

Cooper, William J. and Tom E. Terrill, *The American South: A History*. Lanham: Rowman & Littlefield, 2009.

Cortner, Richard C. *A "Scottsboro" Case in Mississippi: The Supreme Court and* Brown v. Mississippi. Jackson: University of Mississippi, 1986.

Cover, Robert M. "The Origins of Judicial Activism in the Protection of Minorities." *Yale Law Journal* 91, no. 7 (1982): 287–316.

Cuntz, Michael, Barbara Nitsche, Isabell Otto, and Marc Spaniol, eds. *Die Listen der Evidenz*. Cologne: DuMont, 2006.

Dale, Elizabeth. *Robert Nixon and Police Torture in Chicago, 1871–1971*. DeKalb: Northern Illinois University Press, 2016.

Deleuze, Gilles. *Foucault*. Minneapolis: University of Minnesota Press, 1988.

Dollard, John. *Caste and Class in a Southern Town*. Madison: University of Wisconsin Press, 1988. First published 1937 by Yale University Press.

Dorr, Lisa Lindquist. *White Women, Rape, and the Power of Race in Virginia, 1900–1960*. Chapel Hill: University of North Carolina Press, 2004.

Drake, Frederick D., and Lynn R. Nelson. Introduction to *States' Rights and American Federalism: A Documentary History*, edited by Frederick D. Drake and Lynn R. Nelson, xiii–xxv. Westport: Greenwood Press, 1999.

Dube, Leela, Eleanor Leacock, and Shirley Ardener, eds. *Visibility and Power: Essays on Women in Society and Development*. Delhi: Oxford University Press, 1986.

Du Bois, W. E. B. *Dusk of Dawn: An Essay Toward an Autobiography of a Race Concept*. New York: Harcourt, Brace and Company, 1940.

———. "The Negro since 1900: A Progress Report." *New York Times Magazine*, November 21, 1948, 24, 54–57, 59.

Dudziak, Mary L. *Cold War Civil Rights: Race and the Image of American Democracy*. Princeton, NJ: Princeton University Press, 2000.

Dulaney, W. Marvin. *Black Police in America*. Bloomington: Indiana University Press, 1996.

Egerton, John. *Speak Now against the Day: The Generation before the Civil Rights Movement in the South*. New York: Alfred A. Knopf, 1994.

Elliff, John T. "Aspects of Federal Civil Rights Enforcement: The Justice Department and the FBI, 1939–1964." In *Law in American History*, edited by Donald Fleming and Bernhard Bailyn, 604–73. Boston: Little, Brown, 1971.

———. *The United States Department of Justice and Individual Rights, 1937–1962*. New York: Garland, 1987.

Estes, Steve. *I am a Man! Race, Manhood, and the Civil Rights Movement*. Chapel Hill: University of North Carolina Press, 2005.

Finkelman, Paul. "Racial Desgregation (U.S.)." In *Encyclopedia of Racism in the United States*, edited by Pyong Gap Min, 447–59. Westport: Greenwood Press, 2005.

Finzsch, Norbert. "Conditions of Intolerance: Racism and the Construction of Social Reality." *Historical Social Research* 22, no. 1 (1997): 3–28.

———. "Male Gaze and Racism." *Gender Forum* 23 (2008): 23–40. http://genderforum.org/face-to-race-issue-23-2008/.

———. "'Picking up the Gun'. Die Black Panther Party zwischen gewaltsamer Revolution und sozialer Reform." *Amerikastudien/American Studies* 44, no. 2 (1999): 223–54.

Flanigan, Daniel J. "Criminal Procedure in Slave Trials in the Antebellum South." *Journal of Southern History* 40, no. 4 (1974): 537–64.

Foner, Eric. *Reconstruction: America's Unfinished Revolution, 1863–1877.* New York: Harper & Row, 1988.

Foucault, Michel. *Discipline and Punish: The Birth of the Prison.* Translated by Alan Sheridan. New York: Penguin Books, 1977.

———. "Of Other Spaces." *Diacritics* 16, no. 1 (Spring 1986): 22–27.

Frederickson, Kari A. *The Dixiecrat Revolt and the End of the Solid South, 1932–1968.* Chapel Hill: University of North Carolina Press, 2001.

Garland, David. "Penal Excess and Surplus Meaning: Public Torture Lynchings in Twentieth-Century America." *Law and Society Review* 39, no. 4 (2005): 793–833.

Gilbert, William Harlan, Jr. "Memorandum concerning the Characteristics of the Larger Mixed-Blood Racial Islands of the Eastern United States." *Social Forces* 24, no. 4 (1946): 438–77.

Gilroy, Paul. "'. . . To Be Real': The Dissident Forms of Black Expressive Culture." In *Let's Get It On: The Politics of Black Performance,* edited by Catherine Ugwu, 12–33. Seattle: Bay Press, 1995.

Goldsby, Jacqueline. *A Spectacular Secret: Lynching in American Life and Literature.* Chicago: University of Chicago Press, 2006.

———. "The High and Low Tech of It: The Meaning of Lynching and the Death of Emmett Till." *Yale Journal of Criticism* 9, no. 2 (1996): 245–82.

Goodman, James E. *Stories of Scottsboro.* New York: Pantheon Books, 1994.

Green, Ben. *Before His Time: The Untold Story of Harry T. Moore, America's First Civil Rights Martyr.* New York: Free Press, 1999.

Greenberg, Karen J., ed. *The Torture Debate in America.* Cambridge: Cambridge University Press, 2006.

Greenberg, Karen J., and Joshua L. Dratel, eds. *The Torture Papers: The Road to Abu Ghraib.* Cambridge: Cambridge University Press, 2005.

Hadden, Sally E. *Slave Patrols: Law and Violence in Virginia and the Carolinas.* Cambridge: Harvard University Press, 2001.

Hale, Grace Elizabeth. *Making Whiteness: The Culture of Segregation in the South, 1890–1940.* New York: Pantheon Books, 1998.

Hall, Jacquelyn Dowd. "The Long Civil Rights Movement and the Political Uses of the Past." *Journal of American History* 91, no. 4 (2005): 1233–63.

———. "'The Mind That Burns in Each Body': Women, Rape, and Racial Violence." In *Powers of Desire: The Politics of Sexuality,* edited by Ann Snitow, Christine Stansell, and Sharon Thompson, 328–49. New York: Monthly Review Press, 1983.

──────. *Revolt against Chivalry: Jessie Daniel Ames and the Women's Campaign against Lynching.* New York: Columbia University Press, 1979.

Hall, Stuart. "The Spectacle of the 'Other.'" In *Representation: Cultural Representations and Signifying Practices,* edited by Stuart Hall, 223–90. London: SAGE, 1997.

Hamera, Judith. Introduction to *Opening Acts: Performance in/as Communication and Cultural Studies,* edited by Judith Hamera, 1–10. Thousand Oaks: SAGE, 2006.

Harris, J. William. Introduction to *The New South: New Histories,* edited by J. William Harris, 1–11. New York: Routledge, 2008.

Harris, Trudier. *Exorcising Blackness: Historical and Literary Lynching and Burning Rituals.* Bloomington: Indiana University Press, 1984.

Hill, Marc Lamont. *Nobody: Casualties of America's War on the Vulnerable, from Ferguson to Flint and Beyond.* New York: Atria Books, 2016.

Hobbs, Tameka Bradley. "'Hitler Is Here': Lynching in Florida during the Era of World War II." PhD diss., Florida State University, Tallahassee, 2004. https://diginole.lib.fsu.edu/islandora/object/fsu:182219/datastream/PDF/view.

Hodes, Martha. "The Power of Indifference: Violence, Visibility, and Invisibility in the New York City Race Riot of 1900." In *Violence and Visibility in Modern History,* edited by Jürgen Martschukat and Silvan Niedermeier, 73–90. New York: Palgrave Macmillan, 2013.

──────. "The Sexualization of Reconstruction Politics: White Women and Black Men in the South after the Civil War." *Journal of the History of Sexuality* 3, no. 3 (1993): 402–17.

──────. *White Women, Black Men: Illicit Sex in the Nineteenth-Century South.* New Haven, CT: Yale University Press, 1997.

hooks, bell. *Black Looks: Race and Representation.* Boston: South End Press, 1992.

──────. "In Our Glory: Photography and Black Life." In *Picturing Us: African American Identity in Photography,* edited by Deborah Willis, 42–53, New York: New Press, 1994.

──────. "Performance Practice as a Site of Opposition." In *Let's Get It On: The Politics of Black Performance,* edited by Catherine Ugwu, 210–21. Seattle: Bay Press, 1995.

Hopkins, Ernest Jerome. *Our Lawless Police: A Study of the Unlawful Enforcement of the Law.* New York: Viking Press, 1931.

Horton, James Oliver, and Lois E. Horton. *Slavery and the Making of America.* Oxford: Oxford University Press, 2005.

Houck, Davis W., and Matthew A. Grindy. *Emmett Till and the Mississippi Press.* Jackson: University of Mississippi Press, 2008.

Hume, Richard L., and Jerry B. Gough. *Blacks, Carpetbaggers, and Scalawags: The Constitutional Conventions of Radical Reconstruction.* Baton Rouge: Louisiana State University Press, 2008.

Hunt, Lynn Avery. *Inventing Human Rights: A History.* New York: W. W. Norton, 2007.

James, Rawn, Jr. *Root and Branch: Charles Hamilton Houston, Thurgood Marshall, and the Struggle to End Segregation.* New York: Bloomsbury Press, 2010.

Jarvis, Christina S. *The Male Body at War: American Masculinity during World War II.* DeKalb: Northern Illinois University Press, 2004.

Jefferson, Robert F. *Fighting for Hope: African American Troops of the 93rd Infantry Division in World War II and Postwar America.* Baltimore: Johns Hopkins University Press, 2008.

Jeffreys-Jones, Rhodri. *The FBI: A History.* New Haven, CT: Yale University Press, 2007.

Jobs, Sebastian. *Welcome Home, Boys! Military Victory Parades in New York City, 1899–1946.* Frankfurt am Main: Campus Verlag, 2012.

Johnson, Guy B. "The Negro and Crime." *Annals of the American Academy of Political and Social Science* 217 (September 1941): 93–104.

Johnson, Marilynn S. *Street Justice: A History of Police Violence in New York City.* Boston: Beacon Press, 2003.

Kelley, Robin D. G. *Race Rebels: Culture, Politics, and the Black Working Class.* New York: Free Press, 1994.

———. "'Slangin' . . . Rocks Palestinian Style': Dispatches from the Occupied Zones of North America." In *Police Brutality: An Anthology*, edited by Jill Nelson, 21–59. New York: W. W. Norton, 2001.

———. "'We Are Not What We Seem': Rethinking Black Working-Class Opposition in the Jim Crow South." *Journal of American History* 80, no. 1 (1993): 75–112.

King, Gilbert. *The Execution of Willie Francis: Race, Murder, and the Search for Justice in the American South.* New York: Basic Civitas Books, 2008.

Kinshasa, Kwando Mbiassi, ed. *The Man from Scottsboro: Clarence Norris and the Infamous 1931 Alabama Rape Trial, in his Own Words.* Jefferson, NC: McFarland, 1997.

Klarman, Michael J. *From Jim Crow to Civil Rights: The Supreme Court and the Struggle for Racial Equality.* Oxford: Oxford University Press, 2004.

———. "Is the Supreme Court Sometimes Irrelevant? Race and the Southern Criminal Justice System in the 1940s." *Journal of American History* 89, no. 1 (2002): 119–53.

Knauer, Christine. *Let Us Fight as Free Men: Black Soldiers and Civil Rights.* Philadelphia: University of Pennsylvania Press, 2014.

Kozol, Wendy. "Marginalized Bodies and the Politics of Visibility." *American Quarterly* 47, no. 1 (2005): 237–47.

Kramer, Paul. "The Water Cure." *New Yorker*, February 25, 2008, http://www .newyorker.com/reporting/2008/02/25/080225fa_fact_kramer?currentPage=all.

Krasmann, Susanne. "Andere Orte der Gewalt." In *Die Gewalt in der Kriminologie, Kriminologisches Journal, Beiheft no. 6*, edited by Susanne Krasmann and Sebastian Scheerer, 85–102. Weinheim: Juventa Verlag, 1997.

Langbein, John H. *Torture and the Law of Proof: Europe and England in the Ancien Régime.* Chicago: University of Chicago Press, 1977.

Lavine, Emanuel Henry. *The Third Degree: A Detailed and Appalling Exposé of Police Brutality.* New York: Vanguard Press, 1930.

Lawson, Steven F. *Civil Rights Crossroads: Nation, Community, and the Black Freedom Struggle.* Lexington: University Press of Kentucky, 2015.

———. "Introduction: Setting the Agenda of the Civil Rights Movement." In *To Secure These Rights: The Report of Harry S. Truman's Committee on Civil Rights*, edited by Steven F. Lawson, 1–41. Boston: Bedford/St. Martin's, 2003.

————, ed. *To Secure These Rights: The Report of Harry S. Truman's Committee on Civil Rights.* Boston: Bedford/St. Martin's, 2003.

Leo, Richard A. *Police Interrogation and American Justice.* Cambridge, MA: Harvard University Press, 2008.

Levinson, Sanford, ed. *Torture: A Collection.* Oxford: Oxford University Press, 2004.

Lhamon, W. T., Jr. Introduction to *Jump Jim Crow: Lost Plays, Lyrics, and Street Prose of the First Atlantic Popular Culture,* 1–93. Cambridge, MA: Harvard University Press, 2003.

Lindenberger, Thomas, and Alf Lüdtke. "Physische Gewalt—eine Kontinuität der Moderne." In *Physische Gewalt: Studien zur Geschichte der Neuzeit,* edited by Thomas Lindenberger and Alf Lüdtke, 7–38. Frankfurt am Main: Suhrkamp, 1995.

Lippman, Theo. "McGill and Patterson: Journalists for Justice." *Virginia Quarterly Review* 79, no. 3 (2003): 707–17. http://www.vqronline.org/essay/mcgill-and -patterson-journalists-justice.

Litwack, Leon F. *Trouble in Mind: Black Southerners in the Age of Jim Crow.* New York: Alfred A. Knopf, 1998.

Lovell, George. "Imagined Rights without Remedies: The Politics of Novel Legal Claims." *Loyola of Los Angeles Law Review* 44, no. 1 (2010): 91–119.

Lüdtke, Alf. "Einleitung. Herrschaft als soziale Praxis." In *Herrschaft als soziale Praxis: historische und sozial-anthropologische Studien,* edited by Alf Lüdtke, 9–63. Göttingen: Vandenhoeck & Ruprecht, 1991.

Maasen, Sabine, Torsten Mayerhauser, and Cornelia Renggli. "Bild-Diskurs-Analyse." In *Bilder als Diskurse—Bilddiskurse,* edited by Sabine Maasen, Torsten Mayerhauser, and Cornelia Renggli, 7–26. Weilerswist: Velbrück Wissenschaft, 2006.

Mangum, Charles Staples. *The Legal Status of the Negro.* Chapel Hill: University of North Carolina Press, 1940.

Martschukat, Jürgen. "'The Art of Killing by Electricity': The Sublime and the Electric Chair." *Journal of American History* 89, no. 3 (2002): 900–21.

————. *Geschichte der Todesstrafe in Nordamerika: von der Kolonialzeit bis zur Gegenwart.* Munich: C.H. Beck, 2002.

————. *Inszeniertes Töten: Eine Geschichte der Todesstrafe vom 17. bis zum 19. Jahrhundert.* Cologne: Böhlau, 2000.

————. "Lynching und Todesstrafe in den USA im frühen 20. Jahrhundert." In *Wahrheit und Gewalt. Der Diskurs der Folter in Europa und den USA,* edited by Thomas Weitin, 209–23. Bielefeld: transcript Verlag, 2011.

————. "Strafgewalten und Zivilisationsentwürfe in den USA um 1900." In *Rationalitäten der Gewalt: Staatliche Neuordnungen vom 19. bis zum 21. Jahrhundert,* edited by Jürgen Martschukat and Susanne Krasmann, 239–64. Bielefeld: transcript Verlag, 2007.

Martschukat, Jürgen, and Silvan Niedermeier. "Violence and Visibility: Historical and Theoretical Perspectives." In *Violence and Visibility in Modern History,* edited by Jürgen Martschukat and Silvan Niedermeier, 1–23. New York: Palgrave Macmillan, 2013.

————, eds. *Violence and Visibility in Modern History.* New York: Palgrave Macmillan, 2013.

Martschukat, Jürgen, and Steffen Patzold, eds. *Geschichtswissenschaft und "performative turn": Ritual, Inszenierung und Performanz vom Mittelalter bis zur Neuzeit.* Cologne: Böhlau, 2003.

Mason, Gail. *The Spectacle of Violence: Homophobia, Gender, and Knowledge.* London: Routledge, 2002.

McAdam, Doug. *Political Process and the Development of Black Insurgency, 1930–1970.* Chicago: University of Chicago Press, 1999.

McCoy, Alfred. *Torture and Impunity: The U.S. Doctrine of Coercive Interrogation.* Madison: University of Wisconsin Press, 2012.

McGuire, Danielle L. *At the Dark End of the Street: Black Women, Rape, and Resistance; A New History of the Civil Rights Movement from Rosa Parks to the Rise of Black Power.* New York: Alfred A. Knopf, 2010.

———. "'It Was Like All of Us Had Been Raped': Sexual Violence, Community Mobilization, and the African American Freedom Struggle." *Journal of American History* 91, no. 4 (2004): 906–31.

McMahon, Kevin J. *Reconsidering Roosevelt on Race: How the Presidency Paved the Road to Brown.* Chicago: University of Chicago Press, 2004.

McPherson, Tara. *Reconstructing Dixie: Race, Gender, and Nostalgia in the Imagined South.* Durham, NC: Duke University Press, 2003.

Meier, August, and Elliott Rudwick. "Attorneys Black and White: A Case Study of Race Relations within the NAACP." *Journal of American History* 62, no. 4 (1976): 913–46.

Metress, Christopher. *The Lynching of Emmett Till: A Documentary Narrative.* Charlottesville: University of Virginia Press, 2002.

Miller, James A. *Remembering Scottsboro: The Legacy of an Infamous Trial.* Princeton, NJ: Princeton University Press, 2009.

Mixon, Gregory. "'Good Negro—Bad Negro': The Dynamics of Race and Class in Atlanta during the Era of the 1906 Riot." *Georgia Historical Quarterly* 81, no. 3 (1997): 593–621.

Moore, Leonard N. *Black Rage in New Orleans: Police Brutality and African American Activism from World War II to Hurricane Katrina.* Baton Rouge: Louisiana State University Press, 2010.

Mulvey, Laura. "Visual Pleasure and Narrative Cinema." In *Narrative Apparatus, Ideology: A Film Theory Reader,* edited by Philip Rosen, 198–209. New York: Columbia University Press, 1975.

Myers, Andrew. "Resonant Ripples in a Global Pond: The Blinding of Isaac Woodard." Accessed April 25, 2018. http://faculty.uscupstate.edu/amyers /conference.html.

Myrdal, Gunnar. *An American Dilemma: The Negro Problem and Modern Democracy.* New York: Harper & Brothers, 1944.

Nagel, Caroline, and Lynn A. Staeheli. "Integration and the Politics of Visibility and Invisibility in Britain: The Case of British Arab Activists." In *New Geographies of Race and Racism,* edited by Claire Dwyer and Caroline Bressey, 83–94. Aldershot; Burlington, Ashgate, 2008.

Napson-Williams, Theresa. "Violating the Black Body: Black Women, White Men and Sexual Violence, 1920–1952." PhD diss., Rutgers University, New Brunswick, 2007.

Nevels, Cynthia Skove. *Lynching to Belong: Claiming Whiteness through Racial Violence.* College Station: Texas A & M University Press, 2007.

Niedermeier, Silvan. "Police Brutality." In *The New Encyclopedia of Southern Culture*, vol. 19, *Violence*, edited by Amy Louise Wood, 130–32. Chapel Hill: University of North Carolina Press, 2011.

———. "Violence, Visibility, and the Investigation of Police Torture in the American South, 1940–1955." In *Violence and Visibility in Modern History*, edited by Jürgen Martschukat and Silvan Niedermeier, 91–111. New York: Palgrave Macmillan, 2013.

Norrell, Robert J. *Reaping the Whirlwind: The Civil Rights Movement in Tuskegee.* Chapel Hill: University of North Carolina Press, 1998.

O'Brien, Eileen. "Race." In *International Encyclopedia of the Social Sciences*, vol. 7, edited by William A. Darity, 3–8. Detroit: Macmillan Reference, 2008.

Ogletree, Charles J., Jr., and Austin Sarat, eds. *From Lynch Mobs to the Killing State: Race and the Death Penalty in America.* New York: New York University Press, 2006.

O'Reilly, Kenneth. *"Racial Matters": The FBI's Secret File on Black America, 1960–1972.* New York: Free Press, 1989.

Parker, Christopher S. *Fighting for Democracy: Black Veterans and the Struggle against White Supremacy in the Postwar South.* Princeton, NJ: Princeton University Press, 2009.

Pennybacker, Susan D. *From Scottsboro to Munich: Race and Political Culture in 1930s Britain.* Princeton, NJ: Princeton University Press, 2009.

Peters, Edward. *Torture.* Philadelphia: University of Pennsylvania Press, 1996.

Pfeifer, Michael. "At the Hands of Parties Unknown? The State of the Field of Lynching Studies." *Journal of American History* 101, no. 3 (December 2014): 832–46.

———, ed. *Global Lynching and Collective Violence.* 2 vols. Champaign: University of Illinois Press, 2017.

———. *Rough Justice: Lynching and American Society, 1874–1947.* Urbana: University of Illinois Press, 2004.

Plummer, Brenda Gayle. *Rising Wind: Black Americans and U.S. Foreign Affairs, 1935–1960.* Chapel Hill: University of North Carolina Press, 1996.

Pomata, Gianna. "Close-Ups and Long-Shots: Combining Particular and General in Writing the Histories of Women and Men." In *Geschlechtergeschichte und allgemeine Geschichte: Herausforderungen und Perspektiven*, edited by Hans Medick and Anne-Charlott Trepp, 99–124. Göttingen: Wallstein-Verlag, 1998.

Potter, Claire Bond. *War on Crime: Bandits, G-Men, and the Politics of Mass Culture.* New Brunswick, NJ: Rutgers University Press, 1998.

Raper, Arthur Franklin. *The Tragedy of Lynching.* Chapel Hill: University of North Carolina Press, 1933.

Reemtsma, Jan Philipp. "'Wir sind alles für dich!' An Stelle einer Einleitung: Skizze eines Forschungsprogramms." In *Folter: zur Analyse eines Herrschaftsmittels*, edited by Jan Philipp Reemtsma, 7–23. Hamburg: Junius Verlag, 1991.

Rejali, Darius M. *Torture and Democracy*. Princeton, NJ: Princeton University Press, 2007.

Rhodes, Jane. *Framing the Black Panthers: The Spectacular Rise of a Black Power Icon*. New York: New Press, 2007.

Rosenhaft, Eve, James A. Miller, and Susan D. Pennybacker. "Mother Ada Wright and the International Campaign to Free the Scottsboro Boys." *American Historical Review* 106, no. 2 (2001): 387–403.

Ross, Jeffrey Ian. *Making News of Police Violence: A Comparative Study of Toronto and New York City*. Westport: Praeger, 2000.

Roth, Mitchel P. "Blackjack" In *Historical Dictionary of Law Enforcement*, edited by Mitchel P. Roth, 31. Westport, CT: Greenwood Press 2001.

Samuels, Jean Ellen. "My Body, My Closet: Invisible Disability and the Limits of Coming-Out Discourse." *GLQ: A Journal of Gay and Lesbian Studies* 9, no. 1–2 (2003): 233–55.

Scarry, Elaine. *The Body in Pain: The Making and Unmaking of the World*. New York: Oxford: Oxford University Press, 1985.

Schneck, Peter. "Wort und Bild im Kreuzverhör: Rhetorik, Evidenz und Intermedialität im Gerichtsdrama." In *Zwischen Text und Bild: zur Funktionalisierung von Bildern in Texten und Kontexten*, edited by Annegret Heitmann and Joachim Schiedermair, 43–64. Freiburg im Breisgau: Rombach, 2000.

Schumacher, Frank. "'Marked Severities': The Debate over Torture during America's Conquest of the Philippines, 1899–1902." *Amerikastudien/American Studies* 51, no. 4 (2006): 475–98.

Scott, James C. *Domination and the Arts of Resistance: Hidden Transcripts*. New Haven, CT: Yale University Press, 1990.

Senechal de la Roche, Roberta. *The Sociogenesis of a Race Riot: Springfield, Illinois, in 1908*. Urbana: University of Illinois Press, 1990.

Sielke, Sabine. *Reading Rape: The Rhetoric of Sexual Violence in American Literature and Culture, 1790–1990*. Princeton, NJ: Princeton University Press, 2002.

Sitkoff, Harvard. "Racial Militancy and Interracial Violence in the Second World War." *Journal of American History* 58, no. 3 (1971): 661–81.

———. *Toward Freedom Land: The Long Struggle for Racial Equality in America*. Lexington: University Press of Kentucky, 2010.

Smith, Jessie Carney, and Carrell Horton, eds. *Historical Statistics of Black America*. New York: Gale Group, 1995.

Smith, Mark M. "Getting in Touch with Slavery and Freedom." *Journal of American History* 95, no. 2 (2008): 381–91.

Sofsky, Wolfgang. *Traktat über die Gewalt*. Frankfurt am Main: Fischer, 2005.

Sontag, Susan. *Regarding the Pain of Others*. New York: Farrar, Straus and Giroux, 2003.

Spivak, Gayatri Chakravorty. "Can the Subaltern Speak?" In *Marxism and the Interpretation of Culture*, edited by Cary Nelson and Lawrence Grossberg, 271–316. Urbana: University of Illinois Press, 1988.

Sullivan, Patricia. *Lift Every Voice: The NAACP and the Making of the Civil Rights Movement.* New York: New Press, 2009.

———. "Prelude to Brown: Education and the Struggle for Racial Justice during the NAACP's Formative Years, 1909–1934." In *From the Grassroots to the Supreme Court: Brown v.* Board of Education *and American Democracy,* edited by Peter F. Lau, 154–72. Durham: Duke University Press, 2004.

———. "Southern Seeds of Change, 1931–1938." In *The New South: New Histories,* edited by J. William Harris, 210–38. New York: Routledge, 2008.

Tagg, John. *The Burden of Representation: Essays on Photographies and Histories.* Minneapolis: University of Minnesota Press, 1993.

Taylor, Keeanga-Yamahtta. *From #BlackLivesMatter to Black Liberation.* Chicago: Haymarket Books, 2016.

Teel, Leonard Ray. "W. A. Scott and the Atlanta World." *American Journalism* 6, no. 3 (1989): 158–78.

Tolnay, Stewart E., and Elwood M. Beck. *A Festival of Violence: An Analysis of Southern Lynchings, 1882–1930.* Urbana: University of Illinois Press, 1995.

Truman, Harry S. "Special Message to the Congress on Civil Rights, February 2, 1948." In *Public Papers of the Presidents of the United States: Harry S. Truman,* vol. 4, *1948,* 121–26. Washington, DC: Office of the Federal Register, 1964.

Tushnet, Mark V. *Making Civil Rights Law: Thurgood Marshall and the Supreme Court, 1936–1961.* New York: Oxford University Press, 1994.

———. *Making Constitutional Law: Thurgood Marshall and the Supreme Court, 1961–1991.* New York: Oxford University Press, 1997.

Tyson, Timothy B. *Blood of Emmett Till.* New York: Simon & Schuster, 2017.

Ugwu, Catherine, ed. *Let's Get It On: The Politics of Black Performance.* Seattle: Bay Press, 1995.

Valverde, Mariana. *Law's Dream of a Common Knowledge.* Princeton, NJ: Princeton University Press, 2003.

Vandiver, Margaret. *Lethal Punishment: Lynchings and Legal Executions in the South.* New Brunswick, NJ: Rutgers University Press, 2006.

Waldrep, Christopher. *The Many Faces of Judge Lynch: Extralegal Violence and Punishment in America.* New York: Palgrave Macmillan, 2002.

———. "National Policing, Lynching, and Constitutional Change." *Journal of Southern History* 74, no. 3 (2008): 589–626.

———. *Roots of Disorder: Race and Criminal Justice in the American South, 1817–80.* Urbana: University of Illinois Press, 1998.

Walker, Samuel. *In Defense of American Liberties: A History of the ACLU.* New York: Oxford University Press, 1990.

———. Introduction to *Records of the Wickersham Commission on Law Observance and Enforcement, Part 1: Record of the Committee on Official Lawlessness,* edited by Randolph Boehm, v–xiii. Bethesda: University Publications of America, 1997.

Washington, Booker T. *Up from Slavery: An Autobiography.* Garden City: Doubleday, 1901.

Wendt, Simon. *The Spirit and the Shotgun: Armed Resistance and the Struggle for Civil Rights.* Gainesville: University Press of Florida, 2007.

West, Rebecca. "Opera in Greenville." *New Yorker*, June 14, 1947, 31–65.

Wexler, Laura. *Fire in a Canebrake: The Last Mass Lynching in America*. New York: Scribner, 2003.

Williams, Kidada E. *They Left Great Marks on Me: African American Testimonies of Racial Violence from Emancipation to World War I*. New York: New York University Press, 2012.

Williamson, Joel. *The Crucible of Race: Black-White Relations in the American South since Emancipation*. New York: Oxford University Press, 1984.

Wood, Amy Louise. *Lynching and Spectacle: Witnessing Racial Violence in America, 1890–1940*. Chapel Hill: University of North Carolina Press, 2009.

———. "Lynching Photography and the 'Black Beast Rapist' in Southern White Masculine Imagination." In *Masculinity: Bodies, Movies, Culture*, edited by Peter Lehmann, 193–211. New York: Routledge, 2001.

Wright, George C. *Racial Violence in Kentucky, 1865–1940: Lynchings, Mob Rule, and "Legal Lynchings."* Baton Rouge: Louisiana State University Press, 1990.

Zagolla, Robert. *Im Namen der Wahrheit: Folter in Deutschland vom Mittelalter bis heute*. Berlin: be.bra verlag, 2006.

Zangrando, Robert L. *The NAACP Crusade against Lynching, 1909–1950*. Philadelphia: Temple University Press, 1980.

Zirfas, Jörg. "Rituale der Grausamkeit: Performative Praktiken der Folter." In *Die Kultur des Rituals: Inszenierungen, Praktiken, Symbole*, edited by Jörg Zirfas and Christoph Wulf, 129–46. Munich: Wilhelm Fink Verlag, 2004.

Index

Page numbers appearing in italics refer to illustrations.

Till and, 146–47; white resistance to, 133–34, 152–53. *See also* "the long civil rights movement"

civil rights policy, 105–9

Civil Rights Section (CRS). *See* CRS (Civil Rights Section)

civil rights violations and foreign policy, 83, 135–36, 137

Civil War, 16, 69, 133

Clark, Harry Leon, Jr., 142–44

Clark, John, 38, 62–63

Clark, Tom C., 137, 178–79n5

Clarke, James W., 23

Clark University, 89, 112

clemency hearings of Daniels-Robinson case, 51–57

CLU (Civil Liberties Unit), 105–6, 107–8, 120–21, 179n17

coercion to confess. *See* confessions, forced

Cold War, 83, 84, 150

Coleman, Frank, 107

Coley, D. R., Jr., 143

Collins, Leroy, 88

Commission on Interracial Cooperation (CIC), 22, 64, 87

Committee on Civil Rights, 135–38

Communist Party USA (CPUSA), 15, 87

concealment of violence, 1, 8–11, 35, 119, 147, 161n33, 161n40, 161n42

confessions, forced: after 1955, 154; background and overview of, 3, 5–8; Brown, Ellington, and Shields case and, 28, 29–30, 31–36, 38; *Brown v. Mississippi* and, 65–66; of Canty, 42–43, 46; *Chambers v. Florida* and, 69–70; conclusions on, 147–51; Daniels-Robinson case and, 48, 49–50, 52–57; decline in lynchings and, 25–26; of Lyons, 76–80; *Lyons v. Oklahoma* and, 83; NAACP activism and (*See* NAACP campaign against forced confession); Pearson case and, 142; Quintar South case and, 89, 112–13, 117–18; Scottsboro case and,

15–16; swift convictions and, 25–26, 165nn54–55; U.S. Supreme Court and, 65–66, 69–70, 83, 148–50

Congress of Racial Equality, 153

convictions: CRS and, 138; forced confessions and, 3, 8–9, 16, 25–26, 29, 41, 147; Fourteenth Amendment and, 64–65, 69; NAACP and, 71; of police officers, 103, 125–26, 129, 135, 155; of Scottsboro Boys, 15; subaltern status and, 51; "swift," 23, 24, 25, 29–30, 31, 91, 147

Convington, Curvin M., 142–44

Cook, Margaret Green, 138, 139, 141

Cook, Reynold G., 138, 140, 141

Cowan, Lucis, 130

CPUSA (Communist Party USA), 15, 87

Crawford, Charles A., 117

CRD (Civil Rights Division), 186n166

credibility: in cases with women as plaintiffs, 141, 142, 143, 152; Daniels-Robinson case and, 50, 51, 52, 54–55, 57–58; Evans-Faucett trial and, 127–28; Lyons case and, 79; Sutherland trial and, 118

Criminal Division of Department of Justice, 105, 108

Crisis: Brown, Ellington, and Shields case and, 59, 60, 64, 67; *Chambers v. Florida* and, 70; fundraising and, 80–82, *81*; NAACP legal strategy in, 61; visual discourse of, 97

Crongeyer, Robert L., 143

CRS (Civil Rights Section): about, 106, 107–8, 186n166; investigations of women by, 138, 139–40; limits of, 134–35, 136, 138, 145. *See also* CLU (Civil Liberties Unit)

"culture of segregation," 17

Cummings, Homer S., 105

current police violence, 155–56

Dailey, Joseph T., 133

Daily Clarion-Ledger, 27

Dale, Elizabeth, 6–7

Daniels, Henry, Jr., 56, 148. *See also* case of Daniels-Robinson
Danner, R. G., 109, 114, 120
Davis, Charles, 68–70
Davis, Hartwell, 139–40, 141–42
Deacons for Defense and Justice, 153
death penalty, 8–9, 23–25, 86
democracy, 82–83, 101, 104, 107, 146, 150
Dennison, A. C., 43–44
Denny, Charlie, 131
Department of Justice: CRS and, 136, 186n166; Groveland Four and, 86; lynching investigations and, 61, 104, 105; NAACP and, 134–35, 136; police brutality investigations and, 4, 104–9, 151 (*See also* FBI investigations); prosecution of state violations and, 107–8, 120; Sutherland investigation and, 99, 103, 114, 120–22. *See also* FBI (Federal Bureau of Investigations)
Dial, Cliff, 32–34, 35, 37
digitalization, 155
Discipline and Punish (Foucault), 9
discrimination: black activism and, 153; black press and, 98, 99; Committee on Civil Rights and, 136; conclusions on, 151; in jury selection, 62, 117; NAACP and, 61, 62, 67, 68, 75, 80, 82–84, 87, 137; practice of torture and, 7, 8–9; U.S. Supreme Court and, 65, 67, 69, 71; voting rights and, 17, 126
Dixiecrats, 138
Dodd, M. R., 103, 111
Dorr, Lisa Lindquist, 25, 40–41, 57–58, 164n46
Doyle, Oscar Henry, 129, 132
Du Bois, W. E. B., 18, 21, 84
Dudziak, Mary L., 83, 137
due process clause of Fourteenth Amendment, 63, 64–65, 69
Dunjee, Roscoe, 76–77

Edington, David H., 49, 53
Edwards, George, Jr., 71–72

Eisenhower, Dwight D., 138
electric chairs, 7–8, 24–25, 161n29
electrocutions, 14, 47, 51, 58, 68, 72, 86
Ellington, Arthur. *See* case of Brown, Ellington, and Shields
Ellis, C. Neal, 89, 93–95
emasculation, 19, 21
Enforcement Acts of 1870 and 1871, 107
Erskine, William J., 129–33, 151–52
Evans, Edwin E., 122–29, 151–52
evidence: Daniels and Robinson trial and, 48–49; FBI reporting and, 110, 112, 114–15, 117, 119, 151; forced confessions as, 3–4, 31, 38, 63, 65, 68, 83, 150; power structures and, 11, 119
executions: of Daniels and Robinson, 58; of Edwards, 72; rationalization of, 9; transition from lynching to, 23–25, 29, 30, 164n46

Faucett, Henry F., 122–29, 151–52
FBI (Federal Bureau of Investigations): about, 109, 179–80n22; investigative manuals of, 110, 114, 115; reports of, 110–11
FBI (Federal Bureau of Investigations) investigations: of African American tortured women, 142–43; background and overview of, 4, 104, 108–9; of Erskine, 129–31; of Evans and Faucett, 122–26; in Groveland, 86; of McMillan torture, 140–41; of Monroe lynching, 136; of Shull, 84–85; of Sutherland, 99, 103, 109, 110–16, 119–22, 178n43
FBI Technical Laboratory, 110
federal jurisdiction, 104, 106, 107–9, 121, 129. *See also* state sovereignty
Florida Supreme Court, 69, 88
forced confessions. *See* confessions, forced
foreign policy and civil rights violations, 83, 135–36, 137
Foucault, Michel, 9, 10
Fountain, Percy C., 144

Kraft, Jack G., 132
Ku Klux Klan, 17, 70, 86, 153, 176n133

language of torture, 35–36, 166n105
Lauderdale County, Mississippi, 26, 28
law enforcement institutions. *See* police, institution of
leaks of torture acts, 35, 42
Legal Defense and Education Fund, 171n8
legal lynchings, term of, 15, 24, 66–67
limited impact of initiatives against torture, 152; African American testimony and, 47, 51; federal government and, 4, 108–9, 120, 133–34, 135, 138; NAACP and, 75, 134, 149
Lincoln, Abraham, 69, 70
local self-governance, 129, 132–34
Lockett, Pig, 26–27
Lockwood, Mary, 134–35
Lockwood, Willie P. M., 134–35
"long civil rights movement, the," 3–4
Lovell, George, 179n17
Lundy, Mary Elza, 124
lynchings: background and overview of, 3, 10, 19–21, 163n25, 163n27; campaigns against, 21–22; of Cleo Wright, 107; criminal justice system replacement of, 14–16; decline in, 22–26, 27–30, 147, 164n39, 164n41; FBI investigations of, 104, 105; legislation against, 105, 137; of Lockett and White, 26–27; of Monroe, 136; NAACP and, 61, 67, 80
lynch mobs: background and overview of, 19, 20–21, 23, 24, 163n27, 164n41; images of, 80–81; investigations of, 61, 136; in Kemper County, 27, 28–30
Lyons, W. D., 76–83, 81, 149, 175n112
Lyons v. Oklahoma, 83, 175n118

Macon County, 122–28, 134
Marshall, Thurgood: about, 61, 149, 170nn7–8; Canty case and, 68, 72–73,

75; CRS and, 134; Lyons case and, 77–80; on NAACP legal achievements and approach, 61–62, 68, 84
Martin, Harold, 93, 103, 117
Martin, Raymond W., 116, 117, 120
Martschukat, Jürgen, 24
masculinity, 20–21
McCall, Willis V., 85, 88
McCoy, Corine, 131
McGranery, James P., 179n5
McGrath, J. Howard, 179n5
McGuire, Danielle, 3, 144
McGuire, Matthew, 120–21
McMillan, Arthurene, 140
McMillan, Martha K., 138–42, 152
Meridian, Mississippi, 26, 27–28, 29, 32, 33–34
Meridian Star, 28, 29
Milam, J. W., 146
Miranda v. Arizona, 149
Mississippi, 26. *See also specific cities and counties of*
Mississippi Supreme Court, 63–64
Mobile, Alabama, 39, 42, 48, 53, 143
Mobile Register, 48
mob law, 38, 105
mobs, 33, 37, 64, 85, 104. *See also* lynch mobs
monopoly on use of force, states', 15, 22, 23, 26, 30, 35, 38, 147
Montgomery, Alabama, 3, 41–43, 51, 72, 73–76, 147, 149
Montgomery Advertiser: Canty case and, 42–44, 46, 73; Daniels-Robinson case and, 51; Evans and Faucett trial and, 126, 127, 128, 129; McMillan case and, 141
Montgomery Bus Boycott, 3, 147
Montgomery Circuit Court, 43, 75–76
Moore v. Dempsey, 64–65
Murphy, Frank, 105–6, 178n5
mutilation, 19, 21, 80
Myrdal, Gunnar, 18, 41, 161n35
myth of black rapist, 20–21

NAACP (National Association for the Advancement of Colored People): about, 59–62, 83–84, 88; Birmingham branch of, 72–74; Brown, Ellington, and Shields case and, 38; conclusions on, 148–50; CRS and, 134; Daniels-Robinson case and, 39, 51; federal government and, 105, 106, 134–36; fundraising by, 80–82, 81, 86–87; lynchings and, 21–22, 25–26, 61, 67, 80; Montgomery branch of, 74–75, 149, 173n83; Scottsboro case and, 15; strategies of, 82–83; UN Commission on Human Rights and, 137; Woodard case and, 84–85. See also *Crisis*; NAACP campaign against forced confession

NAACP campaign against forced confession: background and overview of, 3–4, 59–62; *Brown v. Mississippi* and, 62–65, 67, 68; Canty case and, 72–76, 168n18; case selection of, 71–72, 76–77; *Chambers v. Florida* and, 68–69, 70; Groveland Four and, 1–2, 85–88; Justice Department and, 134–35; Lyons case and, 76–83

National Commission on Law Observance and Enforcement, 6, 7–8, 160n23

National Guard, 14, 28

Nazis, 69, 82, 141, 160n20

"Negro 'Confesses' to 'Rape,'" 1–2, 2

New Deal, 3, 65, 106

New South, 22, 164n35

New South: New Histories, The (Harris), 159n4

New York City, 6–7, 84, 154

New York Post, 66–67

night riding, 86, 176n133

nonverbal means of testimony, 44–46

Norrell, Robert J., 123

Norris, Clarence, 15

Norris v. Alabama, 65

O'Brien, Eileen, 159n3

Oglesby, Stuart R., 92–93

Oklahoma Supreme Court, 83

Opelika, Alabama, 126, 141

Orso, Cleve, 57

Padgett, Norma, 85

pain, 5, 9, 37, 112

Paint Rock, Alabama, 14

Parker, E. Burns, 125, 139

Parker, James C., 154

Parkman, Edgar M., 54–55

Parks, Rosa, 147

paternalism, 91–92, 93

patriarchal order, 21, 40, 50, 52, 127, 148, 152

Pearson, Mallie, 142–44, 146, 152

Pendleton, Marie, 141

Petty, M. B., 118

Pfeifer, Michael J., 24

photographs, 151; Daniels-Robinson case and, 53–54, 55–56; of lynchings, 20, 94; NAACP use of, 80–82, 81, 86–87, 94; South case and, 89, 93–94, 95–96, 96, 100, 100–101, 178n43; Sutherland and, 113–16, 114–15, 117; of Till, 146

physical gestures in testimony, 44–46

Pickett, Joseph L., 138–39, 140, 141

Pittsburgh Courier, 70, 94, 97, 100, 100–102, 115, 141

Plessy v. Ferguson, 17, 144, 152, 162n12

politics of respectability, 144

police, institution of: accountability of, 1, 6, 88, 108, 119, 135; Committee on Civil Rights and, 136–37; denial of torture, 150; federal versus local authority and, 119, 129, 132–33, 151–52; lynchings and, 22–23; role of, 18–19; social customs and hierarchies and, 18–19, 155. *See also specific police institutions*

police brutality/violence: after 1955, 153–56; background and overview of, 5–8; black versus white press and, 90, 93–102, 96, 100, 150; investigation of, 4, 104–9, 151 (*See also* FBI investigations); lynchings and, 15, 16,

police brutality/violence (cont.)
22–23, 28–29; social order and, 18–19,
147, 148. *See also specific cases of*
police killings, 88, 123–24, 134, 146–47,
155
Porter, William G., 72, 74, 173n83
Powell v. Alabama, 65
power of indifference, 11
power structures: Canty case and, 72, 75;
conclusions on, 147, 152, 155;
Daniels-Robinson case and, 52; Evans
and Faucett case and, 126, 129;
evidence and, 11; Lyons case and, 149;
southern court proceedings and, 40;
Sutherland case and, 109, 116, 119, 122
Pratt, Pierce A., 141
protests, civil rights, 3, 15, 84, 147, 149,
152–53, 155, 156, 176n8

race, term of, 159n3
racial purity, 20
Ransom, Leon A., 75
rape. *See* sexual assault
Raper, Arthur F., 18, 24, 164n41
Rapport, Paul, 43–44, 73
Reconstruction era, 16, 17, 132–33
Reed, Junior, 140
Reemtsma, Jan-Philipp, 35
Rejali, Darius, 161n40
Reynolds, J. P., 99
Robertson, Ralph, 90
Robinson, Curtis C., *55*, 148. *See also*
case of Daniels-Robinson
Roosevelt, Franklin D., 82, 106, 178n5
Ryan, George, 154

Santana, Feidin, 155
Scarry, Elaine, 166n105
Schneck, Peter, 167n6
Schweinhaut, Henry, 121
Scott, Alexander, II, 97
Scott, Emel, 95–96
Scott, Walter, 155
Scottsboro case, 14–16, 65, 66, 147, 162n4

Screws, M. Claude, 135
Screws, William P., 73
Screws et al. v. United States, 135
segregation: conclusions on, 148, 153;
juries and, 122; NAACP and, 62, 84;
Plessy v. Ferguson and, 162n12; in
public schools, 144, 152; of public
transportation, 153; torture and, 36,
167n110; violence and culture of,
16–21, 162nn11–12
Segrest, Henry Neill, 123, 124, 127
Seibel, W. T., 43, 45–46
selective awareness, 90, 99, 102,
176n8
self-representation, black, 102, 178n52
separate but equal, 144, 152, 162n12
sexual assault: execution for, 24; fear of,
20–21, 22, 48; forced confessions and,
25, 31; Groveland Four case and, 1–2,
2, 85–88; Scottsboro case and, 14–16,
65, 66, 147; trials of, 40–41, 144; of
whites against blacks, 3, 144. *See also*
case of Daniels-Robinson
Shepherd, Samuel, 85–86, 88. *See also*
Groveland Four
Shields, Henry. *See* case of Brown,
Ellington, and Shields
Sheriffs, role of, 19
Shull, Lynwood, 84–85, 136
Slager, Michael T., 155
Slate, Henry, 141
slave patrols, 163n16
slavery, 8, 16, 18, 20, 37–38
Slayton, H. J., 93, 100
Smith, Murray, 124
Socialist Party of America, 87
social order: about, 10–11, 17–18; black
women and, 152; executions and, 25;
South case and, 91–92, 98–99, 102;
white support of, 29, 41
Sofsky, Wolfgang, 166n105, 167n109
sources for this study, 4
South, Quintar, 122, 176n1; case of
(*See* case of Quintar South); FBI inves-

trials as a forum for African Americans, 41, 148
Truman, Harry S., 135, 136–38
Tushnet, Mark V., 71
Tuskegee, Alabama, 123–24, 127
Tuskegee Civil Association, 123–24
Tuskegee Institute, 163n25
Tuskegee University, 123–24

Underwood, E. Marvin, 119
Union troops, 16
United Nations Commission on Human Rights, 137
United Nations Convention Against Torture, 5
United States Code (USC), 107–8, 135, 141, 179n14
United States Supreme Court: about, 178–79n5; Brown, Ellington, and Shields case and, 38, 51, 59, 64–65, 67–68; *Brown v. Board of Education* and, 3, 144, 152; *Brown v. Mississippi* and, 64–65; Canty case and, 72, 74, 75–76; *Chambers v. Florida* and, 69–70; civil rights initiative of U.S. government and, 106; conclusions on, 148–49; Daniels-Robinson case and, 51; Groveland Four and, 87–88; Lyons case and, 83; *Lyons v. Oklahoma* and, 83; NAACP and, 61–62, 64–65, 68–72, 75–76, 83, 87; *Plessy v. Ferguson* and, 17; Scottsboro case and, 162n4; *Screws et al v. United States* and, 135
United States v. Dailey, 133

Vaughan, Henry Asa, 124
video images, 155
violence and culture of segregation, 16–21, 162nn11–12
violence and visibility, 9–12, 161n40, 161n42, 179n8
visibility, concept of, 9, 10, 161n42
Voluntary Defenders Committee, 7

voters, African American, 97, 106, 153
voting rights, 16, 17, 108, 153

Wadsworth, Edward W., 43, 45, 74
Wainright, Ottis G., 142–44
Waldrep, Christopher, 4
Walker, Jake, 127
war against terror, 5
Ward, Eunice, 41–42
Ward, Lillian, 41–42, 43
Wartime Conference of NAACP, 134
Washington, Booker T., 124, 163n23
Washington Post, 66, 100
waterboarding, 7, 154
water cure, the, 7
Watkins, Garland, 89, 93
Wells, Ida B., 21, 67
West, Rebecca, 40
White, Holly, 26–27
White, Walter, 39, 69, 76, 77
white opposition to police trials and federal investigations, 125–26, 138, 140, 151–52
white press: case of Quintar South and, 90–95, 103; police misconduct and, 102. *See also specific newspapers*
whites, support of African Americans by: anti police brutality and, 63, 151; Canty case and, 75; Erskine case and, 130–31; Evans-Faucett case and, 123–24, 127; lynching criticism and, 21–22; Lyons case and, 77; South case and, 90–95
white supremacy: black challenge to, 17; in photography, 80–81; racial violence and, 20, 35–36, 148; social order and, 16, 18, 167n110; torture concealment and, 9; trials of blacks and, 40
Wickersham Commission, 6, 7–8, 160n23
Wilkins, Roy, 70
Williams, Franklin H., 85–86
Williams, Mattie, 55–56
Williamson, Jack, 68–70
Willingham, George W., 93